Observations IN LOWER CALIFORNIA

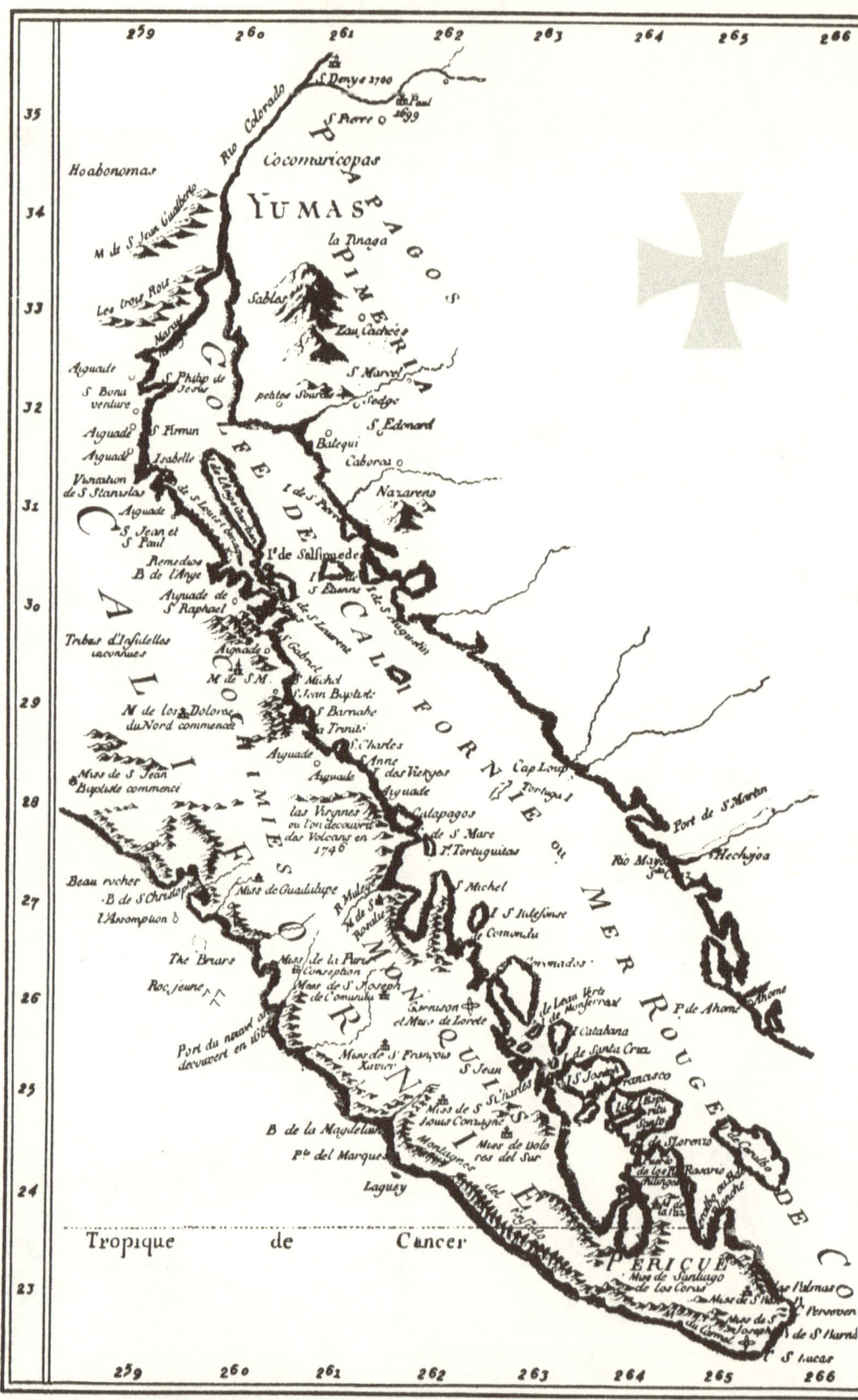

Observations in Lower California

✠ ✠ by Johann Jakob Baegert, S.J., translated from the Original German, with an Introduction and Notes, by M. M. Brandenburg and Carl L. Baumann ✠ University of California Press ✠ Berkeley, Los Angeles, London

UNIVERSITY OF CALIFORNIA PRESS, BERKELEY AND LOS ANGELES, CALIFORNIA

UNIVERSITY OF CALIFORNIA PRESS, LTD., LONDON, ENGLAND

COPYRIGHT, 1952, BY THE REGENTS OF THE UNIVERSITY OF CALIFORNIA

CALIFORNIA LIBRARY REPRINT SERIES EDITION 1979

ISBN: 0-520-03873-8

DESIGNED BY JOHN B. GOETZ

TRANSLATORS' PREFACE

After almost two decades (1751–1768) spent in missionary labors among the Indians of Baja California, the Jesuit father, Johann Jakob Baegert, returned to Europe. He occupied his leisure in the last four years of his life in writing a realistic and firsthand account of the California he knew. His *Nachrichten von der Amerikanischen Halbinsel Californien* was first published at Mannheim, Germany, in 1771, and Father Baegert lived just long enough to make some corrections and additions for the second edition of his famous book in 1772.

The present work is the first complete English translation of the original German text. We have tried to adhere to the original as closely as possible, but many of the expressions and idioms common to eighteenth-century German are no longer in use and we have given, as best we can, English approximations. This difficulty, together with Father Baegert's stylistic peculiarities, we have been at pains to overcome in our attempt to present a good, readable English text. In following the German original we have studiously translated Father Baegert's often very frank personal observations as well as his attacks on the Protestant clergy; these last, of course, based on long-forgotten controversies of little interest to the twentieth-century reader of the *Nachrichten*.

We wish to thank those who have generously given us their time and assistance: the late Charles Yale of Pasadena, who first suggested the translation and later aided with advice; Dr. Henry R. Wagner of San Marino; Dr. Peter M. Dunne, S.J., of the University of San Francisco; Presbítero Don José Trinidad Laris of Guadalajara, Mexico; and Père L. Münch, S.J., of Colmar, France, for assisting us in editing the book; and Messrs. Herbert Burke of Palo Alto, California, and Ray Jahn of New York City, who gave valuable help on the manuscript. We are also indebted to the courteous and helpful staff of the Henry E. Huntington Library, San Marino; and to Claremont College, Claremont, California, for financial aid given us for the typing of the manuscript.

M. M. B. and C. L. B.

CONTENTS

TRANSLATORS' INTRODUCTION	xi
FATHER BAEGERT'S INTRODUCTION	5
PART ONE: *Of California Itself, Its Characteristics, Climate, and Products*	9
PART TWO: *Of the Inhabitants of California*	51
PART THREE: *Of the Arrival of the Spaniards, Introduction of the Christian Faith, and of the Missions*	105
APPENDIX ONE: *False Reports about California and the Californians*	173
APPENDIX TWO: *False Reports about the Missionaries in California*	185
JESUIT MISSIONARIES IN BAJA CALIFORNIA, 1697–1768	201
TRANSLATORS' NOTES	203
INDEX	213

ILLUSTRATIONS

Father Baegert's Mission San Luis Gonzaga	135
Nuestro Padre San Ignacio de Kadakaamang	136
Santa Rosalía de Mulegé	136
San Francisco Xavier de Biaundo	137
Side Door of Mission San Francisco Xavier	138
Tower of Mission San Francisco Xavier	139
Father Baegert's Profession, August 15, 1754	140
Nuestra Señora de Loreto, Mother Mission of the Californias	141
Ruins of the Chapel of Mission San Juan Londó	142

TRANSLATORS' INTRODUCTION

Two hundred years have passed since Father Johann Jakob Baegert, S.J., arrived at Mission San Luis Gonzaga in Lower California. He remained in charge of that lonely outpost for seventeen years, leaving it when forced to do so by the royal decree of June, 1767, which expelled all members of the Society of Jesus from the possessions of the Spanish Crown in the New World.

After Father Baegert returned to Europe in April, 1769, he spent a short time in his native city Schlettstadt (Sélestat), in Alsace, then went to live at the collegium at Neustadt in the Rhenish Palatinate, where he served as "spiritual adviser and father confessor." He died at Neustadt, September 29, 1772.[1]

With the impressions of his recent experiences still fresh in his memory, Father Baegert wrote an account of his observations in Lower California entitled *Nachrichten von der Amerikanischen Halbinsel Californien*. This book was first published in Mannheim, Germany, in 1771; a year later a second edition appeared for which Father Baegert made some corrections and added a map of the peninsula of California, the work of another Jesuit, Father Ferdinand Konschak, California missionary and explorer.

Father Baegert was born in Schlettstadt, Alsace, on December 22, 1717. The register of baptism of the Parish of St. Georges, Sélestat, shows that Joannes Jacobus Baegert, son of Michaelis Joannes Baegert, maker of gloves and leathergoods, and Maria Magdalena (Scheideck) Baegert, was baptized on December 23, 1717, in the presence of the god parents Josephus Wirth, merchant, and Anna Maria (Scheideck) Stahl.[2]

There were seven children in the Baegert family: four sons and three daughters. One son became a secular priest, one joined the Capuchin

---

[1] *Jahreskatalog der oberrhein. Prov. Totenverzeichnis*, p. 34.
[2] The record of baptism was obtained through the courtesy of Mr. P. Adam, of the Bibliothèque et Archives de Sélestat, France.

order, two entered the Society of Jesus. Two daughters also entered religious orders; the third one married.

Johann Jakob,[3] youngest of the brothers, received his early schooling at Schlettstadt, and began his novitiate in Mainz, Germany, on September 17, 1736. From 1740 to 1743 he taught grammar, syntax, and poetics at the collegium at Mannheim. The next four years he spent at Molsheim where he received his training in theology. During the fourth year at Molsheim he was admitted to Holy Orders. In 1747 and 1748 Father Baegert was professor at the collegium at Hagenau, Alsace, where he also acted as president of the Young Workers' Association (Arbeiterjugend). Late in 1748 he was assigned as missionary to the West Indies, and was sent to Bockenheim (Bouquenon), Lorraine, to await further directions.[4]

On February 10, 1749, Father Baegert left Bockenheim to begin the long journey to the New World. He traveled by mailcoach via Ettlingen, Augsburg, Innsbruck, and Milan to Genoa, where he arrived on March 20, 1749.[5]

Ten weeks later he left the Italian port to proceed to Puerto Santa María (Cadiz), Spain. The British merchant vessel which carried Father Baegert was slowed down by unfavorable weather, and instead of the usual ten days or less, it took forty-two days to reach Cadiz.

At the Hospitium de las Indias, in Cadiz, the young missionary received the information that he was to go to Mexico. This, he wrote, was welcome news, because "several provinces in the temperate zone, as for instance California, New Mexico, and others belonged to the Kingdom of Mexico. Also the exchange of letters [with Europe] was much easier." [6]

But the young missionary had to wait for nearly a year before he could continue his journey to Mexico. Moorish pirates had seized several ships, and fear of capture kept most of the merchant vessels in port until about

---

[3] Probably in honor of his admired uncle, Father Jakob Baegert, S.J., of Kaysersberg, Alsace.

[4] From the work of Dr. J. Gass, *Elsässische Jesuiten* (Strassburg, Le Roux, 1918), pp. 43–79.

[5] Letter written by "Pater Jacobi Begert [Latin spelling], Selestadiensis Soc. Jesu, Missionarii" to his brother Father Georg Baegert, S.J., Genoa, March 29, 1749.

[6] Letter written by Father Baegert to his brother, Puerto Santa María, Spain, August 11, 1749.

Translators' Introduction

twenty ships were assembled in Cadiz. Convoyed by two warships, each armed with twenty-eight cannons, the fleet finally sailed from Puerto Santa María on June 16, 1750.

Father Baegert was passenger on the *Condé*, a trading-ship, built and owned by French merchants, but sailing under the Spanish flag while trading with Mexico. The *Condé* just missed being sunk at the very beginning of the voyage when it was rammed by another vessel of the fleet, the *Loreto*. After that incident there were no further mishaps and the journey to Mexico was accomplished in "only seventy-two days." On August 23, 1750, Father Baegert landed at Vera Cruz, Mexico.

In September of the same year he completed his third year of probation at the Collegium San Gregorio in Mexico City. Two months later the Provincial, Father Johann Balthasar, of Lucerne, Switzerland, informed Baegert that he was to go "almost immediately to Blessed California." [7]

From the reports of another Jesuit the reader can get a general idea of the missionary field in Lower California several years before Father Baegert was sent there. Father Lambert Hostel of Münstereifel, Germany, had journeyed in 1737 over the same road Baegert was to take thirteen years later and had done the pioneer work at Mission San Luis Gonzaga. In letters to his family, dated San Luis, September 27, 1743, Father Hostel wrote that he had been ordered to start a new mission among the Guaicura tribe. To prepare him for this task he was sent to Mission Dolores to assist the aged Father Guillén and to learn the Guaicura language, "which was different from the other California languages." Father Hostel described California as "a land, savage, rough, dry and unproductive throughout." The inhabitants, he wrote, were a barbarous nation, chestnut-brown, with pierced ears and noses.

A year later, in 1740, he had gathered seven hundred Guaicuras and could begin with the foundation of the new mission. Marqués Luis de Velasco had donated ten thousand Mexican pesos. This sum was sufficient to build and decorate the church and to purchase food and clothing for the missionary and his Indians. All the necessary supplies for the California missions were, at that period, brought from the Mexican mainland, carried by two ships which made the crossing once a year.

---

[7] Letter written by Father Baegert to his brother, Mexico City, October 21, 1750.

Observations in Lower California

"Should one or the other of these ships fail to reach our shores, we would suffer great hunger in this infertile and dry land." [8]

There is a later informative letter, written by Father Hostel in 1758, which contains some facts of a general nature; although it does not deal exclusively with the work and conditions at San Luis, we thought parts of it should be included in this introduction.

Father Hostel had spent some of the intervening years trying to lay the foundation for a new mission on the west coast of the peninsula. This mission was to be called "Holy Trinity." But lack of funds had forced him to abandon this project. He also mentioned that the failure to send additional missionaries to California had hindered the expansion toward the northern part of the peninsula.

In his opinion, the persistent shortage of water was the cause of all the misery in Lower California. Because of this everlasting drought "the cautious Originator of all nature appears to have provided most wisely that the inhabitants of this peninsula do not increase as rapidly as the human race does elsewhere." In 1758 there were eight German and four Spanish missionaries in Lower California. Half of that number would have been enough to take care of the spiritual needs of the Indians. But the great number of different dialects spoken by the natives complicated the work. The Guaicuras, for instance, spoke four different dialects. In many families the husband spoke one language, the wife another. Older missionaries ascribed this difference to a constant influx of heathen from the north. These migrants also reported that their own country was much more fertile and more densely populated. But although the Jesuits had hoped, since the time of Father Salvatierra, to extend the chain of missions northward, they had not yet been fortunate enough to cross the border of the peninsula where it joins the continent.[9]

Father Baegert left Mexico City on November 16, 1750. A detailed account of his trip to San Luis Gonzaga [10] is to be found in a letter to

---

[8] Father Hostel's letters were published in *Der Neue Welt-Bott, Allerhand so Lehr- als Geistreiche Brief-Schrifften und Reis-Beschreibungen von denen Missionariis der Gesellschaft Jesu* (5 vols., 40 parts, Augsburg and Graz, 1642–1758). Photostat copies of these letters were obtained through the Reverend Peter M. Dunne, S.J.

[9] *Ibid.*

[10] Mission San Luis Gonzaga was founded by Father Hostel, later administered by Father Baegert. It ended its existence as a mission in 1768, shortly

Translators' Introduction

his brother, Stanislaus Ignaz Baegert, a Capuchin monk at Schlettstadt. It was written at San Luis Gonzaga, and dated September 11, 1752.[11] He wrote that he traveled with nine other missionaries (seven Germans, one Mexican, one Spaniard). They had been supplied with mules to ride and to carry the baggage, and were accompanied by twelve drivers, both Indians and Spaniards. On December 19, the caravan entered Guadalajara. "After Mexico [City]," Baegert wrote, Guadalajara is the best city on the whole fearful journey." The "Royal Road" to California wound through Tepíc, Rosario, Culiacán, Los Alancos (or Los Frayles). After leaving Guadalajara the missionaries traversed the present Mexican states of Nayarít, Sinaloa, and Sonora, and arrived at Yaqui, at the mouth of the Río Yaqui, south of Guaymas, on March 9, 1751.

Of the long journey on muleback Father Baegert wrote: "Except for Guadalajara and one or two other towns, the rest of the architecture consisted only of one-story adobe construction. The roads in general are still as they were in the year One after creation of the world. From Guadalajara to Yaqui one sees fewer villages, houses, or people than in the open country in Alsace, on half a day's ride on the mailcoach." He saw twelve or fifteen hamlets, of two or three dozen scattered huts, no larger than the pigsties in Alsace. These, and six small towns inhabited by Spaniards were all the settlements he had seen. The houses were very simply constructed and on a level with the open field. In contrast with the poor housing was "such a display of female finery, especially in Culiacán and Los Frayles as can hardly be found in Mexico City, let

---

after the expulsion of the Jesuits from Lower California. On August 20, 1768, Don José de Gálvez sent the Guaicura Indians of San Luis Gonzaga to Mission Todos Santos. On April 24, 1769, he gave the mission "with its house, church, lands, waters and pastures" in perpetuity to the retired Spanish soldier Felipe Romero. But Señor Romero thought the place too lonely and isolated, and returned the property almost immediately in exchange for a land grant in San José del Cabo. San Luis was then given to Señor Pablo de la Toba, whose descendants held it until comparatively recent years. The present owner of the Rancho San Luis Gonzaga is Señor Don Augustín Arreola of La Paz, Baja California. (Historic dates from Pablo L. Martinez' *Efemérides Californianas*, Mexico, D.F., 1950.)

[11] From "Brief eines Elsässers an seinen Bruder in Schlettstadt," *Patriotischer Elsässer* (Strassburg and Colmar, 1777). This letter was addressed to Father Stanislaus Baegert, dated San Luis, September 11, 1752. Father Stanislaus noted at the bottom of the letter that it arrived in Schlettstadt on September 18, 1753.

Observations in Lower California

alone in Alsace." While on the road, the missionaries' meals consisted of sun-dried beef, beans, and "little pancakes made of cornmeal." Sometimes they stopped in one of the towns for six days, or even longer, and received "good and free hospitality from Spanish clergymen and others who considered it an honor and were pleased to have Europeans stay with them."

After his arrival at Yaqui, Father Baegert went to visit the missions of Sonora while waiting for transportation to Lower California. This "transportation" was "a hollow tree, approximately nine ells long, one and a half ells wide, and about as high." In this frail craft Father Baegert left Sonora on May 7, 1751, to cross the Gulf of California. He seems to have been extremely lucky in view of the difficulties encountered by others who made the same voyage before and after him. After two and a half days—sometimes rowing, sometimes sailing—he landed at Loreto, greeted with a salvo by the local garrison.

On May 26, he left Loreto accompanied by a soldier and several Indians. After a ride of thirty hours he arrived at San Luis on May 28, 1751. Here he found "a tiny church which had collapsed during a recent storm," and two small huts which were to serve as his living quarters, also in need of much repair. About his parishioners he wrote that he found "no more than three hundred and sixty souls, children and adults of both sexes. Several missions have even less."

When Father Baegert came to San Luis he noted that most of the Indians were naked, and a year later they still preferred to do without clothing. When the men came to the mission "they covered themselves with a piece of cloth which the missionary gave them, or which they received from the Spanish soldiers in trade for tanned deerskins. They never wash themselves except when they are forced to do so, and lie practically buried in dust and ashes most of the time. And since they perspire freely, one can easily imagine what they look like afterward. Often I do not recognize even those whom I know very well." Speaking of the physical characteristics of the Indians Father Baegert wrote: "I only mention the color or their skin which I promised to test because I find it so puzzling and have not been able to discover what causes it. Of course, if one wanted to say: 'That is how God created them,' the answer would have been found immediately. But it seems to me they are poor philosophers who go straight to the Lord with their wisdom without

Translators' Introduction

first trying to examine the Divine motive. It certainly could not be God's punishment, as some have maintained, because it is the same whether my skin is light or dark. Also, if it were a punishment for paganism, why does it not turn light as soon as they become Christians? Nor can it be just a common natural phenomenon, otherwise, why would the Spaniards and others remain white as before, even after living here two hundred years?"

Every mission had several rancherías where the Indians lived when they were not required to stay at the mission; San Luis Gonzaga had three. Father Baegert explained that the rancherías were not permanent settlements, but rather temporary "encampments" where his parishioners met after spending the day hunting for food. He referred to them as his three "brigades," one camping toward the north, one toward the east, and the third one on the west coast near the Pacific Ocean. The western "brigade" was the "richest," because it had fish and turtles. The location of the nightly gathering place depended on available waterholes. When one "storage tank" went dry, the Indians moved to the next.

The language of the Guaicura Indians, Father Baegert noted, was exceedingly primitive. The translation of the whole Christian doctrine into the Guaicura idiom required only thirty-five sentences, or five handwritten pages.

Before he came to California, Baegert had often wondered why it was necessary to send priests from Europe to become the pastors of the American Indians. But once among the native Californians he understood why they could not yet become priests or scholars, or fill other responsible positions. There were several natives who had become priests in Mexico City, but they were raised, from early childhood, in Spanish families.

In his letter Baegert also spoke gratefully of Father Hostel, the founder of San Luis, who was then in charge of the neighboring Mission Dolores (Our Lady of Sorrows). Hostel aided his young colleague in every way, gave him valuable advice, sent him fresh fruit and vegetables, and came to visit him at isolated San Luis.

At Mission Dolores, and in the presence of Father Hostel, Baegert made his solemn profession in 1754.[12] The sincere devotion to his work

---

[12] The copy of Father Baegert's solemn profession was obtained from the Archives of the Society of Jesus, in Rome, through the courtesy of the Reverend Josef Teschitel, S.J.

which speaks through the lines of his letters was recognized by his co-workers and superiors. Although he never spoke about it in his *Nachrichten*, the catalogue of the Society of Jesus for the years 1758 and 1764 carried the following short notice: "Pater Jacobus Baegert, S.J., est missionarius, fuit Superior." [13] As Superior of the California missions he visited each establishment on the peninsula. Thus he had the opportunity of becoming well acquainted with the work and progress at the other missions, and with the characteristics of the territory.

When Baegert arrived in California in 1751 there were sixty-two soldiers stationed on the peninsula "maintained by the zeal and generosity of the King of Spain" for the protection of the missionaries. "They were stationed wherever a rebellion might break out. I have five of them here." [14] The salary of each soldier was eight hundred pesos a year. Commenting upon the expenses of maintaining and supplying the soldiers and the missions of Lower California, Father Baegert remarked: "If the money, donations, real property, and interest were divided among the native families they could afford to become Knights of the Holy Roman Empire and ride around in carriages. Good luck and a long life to Ferdinand VI, and Eternal Peace for Philip of Anjou!"

The chief recreation of the missionary of San Luis Gonzaga, the most isolated location on the peninsula, was reading. There were some books at the mission and he had brought more with him from Europe. He

---

Ego Iacobus Begert Professionem facio, et promitto Omnipotenti Deo, coram ejus Virgine Matre, et universa Coelesti curia, ac omnibus circumstantibus; et tibi Reverendo Patri Lamberto Hostell Visitatori vice Propositi Generalis Societatis Iesu, et Sucessorum ejus, locum Dei tenenti; perpetuam Paupertatem, Castitatem et Obedientiam; et Secundum eam peculiarem curam circa puerorum eruditionem, juxta formam vivendi, in litteris Apostolicis Societatis Iesu, et en ejus constitutionibus contentam.

Insuper promitto Specialem Obedientiam Summo Pontificii circa missiones; pro ut in eisdem litteris Apostolicis et Constitutionibus continetur. in Missione a Doloribus B. M. V. in California. Die decima quinta Augusti, Anno Millisimo Septingentesimo Quinquagesimo quarto in Ecclesia dictae Missionis Sanctatis Iesu.

IHS
Jacobus Begert
(rubric)

[13] *Carta Anua*, 1768 and 1764 (Mex. 8, fol. 135, n. 674; fol. 198, n. 579).
[14] "Brief eines Elsässers an seinen Bruder in Schlettstadt," *Patriotische Elsässer*, 1777.

Translators' Introduction

informed his brother that he had seventy-eight volumes and pamphlets, forty-six of them were French, and nearly all on religious subjects. He asked for more books "the kind one likes to read several times, because they are important companions in such complete isolation." The type of reading matter he requested shows clearly the wide scope of his interests: "the works of Huet,[15] some good new French historians, Bossuet, and above all some poetry, comedies, dramas, and the like." He also would like to be informed of new developments in the scientific world, and recent publications about the Church and theology, and asked for a history of Jansenism.

Father Baegert confides in his letter that the life of a missionary, at least in California, was far different from what he had thought it to be when he lived in Alsace. In Europe it was generally assumed that a missionary "lived in a hollow tree, or in a green bower, slept on tigerskins, walked barefooted, the pilgrim's staff in hand, and lived exclusively on roots." The books he had consulted before he left home proved to be full of misinformation. He had believed an established mission was "an organized, settled, and civilized group of natives, wearing clothes, living in a community of small homes, working at agriculture, and other necessary trades." He had thought that a missionary, who was ordered to start a new mission, "could complete a decent little village in a few years." All this was far from the truth. Nor was he the only one who found that the reality had little in common with the earlier dreams and descriptions. Nearly all missionaries in California had been equally duped. But this, he added "was really no one's fault, because who, in Europe, would ever look for a land like California on the face of the globe?"

Since he left his native soil, however, he was in good spirits and content with his lot; he had never been sick or melancholy for an hour. "Health is necessary here, and melancholy is useless."

He concluded his report about the Indians, their way of life and struggle for existence with the words: "Yet this should not deter anyone in Europe from seeking to serve in American missions. Just because the Indians are less numerous, they must not be left helpless. The more forsaken a people is, the more miserable the land it lives on, the more worthy it is of compassion: so it would not come from the rain into the

---

[15] Pierre Daniel Huet, Bishop of Avranches, 1691; editor of Origen's *Commentaries* and well known for his writings on Descartes.

Observations in Lower California

brook, from a temporal hell to an eternal one. I confess that up to now I have felt no regrets, nor do I see how I should ever have any. I am happy, especially because I realize daily more and more how many who are working in Europe may appear very important, but they achieve nothing, neither for themselves nor for others. Self-love has absolutely no value here."

Nachrichten

von der

Amerikanischen Halbinsel

Californien:

---

mit einem

zweyfachen

Anhang falscher Nachrichten.

Geschrieben

von einem

Priester der Gesellschaft Jesu,

welcher lang darinn diese letztere Jahr
gelebt hat.

Mit Erlaubnuß der Oberen.

Mannheim,
gedruckt in der Churfürstl. Hof- und Academie-
Buchdruckerey 1772.

Reports

from the
American Peninsula

California

With a

twofold

Appendix of False Reports

===

Written

by a

Priest of the Society of Jesus
Who Has Lived There in the
Years Past

With Permission of the Superiors

Mannheim

Printed by the Electoral Court and Academy Press

1772

CONTENTS

INTRODUCTION 5

PART ONE: *Of California Itself, Its Characteristics, Climate, and Products*

CHAPTER
1. Of the Location, Longitude, Latitude, and Size of California, and of the Gulf 11
2. Of the Heat, the Cold, and the Four Seasons of the Year in California 15
3. Of the Rainfall, the Rivers, and Other Waters of California 19
4. Of the Character, Fertility, and Barrenness of the Soil of California 24
5. Of the Trees, Shrubs, and Thorn Bushes of California 30
6. Of the Fruits of California 34
7. Of the Quadrupeds, Fish, Fowl, and Birds of California 37
8. Of the Vermin of California 40
9. Of the Pearl Fisheries and the Mines of California 44

PART TWO: *Of the Inhabitants of California*
1. Of the Physical Appearance of the Californians, Their Color and Number, When and How They Might Have Come to California 53
2. Of the Habitations and Shelters of the Californians 58
3. Of the Manner of Dress and Decoration of the Californians 61
4. Of Property and Utensils, of Labor and Occupations of the Californians 63
5. Of Food and Drink, of Cooking and the Voracity of the Californians 65

Contents

6. Of Marriage and the Education of Children in California   72
7. Of Diseases and Medicines, of Death and the Burial Customs of the Californians   76
8. Of the Character, Nature, and Customs of the Californians   80
9. Of Certain Mores and Manners of Living of the Californians   87
10. Of the Language and the Manner of Speech of the Californians   94

PART THREE: *Of the Arrival of the Spaniards, Introduction of the Christian Faith, and of the Missions*

1. Futile Expeditions of the Spaniards to California. Father Salvatierra Gains a Firm Footing and Establishes Mission Loreto   107
2. Of the Progress of the Established Missions and of the Founding of New Ones   110
3. Of the Revenues and the Administration of the Missions   119
4. Of the Churches in California, Their Furnishings and Ornaments   124
5. Of Agriculture in California   128
6. Of the Livestock in California   131
7. Of the Soldiers, Sailors, Craftsmen, as well as of Buying and Selling in California   145
8. Of the Death of the Two Jesuit Fathers, Támaral and Carranco   150
9. Some Questions Directed to Protestants and Particularly to Protestant Ministers   156
10. Of the Arrival of Don Gaspar Portolá and the Departure of the Jesuits from California   165

APPENDIX ONE: *False Reports about California and the Californians*   175

APPENDIX TWO: *False Reports about the Missionaries in California*   187

INTRODUCTION

Everything concerning California [1] is of such little importance that it is hardly worth the trouble to take a pen and write about it. Of poor shrubs, useless thorn bushes and bare rocks, of piles of stone and sand without water or wood, of a handful of people who, besides their physical shape and ability to think, have nothing to distinguish them from animals, what shall or what can I report? However, because California forms no small part of that New World about which the Old World desires information; and because all the modern geographers and cosmologists tell about it, and none of them tells the truth; furthermore, because a short time ago the same California caused (in Mexico as well as in Madrid) a great deal of clamor because of its imaginary riches, some of which may even have been heard in Germany; and finally, because in Europe one hears and reads with equal interest of the poverty and misery as of the abundance and wealth, of the stupidity and animal-like existence as well as of the accomplishments and good government of peoples beyond the ocean; I decided to accede to the demands of my good friends and other respected persons and, through a short description of the land and other things connected with it, to satisfy the craving curiosity of the public, as well as to refute the falsehoods and defamations of some of the writers.

I am able to do this without difficulty, since it was my lot to live in California for seventeen years. During that time I have wandered up and down its length for a distance of eighty hours, and have seen both coasts several times. Also I have talked with others who have lived there for more than thirty years, and who have more than once (as far as the land is explored) [2] wandered from one end of it to the other, or who have lived for a considerable length of time in various parts of the country: toward the south, in the north, or in the central part.

---

[1] For the translators' numbered notes, see pages 203–211.

Observations in Lower California

About twelve years ago reports concerning California had already appeared in Madrid—three rather bulky volumes in folio, which have been translated into English (much abbreviated, as a recent translation from this same English text into the French language seems to indicate).[3] Now I hear, and received news from Austria only a few days before I started to write, that a German translation of this same English text has also appeared; wherefore this little work would seem superfluous.

However, if the French version of the original English translation (of which the German must be an echo) is exact, the English translation contains two principal faults. 1. It contains (the high-sounding title included) various falsehoods which could not have been in the Spanish original, or if they were, should have been deleted. 2. Although it is only half the size of the large Spanish work, another half could have and should have been omitted if the purpose of the book was to report to the public what it wishes to know about California. And to make such a report is exactly what I shall endeavor to do.

The worthy Spaniards enjoy writing extensive volumes and at times fill their books with all sorts of unnecessary descriptions, dragged in by the hair and augmented by superfluous torrents of words, which the first English translator should have pushed aside and eliminated even more than he did. For instance: What good are long-winded introductions to almost every chapter? Or the lengthy and dry narrations which do not interest anyone in England, France, or Germany? What good, say I, serve such ramblings except to raise the price of books? Instead of pleasure and interest, they give boredom and drowsiness to the reader. What has Rome and Carthage, Columbus and Marco Polo, the Peruvian quippos[4] or the Peruvian style of writing, or an extensive list of no less than forty-three naturalists to do with California or California's history? Why bring in the fights of the Apaches, the Seris, and the Tepocas, whom a whole ocean separates from California, and who never had anything to do with California? Or the expeditions of a Vásquez Coronado to the legendary Cibola? Or Paratax, king of the fictitious Quivira?[5] Or the travels of a Father Sedelmayr[6] to the Gila and Colorado rivers, which are not in California? What cares an Englishman, Frenchman, or German about the delays and many deliberations of the law courts of Mexico and Guadalajara? Aside from a few short remarks on ethics and chapter nine in the Third Part, the reader will find herein only that which directly

Introduction

concerns California and that which should serve to satisfy and stimulate a laudable curiosity, since the entire little work represents the answer to the many questions asked of me after my return.

I must remind the sympathetic reader to remember the following:

1. In writing these reports, I have used neither the large Spanish book, which I read in part ten years ago while still in California, and which I have long since forgotten; nor the English translation, which language I do not understand; nor the French translation. I have relied exclusively upon my own experience; therefore I cite as proof only what I have seen and encountered in person or what I was told by those who have lived with me in California.

2. In these reports the reader must not expect to find great wonders of nature or other extraordinary occurrences and events. California is not the land to produce the latter, nor has it pleased the Creator to bestow any of the former. The reader must not even expect to find here such things as are described by others in reports about equally small territories and tribes of America in general. Because of the all-too-great infertility, the narrowness of the peninsula, and the very limited number of its inhabitants, the Californians, even those who speak the same language, have never formed a national body or a real republic among themselves. They have remained at all times divided into very small groups which, so to speak, live in a long row from south to north, widely separated, without authority, without commercial or social contacts with one another except only the visits of immediate neighbors. Just as in each one of these groups few things occur worth mentioning, so is there little or nothing remarkable to relate concerning the people as a whole. And again, nothing very edifying can be told about the Californians because the results of our work among them, in terms of the applied toil and diligence, are very poor indeed, though the reason for that must in part be attributed to the inferior quality of the land. After religious instruction, it was not difficult to persuade the majority of the Californians to be baptized; they had no other religion with which to contradict the teachings of Christ. But no human effort was adequate to make them practice what they had promised at baptism. However, had all the labor among the adults been fruitless (which was not always the case), the more than fourteen thousand young Californians who have been sent to heaven during the last seventy years is reward enough for the efforts of the missionaries,

Observations in Lower California

and represents a generous return on the money expended partly by the three Catholic Kings and partly by private citizens for California.*

3. Much of what I shall report is not so completely characteristic of California that it does not equally apply to other districts, inhabitants, or missions of America. But are there not many among my readers who know as little of the one as of the other?

4. California is an extensive land, sparsely populated, but the home of many tribes, which in some instances live thirty hours or more apart. Whosoever detects some discrepancies in reading about the weather, the customs and manners, the language and similar things, told by others who, like myself, have spent many years in California, let him remember what I have just said. It is not strange to find such differences if one considers the remoteness and the many tribal groups, although in general, I can safely say that everything in California is made on the same last.

5. In the following index or contents some things are listed to give the reader information not only about what there is in California, but also about what there is not.

6. Now and then I shall include a bit of moral philosophy, just as it comes to my mind while I write. If that should appear against my intention, since I promised merely to report, may I remind the reader that such is not in conflict with my position and my profession.

7. Throughout this work I am using the word "hour" instead of "miles," since the miles are not everywhere of equal length, not even within Germany; but when I say "one hour" or "one hour's walk," everyone knows that and can easily imagine it.

8. If my style of writing is uneven and somewhat faltering, and when at times the orthography is incorrect, please consider that during seventeen years, from 1751 to 1768, I rarely found an opportunity to speak German and for that reason have nearly forgotten my native language. However, concerning various new expressions which I found when I returned to the Rhineland [in 1769], I wish to say that I have deliberately refused to use these; some of them are affectations and others have needlessly been resurrected from a remote age.

---

* It is related that Philip V, when advised to relinquish the Mariana Islands because they did not provide an income to the Spanish Crown, but caused great expenditures, asked whether children were still baptized in those islands. When answered in the affirmative, he replied, "Then the money which the islands cost us is well spent."

PART ONE : OF CALIFORNIA ITSELF
ITS CHARACTERISTICS, CLIMATE,
AND PRODUCTS

CHAPTER ONE : *Of the Location, Longitude, Latitude, and Size of California, and of the Gulf*

CALIFORNIA, the land in the extreme West, is a part of North America and, as one may see from the maps, constitutes an appendix or tail which is the narrowest of one of the world's longest peninsulas. It is separated from the Mexican Empire by an arm of the Pacific Sea, as Egypt from Arabia by the Red Sea, or Italy from Greece by the Adriatic. This arm has a width of about one hundred and fifty hours at Cabo San Lucas, the southernmost point of California, and becomes narrower the nearer it comes to the Red River (Río Colorado) in the north, where California is joined to the mainland. In 1751, I crossed this California Red Sea, as some call it, in a hollow tree (a small boat of one piece) at the twenty-eighth degree northern latitude without seeing either the shore I had left or the one I was approaching throughout the second day of the journey. This will give an indication of the width of this arm of the ocean.

The aforementioned Red River is, of all the waters which empty into the almost four-hundred-hour-long California ocean, the only one that deserves to be called "river," and near California it is more than a quarter of an hour wide. All the others found on the maps are hardly more than rain-water courses, which during the greater part of the year have very little water, so that it is possible to ride through them without wetting one's shoes. However, in all of them abide alligators of considerable size, and since some of them are capable of devouring a full-grown man, it is necessary to be on guard while drawing water, bathing, or washing. I have seen several of these creatures. As everyone knows, they resemble a lizard, but are completely clad in armor like a turtle. Not many years ago it was discovered in America that the eyeteeth of alligators are a strong antidote. By applying to the wound or swallowing some of the powder scraped from such teeth, the lives of many who have been bitten by snakes have been saved.

Observations in Lower California

Along the California coast, the Gulf of California is studded with islands of various sizes. This fact would indicate that the peninsula was once much wider than it is now, or was possibly at one time part of the Mexican mainland. Some of these islands were still inhabited in this century, especially the three: Catalána, Ceralbo, and the one called San José. Either by trading or by force, the inhabitants of these islands had acquired small boats from the pearl fishers and begun to practice piracy. However, after they were put out of trade in 1715 by California soldiers, some of them died out, and others were transferred to the missions in California. These and other islands are now deserted. They may be regarded as suburbs or anterooms of California, and from the barren appearance of their mountains and rocky cliffs one gets a foretaste of California misery and the poverty of the land.

After Father Ferdinand Konschak,[7] a Jesuit from Hungary, investigated and explored the entire east coast of California as far as the Colorado River (which he followed upstream for several hours in 1746), it can no longer be doubted that California is a peninsula, bounded by the sea on three sides only, rather than completely surrounded as was once believed. Nevertheless, to confirm this conclusion, and because the results of Father Konschak's exploration were questioned by scientists in Mexico and Spain regarding the angles at the left side of the mouth of the Colorado River, where for several miles the low and swampy shore made the close approach of a boat or an attempt to land impossible, Father Wenceslaus Linck of Bohemia (who was in charge of Mission San Borja, the last to the north at that time) was ordered in the year 1766 to proceed overland to the aforementioned river. As the crow flies, the distance from San Borja to the mouth of the Colorado River is only about ninety hours, but he who has not seen California or similar countries in America has no idea what it means to undertake a journey of ninety hours over land without roads, where all is rock and stone, where water reservoirs are unknown, and all provisions and equipment, sometimes water too, have to be lugged along. For instance, in a straight line the distance between Mission San Xavier and the Bay of Santa Magdalena is not more than thirty hours, yet the first traveler required nineteen days in which to complete this journey. Accordingly, Father Linck [8] started on his way in the company of sixteen soldiers and more than a hundred natives, but after four weeks he had proceeded no farther than the region of San Bona-

Of California Itself

ventura, which is still twenty or thirty hours distant from the Red River [Rio Colorado]. Here, as far as the eye could reach, he encountered nothing but pure sand between the north and the east and toward the California Sea.

Many Indians became sick. Horses and mules, shod for the first time with poorly fitted horseshoes, were weary. But especially tired were the soldiers, who saw that aside from hardship and danger the undertaking would provide no profit. They therefore remonstrated and insisted that it was impossible to continue the march to the north. Had there been hope of encountering mountains of gold, they would not have lacked the strength to carry on another hundred miles, barefoot, half-naked, without provisions, as they had done more than once before. It is deplorable that the undertaking should have come to such an end. Now, it may take another half century until someone else reaches the non plus ultra of Father Linck, unless the British conquests in North America during the last war or the expeditions of the Russians from Kamchatka (who already in 1741 made a landing north of California in America) force Spain to it.

The length of California must be considered as far more than three hundred hours, since the ten degrees latitude (counting each degree at fifteen German miles, and each mile at two hours) from Cabo San Lucas (under the twenty-second degree) to the mouth of the Río Colorado (under the thirty-second degree), between which two points I place California, more than account for the three hundred hours. Even if California ran in a straight line from south to north, this would be true; but as a matter of fact, the peninsula shows a marked inclination from east to west, which adds a number of miles to its length.

I said that I place California between Cabo San Lucas and the mouth of the Colorado River, for to extend it beyond this point would mean to enlarge California to immense proportions without need or reason. Many geographers like to extend it to Cabo Blanco,[9] or perhaps even to Mendocino (under the forty-first degree north latitude), especially the Spanish, since under Captain Sebastián de Viscaya the west coast of North America was sighted from the water by the Spaniards as far up as this point. I set the borders of California where nature seems to have placed them; that is, where nature has appended the very long and no less narrow California peninsula to the more than one-thousand-hours-wide continent of North America. I feel justified in doing this, since the soil

Observations in Lower California

and other conditions, as well as the natives and their language, above the thirty-second degree north latitude, are entirely different from those in the already known and explored part of California, as can be read in the diary of the aforementioned Biscayan ship's captain. The two promontories named before (Cabo Blanco and Mendocino) are on the mainland several hundred hours from where the peninsula is joined to the continent.

I know well that the Duchy of Milan and the rest of Lombardy, which is also on the continent, is part of Italy, which is also a peninsula; but I know too that the distance from Genoa and Venice to Tyrol and Carinthia is not very great; that Italy, from Calabria to Lombardy, gradually expands; that the same fertility, the same language, and the same customs prevail with small exceptions in all the provinces which are regarded as part of Italy. In our case, it is exactly the opposite.

The width of California is all out of proportion to its extraordinary length; it is approximately sixteen times narrower than it is long. Nowhere is it more than fifteen to twenty hours wide. I lived in the center of it, at twenty-five degrees latitude, north, opposite the small Bay of Santa Magdalena, and was able to reach either of the two seas between which California rises within eight hours on horseback over a path that was neither straight nor level. Perhaps because of insufficient information, or perhaps because California would otherwise be almost invisible (on universal maps at least), the cartographers have added many more miles to the width of California than it actually possesses.

Concerning the longitude, it is possible that the French astronomer [10] who was sent to California in 1768 to observe the passage of Venus may be able to give us the facts, for until now nobody has considered it worth the effort to establish and determine it. This explains the difference in the longitude of California as noted on the maps. As for the rest, it seems that the sun rises about nine hours later for the Californians than for those who live on the Rhine.

If, from these statements, one may correctly assume that California is only three hundred hours long and twenty hours wide, the area is nearly as large as the entire Swabian and Bavarian Province. This would provide a duchy or kingdom of notable size indeed—if size alone were decisive. But I can assure and solemnly declare that the Catholic King would show no great favor to the man whom he would make feudal lord of California,

Of California Itself

as will become clear from these reports. It would be far more profitable for any man to receive a village of one hundred peasants or to be the mayor of a small market town than to be Grand Duke or Hospodar of California.

As reluctant as we, my colleagues and I, were to leave California, as gladly would the Spanish dragoons and their officers who had come to drive us out have started their homeward journey with us from this afflicted land.

CHAPTER TWO : *Of the Heat, the Cold, and the Four Seasons of the Year in California*

I ASSUME that the weather cannot be exactly alike in all parts of the peninsula, since California extends over a distance of three hundred hours from south to north. However, since it does not go beyond the thirty-third degree latitude, north, and has no forests or particularly high mountains, the winter cannot be long, nor the cold severe. It is known that the fields and gardens of the Spanish province of Andalusia are as green at Christmastide and in January as are the countries on the Rhine at the end of May. Probably no snow has fallen in the region of Cadiz within the memory of man, nor has there been any ice except that brought down from the mountains of Granada, and the women of that region, rich or poor, never have a fan out of their hands; yet Cadiz lies three degrees farther north than the northernmost part of California. On the other hand, since neither the distance from, nor the nearness to, the sun provides the only reason for hot or cold weather in the land, it has sometimes happened at Mission San Borja that the water froze in its containers and snowflakes fell to the ground. Likewise, the south

Observations in Lower California

experiences almost every year several cold nights and frosts which injure the corn. At Mission Todos Santos, which is close to the Tropic of Cancer on the west coast, the grapes would not ripen because of the continuous fresh winds and fog which rise from the Pacific Sea. However, in spite of the occasional cold weather, John Huebner [11] had no right to make defamatory remarks about California and to call it a cold country, thus giving the reader cause to compare California with Norway or Novaya Zemlya. (It would have been well for this gentleman if that had been the only lie he had written; then the Catholic world would have had no reason to nickname him "John Luegner" [John Liar].) Exactly the opposite is true, for California, far from having a cold climate, must be placed among the hot and very warm countries. Some people even want to derive the word "California" from "calida fornax," which means "hot stove"; but I do not agree with this statement. It is certain, however, that the Spaniards did not hear the name of the land from the California natives, as the latter never named the whole peninsula (of which they knew neither whether it was large or small, nor where it started, nor where it ended). Each tribe knew only the region where it lived and wandered, and although each of these regions had a name, none was called "California."

As long as I lived in California, the temperature was seldom cooler than it is along the Rhine at the end of September or April. I felt the cold only a few days of the year if I were inside the house, or until the sun had risen a few yards above the horizon if I chanced to spend a night in the open field. It was different when the north wind blew all day, as happened occasionally; then it became somewhat cool within the house or in the shade. I never had to go near the fire because of being cold, although my garment was only an unlined camlet coat and I wore no underclothing. Once, early in January, when an epidemic of smallpox in a neighboring mission made it necessary for me to go there, I perspired endlessly throughout the journey (from three to eight in the afternoon), although it was a windy day and I did not walk hurriedly. These climatic conditions are most favorable to vegetables sown toward the end of October and the following winter months; since lettuce, beets, cabbages, and the like, sown from the beginning of May onward shoot up too fast and quickly go to seed. Likewise, the wheat which was sown in October

Of California Itself

begins to head out in January, and corn planted in September can be harvested in December or January.

The hottest season of the year begins in July and lasts until about the middle of October. Even after sunset at the beginning of this month, while I was kneeling at the entrance to the church, almost in the open air, reciting the Rosary with the Indians, a profuse perspiration forced me to abandon my place, and I saw several people leaving the vaulted church, half-faint and bathed in sweat, although they were almost naked. Accordingly, I decided in the following years to hold the evening prayer meetings outside the church under the open sky during the summer months. At the beginning of each summer, I had to put aside my underbedding, a mattress of barely three fingers' thickness, and use instead a stretched hide; and though I slept between two open windows, one opposite the other, at times the heat and perspiration kept me awake almost until midnight. During these months, I was careful not to stand hatless in the sun at noontime, not even for a minute. When necessity required me to leave the house or shade and walk but a short distance, everything was immediately damp with perspiration, since the heat reflected from the ground was so intense that it was almost as if I were standing before the open door of a heated stove. In summer when I was called to attend a sick person in a distant place and had to spend the night in the open, I would mount my horse at two in the morning or at midnight to start my return journey in order to be under the shade of the roof before noon, since there was no other shade to be found on the way. I know one priest who assured me that, when at times he was forced for some reason to delay the Sunday morning Mass until ten o'clock, not only his shirt, but also his priestly vestments were wet with perspiration. If, during the heat of the day, it is necessary to make a halt in the open field, it is not possible to sit on a stone without first placing a folded coat or something similar over it. Eight hours are sufficient, even in the shade, to make fresh meat turn green and become alive with maggots. Unless it were possible to butcher every day, one can only preserve the meat for a week by removing the skin and cutting the meat into long, thin, sausage-like strips, which are then well salted and exposed to the sun until hard and dry. Consequently the meat tastes insipid and loses its nutritive value.

Although the heat in California is intense and the summer arid, I have

Observations in Lower California

never heard California natives complain about it, but they certainly do complain about even a light frost in the morning or during the night in winter. This is not surprising, for they are almost naked and without shelter or dwelling. They have no other protection against the cold except the warmth of the fire, about which they lie at full length, turning to roast from side to side all night long, occasionally rising to add fuel. They are not ashamed to lie by the fire until late in the day when other people are already sweating.

Here it is necessary to mention that there are noticeable differences in the temperature in California, not only between the southern and the northern part (as can easily be imagined, and as was stated at the beginning of this chapter), but also between many regions which are situated in the same latitude. On the whole west coast it is considerably cooler throughout the year than on the east coast; this is caused by a strong northwest wind which always makes itself felt on the western shore. Under the same parallel, but on opposite coasts in California, late in November I have had to leave the room at midnight to go out of doors to sleep because of the heat; and on the other hand, in the middle of May I have been compelled, while walking all day, to wear a cap and a coat because of the biting wind and the frost carried with it.

But all days and all seasons are not alike, especially in California. If spring is supposed to be the time when the temperature begins to rise, and fall the time when it starts to diminish, then there is a spring and a fall season in California. But if spring is looked upon as the time of year which breaks the spell of winter and brings forth new grass and hundreds of different flowers to please the eye, the time when meadows and fields cover themselves with pleasing verdure, and fruit and ornamental trees alike lay aside the mourning garb they wore for six months, when nightingales and other birds in field and forest divert us with their singing; or if fall is the time when cellar and fruit loft are stocked for the coming winter, the time to catch larks and other feathered animals, when fogs and chilling rains begin to annoy us, when the fingers become numb with cold, the meadows turn yellow, and the successive frosts cause the forest to shed its leafy adornments; then California knows no spring and no fall. As far as verdure and harvest, clear skies and warm days are concerned, California has continuous winter and everlasting summer. Except for a few, scattered, low-growing evergreen shrubs, no bush will bear

Of California Itself

foliage, nor will the soil bring forth any grass until six to eight days after a good rainfall. This happens rather late in the year (as will be explained in the following chapter) and lasts no longer than three or four weeks, since the excessive heat and the burning sun quickly wilt everything green and cause the leaves to drop.

There is not a day in California that does not bring a rather brisk wind, which surely begins to blow at noon, if not earlier, and continues on into the night. If the wind fails for only a minute during the hottest days of the summer, one is immediately aware of it, for perspiration increases and flows copiously. The prevailing wind in California is from the northwest or from the southwest. A true north wind occurs only now and then during the winter months and lasts only a few days. Not once in seventeen years have I noticed that the wind came from the east (except during a severe storm), which circumstance seems strange in view of the fact that all the clouds in the sky, when there are any, usually come from that direction.

CHAPTER THREE : *Of the Rainfall, the Rivers, and Other Waters of California*

Several years ago the missions of California were accused at the Court of Madrid of trading with the English. Yet there is nothing in California except wacke and other worthless rocks, and it produces nothing but thorns. If the English would accept these and in return import, above all other things, wood and shade, rain and rivers; then to be sure, a trade of great advantage for California could be established with Great Britain. Otherwise, there is nothing to trade. Wood and water, stones and thorns, are four elements of which California has an

Observations in Lower California

unbelievable scarcity of the first two and a great surplus of the others. Nothing is so common in California as rocks and thorns, nothing so rare as moisture, wood, and cool shade. It is not necessary to be afraid of drowning in California, but it is easy to die of thirst. A man only needs to lose his way, which can happen easily, and he may wander whole days or even weeks without finding a drop of water. Only a few years ago, several people whose ship had been wrecked on the coast of California died miserably of thirst, because in spite of their diligent search, they were unable to find water.

Just as the California soil appears to be pure rock, the sky above it seems to be made of steel and bronze; only rarely will it be persuaded to let a beneficial rain fall upon the dry, burned earth. July and August, September and October, are the months in which rain may be hoped for. If there is rain at other times, it is regarded as something extraordinary, and it does not happen every year. But even in the aforementioned months, rain is so scarce that the whole time of rainfall during that period does not add up to much more than three or four hours. Four or five days after the first downpour, everything that can possibly turn green will do so; then for a short time (sometimes in September, but never before the end of that month) there is a faint semblance of spring. However, the same thing happens when, against the established order of things, rainfalls occur unexpectedly in December or January.

These downpours, a rare gift from heaven, are usually accompanied by storms and are by no means widespread or lasting. They cover a territory of about half an hour's to several hours' walk; and since it rains here today and at some other place tomorrow, there are many places in which during three, six, and even more years in succession not even the dust is settled. All the storms I observed (and I could observe them all, partly because in many years not two of them occurred during the night or before eleven o'clock in the morning, and partly because nothing prevented me) came from the east or the north. They are, throughout, not very severe, never two on the same day, and in their greatest force of not more than an hour's duration, after which time the sky is soon as blue as before, the air clear, and the previous quiet restored.

Since the Californians are either insensitive to mortal danger or too devoid of reason to recognize it, they are not afraid of anything. They show no fear of thunder and lightning, but continue to laugh and joke

Of California Itself

even when it seems that the sky is about to fall. This may be due to their ignorance of the causes of thunder and of the effect which lightning has when it strikes anything.

If the storm passes without a cloudburst, as often happens, then it brings only rain. Hail fell only once during my time, and then only a few stones; yet I know of no place where hail could do less damage than in California, where it could neither break windows nor ruin fruit crops and vineyards.

During the four rain months mentioned above, there was never any lack of clouds or other indications of approaching rain, but I have often heard it said that in California it threatens twenty-four times before it rains once. One year, during the month of August, not a single day passed without a storm, but the amount of rain which fell in thirty-one days and as many nights was much less than that which falls in other places in half a forenoon or half an afternoon.

After half an hour or forty-five minutes of good rain, the water, shed by the hard soil, rushes from every side to form a stream, often wide enough to resemble a river, which tears with a great roar of noise (so that one can sometimes hear it at half an hour's distance) and a thousand turns and bends between the rocks and cliffs, only to diminish just as rapidly. In a few hours nothing is left except the former drought, innumerable toads, and a few scattered mud puddles. However, everyone is glad about it, and as they say, the cellars of California are again filled for the year. All water, all swamps and puddles (with few exceptions), of which man or animal can drink and quench his thirst throughout the year are found between the two banks of such temporary rain-water courses. Some of these reservoirs disappear a few weeks or months after the rain, others last throughout the year. If the rains are frequent and those transitory streams flood the ground a number of times, these reservoirs will be well filled, and more water will be available to start the new crops.

These rain-water torrents often cause a great deal of damage, since they break the dikes (which were constructed with much toil to protect a small piece of tillable land) and wash away the earth, or at least a good deal of it, so that nothing is left to the farmer or horticulturist except the bare rocks. Thus it happened that in 1763, when I visited a mission and tried to find an orchard containing fifteen or more very large fig trees and as many pomegranate trees, which I had seen more than a hundred times in the previous year, I could find neither the trees nor the land upon which they had stood only two days before my visit.

From the rains and the rain-caused rivers which occur so infrequently and whose courses are so short, let me now proceed to those nonexistent rivers and other waters whose constant flow is fabled on maps and in some books.

Aside from a very few little trickles (often twenty or more hours apart, some as wide as a straw, others the width of a finger) which spring from rocks but soon lose themselves in the sand, there are in the whole of explored California (a stretch of land more than three hundred hours long) no more than six watercourses. These have only an actual flow of water which can be followed for one or several hours, and they, without doing them injustice, may rightly be called brooks or rivulets. They are to be found in the three missions of San José del Cabo, Santiago, and Todos Santos in the southern end of California, and in the three missions of San José Comondú, Purísima Concepción, and Santa Rosalía toward the north. Of these six little brooks, only four reach the sea, because their source lies not far from the shore. The other two disappear and are lost between the rocks and sand not too far from their origin. It is possible to wade through all six of them or even to jump across their courses without danger of getting water into the mouth.

Thus, after the rain-water freshets have ceased to run, there remains little wet ground or moisture except for the equally scarce swamps, puddles, and in short, still waters of any kind. These still waters are of varied sizes and conditions. A few are as wide, or as long, as a rifle shot and more; others, barely three feet. Some are green with dirt and scum, some are very salty, others, clean and clear and pleasing to the taste; but all of them, whatever they may be, have to be used as drinking fountains. Some will last all year, others will soon dry up. From these storage cellars the natives and other inhabitants of the peninsula draw their Rhine and Moselle wines, their Rosóli and hydromel. In these swamps they bathe; in these waters both man and beast find restoration and refreshment; and before such waters the California Indian lies down on his stomach and drinks like a cow, since as a rule, he has nothing he could use as a dipper. And would to God these communal storage tanks or inns could be found wherever they are needed and were not at times separated by a whole day's journey! If a man has to travel (as I had to do, to a certain place fifteen

Of California Itself

hours from my mission, where now and then some of my parishioners decided to camp), he has to carry water with him in leather containers, for unless he wants to make a long detour, he will find none on the way, and the water at the camp is so brackish that even the horses refuse to drink it. Once, in the middle of October, I was called to another place. I traveled all morning, my thirst growing as intense as the heat. Dismounting, I asked for water. I found it as warm as though it had been kept near a fire; moreover, it tasted extremely salty. But I had to drink, and since there was no other inn near by, I filled a glass bottle and set it to cool in what little shade I could find. After a quarter of an hour, the water was quite refreshing. But the California Indian cannot do likewise. So far nothing is known in California about glass production, and the native has to drink the water, cool or warm, just as he finds it. Yet he is strong and healthy. It seems that much depends on habits, and apparently necessity knows no law.

At the time of the *pitahayas* (they are a juicy fruit which will be discussed in a later chapter) the California Indians can go for several days without drinking water. At other times, while traveling in waterless territory, they carry water with them, either in a turtle bladder or in dried intestines, which are, as a rule, thick as an arm.

Many dense fogs rise in California, but only in the morning, and not only late in the year or in the winter, but sometimes also in the middle of summer and in August. This, however, does not prevent the fogs being followed by an unbearable heat or even a sudden thunderstorm. All these fogs come from the western sea, and they are more frequent in the western part of the peninsula than in the east. Sometimes the fogs carry with them something the Mexicans call *chahuixtle*, which is very damaging to the wheat fields. The dew, which some authors describe as very frequent and copious, does not seem remarkable to me; it does not fall more often nor heavier than in Germany when the sky is clear. As for manna, about which even more fuss was made in some writings, that is just another old fable of the out-dated naturalists. It is a somewhat sweetish dew which very rarely appears upon the leaves of the common cane, and it is as useful in California as the fifth wheel on a wagon in Germany; therefore I have had no desire to see it.

[Pitahaya, *Lemaireocereus thurberi*.]

Observations in Lower California

From what I have said in this and in the preceding chapters, it is clear that: first, there is not sufficient rainfall in the whole country to seed or plant anything except in the vicinity of a swamp or some hidden underground reservoir which keeps the soil moist, or where still or running water is available and can be conveyed to a piece of land, and where the soil (like the meadows in Europe) can be irrigated almost daily. There are very few districts where that is possible, and there were some missions where not even a small garden could be planted and maintained. Also, where there is water, there is often no soil, but merely sand and stones; and where there is soil, there is usually no water, or it lies very deep, or is so situated that it can be used only to drink, wash, or bathe.

Second, according to my observation and experience, California is a healthy and, in its climate, a pleasant country. Three assets which appear beneficial to man's life and his body are a sky that is clear night and day almost throughout the year, an eternal, general aridity, and a gentle, air-cleansing and continuous breeze. Therefore, the only thing I could have wished to carry with me from California was the unique climate. If one perspires there more than any other place, that is easy to bear compared to the unpleasant, unfriendly, cold, wet, foggy, and dark, seven or more, months of winter, late fall, and early spring which have to be endured in many other places.

CHAPTER FOUR : *Of the Character, Fertility, and Barrenness of the Soil of California*

IF I WISHED to describe California (of which it has been said in jest that of the four elements it received only two: air and fire) in a few words, I could say with the prophet in the Sixty-second Psalm that it is

Of California Itself

waterless desert, impassable because of rocks and thorns ("Terra deserta, et invia, et inaquosa"), or that it is a long rock jutting out of the sea, overgrown with extraordinary thorn bushes, and almost devoid of grass, meadows, forests, shade, rivers, and rain. There is no lack of level surfaces, small and large, especially on the west littoral, but it takes, as a rule, only a little digging to strike rock or stone. The soil itself consists mostly of sand and fine gravel. For this reason, I had the four walls of my cemetery filled in almost to the top with soil, to lessen the work of the grave diggers and to spare the iron tools.

The mountains and cliffs of California reach in many places to considerable heights. They are mostly ash-gray and are covered with little or no soil, which is probably only the residue of dried, decayed thorns, leaves, and shrubs, which, miraculously, know how to exist in bare rocks and sometimes even achieve a height of several yards. When, with a great deal of labor, and after removing shrubs and thorn bushes, a path has finally been cleared across such a mountain, the first or second local rainstorm often carries the thin cover of soil away, leaving only bare and uneven stones as the future road. These stones retain a great deal of moisture and are, therefore, so soft that they are easily broken by the blow of an ax. They are useless as cornerstones or as door and window frames in the construction of a building, because they easily split when exposed to the sun and pieces drop off, as happened when I built my new house.

This stone or rock is the center, the heart, the substance, in a word, the principal ingredient of the whole body of California, upon which here and there other species of stone are set and over which the scarce soil or the sand has been scattered. Furthermore, there are:

1. Large bluffs and smaller hills, as well as wide veins on the flat ground, resembling unpolished, hard, white marble. These veins are nothing else than petrified sea shells firmly baked together, which, when burned, furnish excellent lime for mortar. I, and others, have used it to build church and house.

2. Mountains which appear to be a solid mass of flint cast in a single mold.

3. Barrows composed of innumerable large and small wacke stones so solidly held together by a mortar-like substance that almost no force can separate them.

4. Also, and especially north of the twenty-fifth degree latitude, the

mountains and plains show nothing but smooth, polished stones of varying size, which seem to have been brought there intentionally and piled up or laid down by hand. No plant of any kind, or anything else, can be seen between these stones. Where the road leads through such "badlands," it is possible to ride for a quarter of an hour between two parapets of such stones, which almost hide man and horse.

5. Deposits of workable sandstone (in a few places), a great deal of firestone, gypsum, and finally such a mixture, such conglomerations and layers, one on top of the other (neither earth nor stone, neither sand nor clay, nor anything known in Europe), which defy identification and can only be classified as "pieces of California."

More proof that California is mostly rock, or a pile of rocks, is found in the banks of the ravines cut out by the small and large torrents of rain water. The material exposed is not what we commonly call earth, but rather a hard and stony mass. Up to now, no one has attempted to use a coach for traveling in California or to use a cart to move something from one place to another. If one could only use horses and mules everywhere, it would be of great help. Those who are not compelled to travel in California had better stay at home. No real shade is to be found either along the route or at the way station; there is no beautiful scenery to please the eye; the water is often stale; there is no other food except that which is carried along, no other bed but the hard ground. It is easy to imagine the attractive condition of the trails in such stony and mountainous terrain, even though attempts have been made to make the main roads as comfortable and as usable as possible. Therefore, I have never mounted a horse unless there was need for it, nor for seventeen years did I leave the house merely to take a walk. All my promenading during that time had to be done in the little walled court before my house, and only after sunset.

A careful reading of this and the preceding chapter will give some idea of the infertility of California. Hard rocks and soil without water are unproductive. To try seeding and cultivating under such conditions would be like attempting to wash an Ethiopian white; all the toil and labor would be futile.

Because of this barrenness, the bread required to feed the handful of Spaniards who live in California must be found elsewhere and imported; otherwise they must eat their meat without it—if they have meat. The

Of California Itself

natives, excepting those who live on seafood (there are few of these, because that, too, has its difficulties in California), show plainly the effect of black hunger and miserable fare except during the time of the pitahayas. The rest of the time they are forced to find and to devour as delicacies all manner of filth and dirt and to spend their time in sinful idleness.

One result of this infertility is the lack of shade, except behind a mountain or in a cave; another, that all the lumber needed for construction, carpentry, or cabinet work has to be brought across the sea. It is not uncommon that in a whole day's journey not one blade of grass, green or dry, can be found to feed a hungry horse. Animals, both wild and domestic, are small, skinny, and often die in great numbers for lack of pasture. At times the missionary does not even dare to throw a handful of grain to the chicken, for fear of depleting the meager store on hand for the sick and the working Indians. The chicken, in return, repays him the same coin and quits laying for a long time, just when the eggs are most needed.

But wherever there is a piece of land provided with moisture, either by the proximity of a swamp or because it is possible to irrigate, the picture is entirely different. Anything at all can be planted or sown, and everything will do well. The soil bears hundredfold and out-produces the most fertile regions of Europe.[12] There is wheat, corn, rice, melons (watermelons and also other varieties) weighing twenty pounds, pumpkins, cotton,* lemons, oranges, bananas,† pomegranates, delicious honey-sweet grapes, and olives. The fig trees bear fruit twice within one summer. Two or even three crops can be harvested from the same cornfield in one year; the corn grows eight feet high and often bears twelve ears to a

---

* Cotton grows on shrubs which, at least in California, do not grow higher than four French feet. These are pruned annually, like the grapevines or the espaliered fruit trees in Europe. The leaves are round and about an inch wide. The fruit too is round and nearly the size of a walnut. When the cotton inside the fruit matures, the thin hull splits open in four places. At that time it is gathered and the cotton extracted. It adheres to the dark seed, which is rounded and oval and resembles a grain of roasted coffee. The cotton is ready for spinning and is wrapped around the seed like the silk around the worm. Not all cotton is white; some of it is cinnamon colored.

† The fruit which the Spaniards in America call *plátanos* or *plántanos* (bananas) resembles a grapelike cluster, which at times weighs five hundred pounds or much more. There are different varieties, and some of them carry

hill. I have seen grapevines in California which bore a medium-sized basketful of good grapes in the second year and had grown as thick as an arm in the third and fourth year; the new shoots attained a length of forty-five feet and more in one year. It is a pity that such humid soil is so rare and that sufficient water for irrigation is at times sixty hours away. Except for these few small oases, the poorest piece of European land (provided it has sufficient rain or other water) would be regarded as paradise in California.

The English sea captain Woodes Rogers, who landed in California in the year 1710, describes it as follows: "The part of California I have seen is full of mountains, unproductive, with low shrubs here and there. . . . Of all places we have touched since our departure from England, California is least capable of supporting its inhabitants." [13] This was Rogers' impression. Yet he landed on the best piece of California, the southernmost point of the peninsula.

Before I finish this chapter, I wish to add my own thoughts and conjectures which have come to me repeatedly while contemplating poverty-

---

as many as two hundred individual bananas on one stem. The individual fruit (or berry) is long and round, of even thickness from top to bottom like a cylinder, but pointed on both ends. All bananas on one stem are of equal thickness and length. Some are only about a third of a span long, others a span and a half, and are almost as thick as a man's arm. That is the main difference in the bananas, although some do taste better than others. The fruit pulp is enclosed in a rather thick but soft skin which can be pulled off without difficulty. The whole cluster is cut off when the bananas are still green and hard. After it has been kept in the house for some weeks, the skin turns yellow, showing that the fruit is ripe. If it is kept longer, the skin turns black and the pulp golden yellow, like an overripe prune or very yellow may-butter; then it is at its best. Imbedded lengthwise in the center is the tiny, almost invisible seed. The bananas taste good, slightly sweet, but are a little hard to digest. They grow on a tall bush which bears fruit only once and then, as though it had done its duty, dries up and dies. The plant grows three to four fathoms high and is made up of a row of delicate leaves, a fathom long and a span wide. Through the center of the leaf runs a proportionately thick rib. As the plant grows up, the green section of the leaf dries up, but the stems remain alive, gain in thickness, and form the base of the plant, which at times grows to considerable size and is thus able to carry the heavy fruit stem.

It is not necessary to re-seed, because around each base, as the trunk grows higher, many young shoots come up from the same root and can be transplanted. Several years pass before the plant bears fruit. Whether or not these American bananas are the same fruit mentioned three times in the Holy Scriptures, and of which various authors have told, I leave to others to find out.

Of California Itself

stricken California. I have been wondering whether subterranean fires, an earthquake, or some other upheaval did not create this land and cause it in time to rise from the sea, after the creation of the rest of the world. It is well known that such is the origin of several small islands and peninsulas, and there seem to be well-founded reasons to believe that this is also true of other lands. One, the rock I have described as the foundation of the whole of California appears to be nothing more than hardened ocean sand. Two, in this fieldstone, or extremely soft sandstone, there are now imbedded (at times singly, at times in groups) large and small pebbles or stones, some more than a hundred pounds in weight, also pieces of petrified wood, resembling a diamond set in a ring, or as though someone had thrown stones or wood into molten lead or wax. Some of these rocks are several feet above the ground, but solidly immured. From this fact it is possible to conclude that the whole base and body of California consisted in times past of a soft mass, like warm wax, or dough, and that during the process of fermentation rocks and wood were caught in this soft paste, in which they settled. Three, the same could be said of the numerous mountains and rocks described earlier, which are made up of large and small flint and other stones and seem to be held and glued together by a mixture resembling mortar of sand and lime. Four, furthermore, as has been mentioned before, the surface of California is in many places nothing but a conglomeration of divers bodies, pieces, and matter which I do not know how to name or classify. They seem to be the product of a general and violent fermentation which arbitrarily brought these pieces together and piled them one above the other. Five, the great number of petrified marine shells and sea snails, wood, and the like, which lie deep below the surface in some places, not covered with small stones, may prove something too. At one place, an hour from my mission and ten hours inland from the sea, the trail is littered with stones knit to sea shells; all of these shells, even the tiniest, have retained their natural color. I also recall how, on a trip, I pulled a piece of mother-of-pearl from a river bank (two hours inland) about one fathom below the surface; the piece had retained all of its original color and sheen.

If all these points are not conclusive, as I am willing to admit, to prove the emergence of this peninsula from the ocean or even to make it seem probable, the reader can still see that poor California too, together with other parts of the world, offers its body of evidence of the general deluge and stands in line against the zealots who try to deny this strange tale in the Holy Scriptures, calling it a fable; they wish to tell the simple-minded that it is empty fiction, and take pains to prove it in their accursed books. Where else could those sea shells and other things I told about come from, except from a general flood?

CHAPTER FIVE : *Of the Trees, Shrubs, and Thorn Bushes of California*

CONSIDERING the drought and the hard soil, it is surprising to find anything growing in California. It is even more surprising to learn that nearly half of the California plants are full of liquid, like a beet, and that many of them grow so tall and weighty they could easily compete with a well-developed oak tree, and would yield ten times as much sap if anyone would try to press them or in some other way extract the juice.

In speaking of California plant life in general, it is well to know: first, that in the whole territory there is to be found neither forest nor grove. Second, that there is not a single tree which bears fruit, although in other American provinces such trees are found in great numbers and in many varieties. And third, not a single tree (unless perhaps in the mountains near Cabo San Lucas, in the Sierra de la Giganta near Loreto, in the mountains near Guadalupe, or in some districts behind the last mission in the north, which Father Wenceslaus Linck traversed, and where there are a few scattered oaks, firs, and other trees unknown in Europe)—not a single tree, I say, which spreads enough shade to provide a comfortable shelter or furnishes useful wood for carpentry or cabinet

---

[Mesquite, *Prosopis glandulosa.*]

Of California Itself

work, except only the *mesquite*, whose trunk is very short and whose wood is extremely hard and does much damage to saw and plane. The branches are poorly distributed, and the foliage narrow as on a fir tree, but less dense. The mesquite trees do not occur in forests but grow here and there in the path of rain-water drains or on the banks of watercourses.

In addition to the mesquites, some low-growing brazilwood is found in the southern part and at the tip of the peninsula; willows grow in many places, and palms which bear no fruit. There is also the *paloblanco*, as the Spaniards call it, whose bark is used in tanning and is supposed to be a good remedy for certain diseases, the *palohierro*, or ironwood (so called because its wood is even harder than the mesquite), the *chino*, the *uñagato*, and the wild fig tree, which bears no fruit. These trees are scattered, as I said before, one here, one there, and sometimes no tree at all for a distance of ten hours. All of them would look puny alongside a European oak or walnut tree, and all have the same narrow foliage as the mesquite. In addition to these trees, there are scattered low bushes, shrubs, thickets, and little espalier trees, comparable in size to low, misshapen little apple or pear trees; a man on horseback can easily see over their tops. Nearly all of them have more thorns than leaves, and the foliage is long and narrow like that of the mesquite. One of those little dwarf trees secretes a fragrant resin, which is used instead of incense in the churches of California. Another one emits drops of a kind of pitch or wax, which is used to paint the ships.

This small and inadequate stand of wood becomes more scarce, and the growth becomes thinner and more transparent as one goes from south to north. The priest of Mission San Ignacio (under the twenty-eighth degree latitude, north) long delayed the construction of a masonry church because he did not believe it possible to find enough wood to burn the lime. This difficulty, however, was overcome by his successor a short time ago. I was able to find the necessary wood (under the twenty-fifth degree latitude, north) for the lime kilns when I built my church [14] and house, but for the thirty thousand bricks I burned the marrow and skeletons of shrubs and stalks, of which I shall now tell more.

[Paloblanco, *lysilomax candida*.]
[Palohierro, *Olyneya tesota*.]
[Chino, *pithecollobium mexicanum*.]
[Uñagato, *acacia gregii*.]

Observations in Lower California

All other California plants which are conspicuous for their size (not to mention the Indian fig and *agave* plants, which are already well known) are stalks and shrubs of varying size, shape, and thickness, and of many species, some of which may now be seen in the gardens of great lords. But these lack much of the size, height, and thickness, and the number of thorns they achieve in America and particularly in California. I call these plants shrubs because they are neither trees nor bushes; and I call them stalks because they are not wood, but a succulent substance, so soft that even the stoutest of them can easily be split in two with a single stroke. The first place in this group belongs to what the Spaniards in California call *cardón*. It grows at times six fathoms high, and its branches are nothing more than twelve to fifteen green, round beams, three to four spans thick, with channels or furrows running the full length of them, clear around the evenly shaped stems. They are about as high as four or five men; when young these branches are covered with spines. Their substance is not hard and durable, like wood, but decays in a few weeks when cut off, falls apart, and becomes a soft pulp. Nothing is left but a poor, useless skeleton. This terrifying scaffold in the shape of a plant is scaled by the natives either to pick the tasteless fruit which grows out of the sides of those beams or to survey the country in search of game, heedless of the fact that the whole structure shakes and bends from side to side because its substance is so weak and the roots no more than two spans long.

Just as there is no semblance of a forest in California, there is also no trace of a meadow or of a green turf. After a good rain of the California kind, some grass will grow, but as a rule, in most places the growth is so thin that it does not even resemble a meadow. No hay is harvested or stacked, but throughout the year, day and night, the horses, mules, donkeys, cows, and oxen wander through the open field, in the mountains and valleys, to find their feed until they are rounded up or die from hunger.

Among the California herbs, there is one which the natives eat raw, right where it grows and as God created it. I myself have used it as a vegetable. It was the only one I enjoyed several times when I had no garden. Its season is very short; it appears in August and September, but

---

[Cardón, *pachicereus Pringlei Watson*.]

Of California Itself

because of the heat prevailing at that time of the year, it quickly grows rank and goes to seed.

The shrubs and stunted trees which produce not only leaves or thorns (including the mesquite and other trees mentioned before) bear their fruit in long pods, similar to our beans, peas, or horse-beans, but only a few of them furnish food for the Indians.

The thorns in California are surprisingly numerous, and there are many of frightening aspect. It seems as if the curse of the Lord, laid upon the earth after the fall of Adam, fell especially hard on California and had its effect. It is doubtful whether in two thirds of the European continent there are as many prickles and thorns as there are in California alone, of which the following might be proof. I became curious once and took it upon myself to count the thorns on a piece of plant cut from the center of a branch. It was a span as long and as thick as a fist. I counted no less than one thousand six hundred and eighty. The land is full of plants like this up to and beyond the thirtieth degree latitude, north, where they stop. Many of them have sixty, seventy, or more branches. They are all of the same thickness from top to bottom, almost one and a half fathoms high, evenly studded with thorns. The thorns are arranged in little clusters, ten in a group, resembling the face of a compass and pointing in all directions in symmetrical arrangement. These little clusters sit on the ridges which divide the furrows running the whole length and completely around the branch, just as on the cardón. It is easy to see that, according to my calculation, a single one of these shrubs carries more than a million thorns.

Just as a great many of the California thorn bushes are entirely different from those of Europe, so also are the thorns. Nearly all of them are pointed like needles, some white, others red or ash-colored, and they seem to be made of bone or wood. Some of them will puncture shoes or boots as though they were soft wax, if care is not taken to avoid them when passing by on horseback. The place of honor, however, belongs to a plant which the American Spaniards call *bisnága*. This is a single, green, soft shoot, without branches or arms, four to six spans high, three to four spans thick, grooved from top to bottom, and studded all over with red thorns. These become longer and more curved toward the upper part of the plant, and at

---

[Bisnága (viznaga), *echinocactus*.]

the top center, they are as long as a finger and curved like a firehook. These thorns make excellent toothpicks, and one of them will serve many years without repointing or resharpening. Considering the great amount of thorns, I have often wondered, and still wonder, that the always barefooted and very careless California Indians, especially the children, do not get hurt every day, and that of all the Spanish riders not more are injured. This gives me cause to admire the vigilance of their Guardian Angel and the wisdom of Divine Providence.

CHAPTER SIX : *Of the Fruits of California*

THERE ARE only two kinds of fruit, the one called *tunas* by the Spaniards, and known in Germany as "Indian figs" (prickly pears), and the pitahayas, which are divided into two classes, the sweet and the sour. The tunas are not very plentiful; in one year they ripen toward the end of July; in another, later. They last three to four weeks and will keep only a few days, just like the pitahayas. Their color is similar to that of our raspberries, and the flavor too reminds me a little of that fruit. They have a thin skin and many stones or seeds the size of large lentils. Tunas are about as large as figs, oblong, cylindrical, but pointed on one end. They belong to the sweet-sour varieties of fruit, and with a little sugar they would make an excellent addition to a meal of field fare. The skin is covered with many clusters of prickles, so tiny that if some of them stick to the fingers when the fruit is gathered, it will sometimes take several days to get rid of them. The tunas grow radially around the edge of a green leaf the size and shape of a tennis racket and as thick as a finger. This leaf is covered on the upper and lower surface with sharp, white

[Tuna, *platyopuntia*.]

Of California Itself

thorns in symmetrical arrangement. The entire plant is nothing more than a successive growth of such leaves, one growing out of the rim of the other. Upon these leaves are found the so-called cochineal (*Grana* or purpleworm), which is used for the production of scarlet dye. For this purpose the plant is carefully cultivated in Mexico, where in many places it reaches the size and circumference of a medium-sized tree, but in California it merely sprawls on the ground.

The other California fruit is the sweet pitahaya. It is round like a ball and the size of a hen's egg. The skin is green, tough and thick, and covered with sharply pointed thorns, just like a porcupine. The flesh is either blood-red or snow-white, and the black seeds are scattered throughout the pulp like grains of powder. The fruit tastes sweet, but the flavor is not particularly pleasant, except when improved with lemon juice and sugar. It is set upon the end of the branch and grows upon the plant described in the previous chapter, the one with the million thorns. There is no shortage of these plants in the land, and some of them bear abundantly. The pitahayas begin to get ripe about the middle of June, and their season extends over more than eight weeks. The time of the pitahaya harvest is fall, the carnival season for the California Indians; after that the nine months of misery begin again. During that season they can, without labor or expense, eat their fill whenever they desire, and they certainly take advantage of it. With many of them, this sustained period of plenty works wonders to such a marked degree that, at the first meeting when they come to greet me after three or four weeks out in the field feasting on pitahayas, I do not recognize them, although at other times I know them as well as if they were my brothers. The whole body and especially the face is filled out and bloated.

The third fruit, or to be exact, the other variety of the pitahaya, is the *sour* type. Apparently it grows only in California, because I have always been told that it is not found in any other place, except perhaps in the north beyond the limits of the peninsula, where no European has traveled until now. The difference between the sour and the sweet pitahaya lies not only in the taste, for all the fruit of the sour variety is red and incomparably larger. One of them was more than enough for me when I ate it for dessert. I have heard talk of some that weighed two

---

[Sour pitahaya (pitahaya agria), *machaerocereus gummosus*.]

Observations in Lower California

pounds and also of a few yellow ones found in the northern part of California. When the sweet ones are gone, the sour pitahayas begin to get ripe, but there are not nearly so many of the second variety as of the first. Some years I saw or ate hardly more than half a dozen. There are plenty of the plants in the central part of the peninsula, but not one in a hundred bears fruit. If a man is lucky enough to discover some on a plant, they can easily be counted on his fingers. In either of the two coastal regions, however, they are much more plentiful.

The plant which bears this fruit is low, spreads on the ground, and its branches or arms are only as thick as six or seven fingers. But there are often so many of them that they cover a large circle of several fathoms in diameter. In recompense for its slight height and less massive development, as compared with the sweet pitahaya plant, the sour variety is overly compensated by the size and viciousness of the thorns it produces. At first glance one sees nothing but thorns, and it seems as if all the branches were encased in a belt of penance with twelve rows of spikes as long as a finger. Several rows of these shrubs used as a barricade would serve as well as all palisades or *"chevaux de frise."*

This sour pitahaya tastes much better than the sweet one, although it sets the teeth on edge. The California Indians pay no attention to this, or perhaps they do not notice it, since they never eat bread after it. Sprinkled with sugar, this fruit deserves to be set on a princely table.

And that is all about the fruits of California. The Europeans who live in California do not derive a great advantage from them, nor will the reader's memory be confused by the many varieties and great differences.

CHAPTER SEVEN : *Of the Quadrupeds, Fish, Fowl, and Birds of California*

IN THIS chapter too, there is little to report. In a land without rivers, lakes or brooks, without forests, groves or shade, without meadows or grass, how much game, birds, or fishes can exist and find food? Each year at the beginning of the forty days' fast, I had my supply of fish brought from the Pacific Sea. I salted them and tried my best to keep them fresh until Easter, that is, to preserve them without drying them in the sun. Although I should have liked to eat freshly caught fish more often, I could not afford to do so. The ocean is twelve hours away, and I could not afford to pay a day's wages to the carrier for more than one trip. On other days of fasting and abstinence, my meal consisted of a little goat's milk and dried vegetables. If I were able to add a few eggs to this fare, I did not look any farther, but considered myself well, if not splendidly, treated.

It cannot be denied that a few small fish and carp swim around in some of the little bodies of fresh water I described before, but I had the luck to live many hours from such ponds and fish pools. The closest of them was six hours away in the territory of my neighbor, and I am convinced that, if he caught for six succeeding days only enough fish for his own kitchen, he would have eliminated the last trace of fish life in his district. Another and better stocked pond was no less than five days' distant. In the little puddle in front of my door, and therefore in my own territory, I never saw anything that could be mistaken for a fish, but I could hear all night long something, either frogs or toads or some other third species of water animal different from both. I could not tell what they were, because they never showed themselves outside of the water or above the water. They could not have been very good, or they would not have fled from the light as they did.

The Pacific Ocean, the sea to the west of California, is full of fish, but not so the Gulf of California, except perhaps the waters near Mulegé or

Observations in Lower California

Santa Rosalía; or it could be that the Spaniards who live in California, through lack of skill or innate laziness, were unable to catch fish. Because of that, the people of Loreto, on the coast of the Gulf of California and the headquarters of the California soldiers, have nothing but dried beans on their tables during the Lenten season, as well as on Fridays and Saturdays, unless some fish is brought there from Mulegé.

As it is with the fish, so it is also with fowl and game birds. I do not dislike them, but I doubt that the number of birds I ate in California surpassed the number of years I spent there by one or two. It is beyond doubt that a man can travel one or two days at a time in California without seeing or hearing one bird, unless it be a dirty crow or vulture. But still there are a few. I have seen some which are completely red, and therefore called "cardinals," and others which are blue. Other birds are ash-colored and have a long tail like a peacock, with a pretty tuft of feathers on their heads. There are also some of the birds which the French call *moucherons*, partly because of their small size and partly because of the humming sound they make while flying. They are indeed exceptionally small, and one could make three of them out of one bluebonnet. The head is as large as the rest of the body, the bill is excessively long, and their eggs are no larger than peas.

Wild ducks are found in several swamps. The meat of some of these ducks is excellent in flavor, but that of others tastes neither like fowl nor like fish, nor anything else. Now and then a species of swallows can be seen, but not many of them. I believe they are foreigners and come to California only on a visit; otherwise one would see them throughout the year in this land of eternal summer. Nor are they as loquacious by far as their comrades and stepsisters in Europe.

The four-footed wild animals in California are deer, hares, rabbits, foxes, coyotes, wildcats, leopards, ounces, and wild sheep. All of these animals are represented to some extent; of the first named there is a considerable number, but of the last four there are only a few. The hares are only half the size of those seen in Germany. If a newly seeded field of wheat or corn is not constantly watched day and night, deer and rabbits will eat it clean. This must be excused because the extreme and ever-present shortage of food makes it permissible in California to help yourself by using another person's property.

The rabbits are all of the usual rabbit color, as are also the foxes except

Of California Itself

for the tips of the fur, which seems remarkable, but in the tails and the rest of the body they cannot deny the resemblance.

The coyotes are like medium-sized dogs and have a little of everything, that is, of the dogs, the foxes, and the wolves. Everywhere they can be heard howling at night. When more of them get together, one of the pack always sings the tenor, and when the others are through, the same animal will repeat the trills a hundred times. But during the day a man can ride on horseback through the whole countryside and never see a single one of them. That they should be as dangerous to the chickens as the foxes is not surprising because there always were birds in California, but I do not know who taught them to eat melons and grapes, of which their forefathers certainly never dreamed.

The wildcats are much larger than the domestic varieties and have a white skin mottled with black, similar to the tigers. The leopards (that is what the Spaniards in America choose to call these animals) resemble the tigers in almost everything, but their skins show more yellow and have no spots. I have seen one, half-grown and killed by dogs, which was brought to me. I have also observed the forefeet of another one, which seemed to be as big as those of a medium-sized steer, and the claws at the base as thick as a little finger. The ounces have longer bodies than the leopards, but shorter legs, and have only a single intestine. Both are dangerous to man and animal. One ounce dared to invade my neighbor's mission while I was visiting and attacked a fourteen-year-old boy in broad daylight and practically in full view of all the people; and a few years ago another one killed the strongest and most respected soldier in California.

Where the mountain chain, which runs the full length of California from south to north, becomes considerably higher, there are animals which look very much like our rams, only their horns are thicker, longer, and much more curved. When pursued, they throw themselves from the highest cliff and land on their horns without injury. Their number cannot be very great. I have never seen an Indian who had one of these animals or its skin, but they had many skins of leopards and ounces.

Finally, there is in California, as well as in other provinces of America, a very pretty little animal, in appearance not much unlike a squirrel, and called *zorilla*, but—to report with due respect—afflicted with a pestilential, evil-smelling urine. When cornered in a room (in the attempt to chase it out), it will discharge in fear and leave a man breathless; the infernal odor stays on for months afterward. A certain missionary of California could tell a great deal about that.

From what I have already said in this chapter, no one should conclude that there is good hunting in California and that, consequently, the natives of California and their pastors eat roast frequently and have a great supply of game. I never ate myself sick, either on birds or on deer or rabbits. The opportunity never existed. And if an Indian by chance—to send a man out to hunt for game, as we do here, would be useless, and a man could wait from the day of the Three Holy Kings until Ash Wednesday for that roast—if by chance, I say, an Indian kills some game, it happens as a rule far away from the mission, and it would never occur to him to offer a piece of the meat to his missionary.

As far as the natives are concerned, let us suppose that one hundred families killed three hundred deer in one year (which, however, is not the case). This would provide only three meals per family in three hundred sixty-five days and would help very little to relieve the hunger and the poverty of the natives. The hunt after snakes, lizards, mice, and rats, which they practice with much zeal, is far more remunerative and provides their kitchens with a great many more roasts.

CHAPTER EIGHT : *Of the Vermin of California*

To this group belong the snakes, scorpions, centipedes, horrible spiders, toads, bats, wasps, ants, and locusts. Of the first named there are twenty different kinds in California, and every year thousands of them are buried in the stomachs of the California Indians. Some of these snakes are blackish-brown, others ash-gray, others yellow and reddish, large and small. The size of these vermin is not important. The bite of some of them is fatal. Except for two or three other species, the most

Of California Itself

vicious are the ones called *serpents à sonnet* by the French. The head is broad and ugly, the tail not pointed as that of other snakes, but blunt, and it consists of a number of rings, which (as the Indians tell) indicate the age of the snake, one ring for each year. These rings are joined together like the tail of a crayfish. They are hollow and completely dry, and when these snakes hear or see anyone approaching, they produce a loud terrifying noise with the rings; it is terrifying because it announces the proximity of the snake and, consequently, the danger. Once at dawn, I heard that noise five times within half an hour's ride, and close to the place where I had slept in an open field the night before.

The bite of this snake can kill a man within a few hours if the poison which is poured into the wound through the curved fangs mingles with the blood stream. The fangs have a very small opening, visible only through a magnifying glass. They were thoroughly examined by Father Franz Ináma,[15] a Jesuit from Vienna, Austria, and a missionary in California.

Every year several natives are dispatched into eternity by snake bites, and still they have no other protection against it except to tie the injured member between the wound and the heart in order to restrict the blood circulation, or if a finger or hand has been bitten, to cut it off, as I have seen in several cases when someone performed such an operation on himself or on a member of his family. A person is never and nowhere safe from these visitors because they glide up a flight of stairs or the walls of a house. Almost daily I found traces of them in various places around or in my home. Once I discovered one of them, five spans long, on the top shelf of my bookcase when I reached for the scissors. Another time, when I woke up, I found one on the inner ledge of my window, and again, one on the doorstep when I opened the door. This snake was only one span long, but one of the most poisonous; it had a mouse, intact, in its body. This causes me to believe what the Indians say—that young rabbits and hares are often found inside these snakes. I would never have believed how fast they can move from one place to another had I not seen one of them chasing a mouse, and the mouse certainly was not slow. It is a well-known tradition and often-told legend that no missionary died from snake bite in India or was ever bitten by a snake; nevertheless, one is made uncomfortable by such ever-present and uninvited guests.

I am also sure that I am telling the truth when I state that in thirteen

Observations in Lower California

years I have killed more than half a thousand scorpions in a new house built of stone and brick. This indicates what a surplus of these pretty little animals is to be found in some districts of California. Because of that I always had an awl in readiness, so I could use it as a spear whenever I saw one on the wall. Nor is it a miracle when one of those neat native cooks brings, among other delicacies, some scorpions to the table. It is a lucky thing indeed, considering the great number of scorpions, that its bite is not fatal in California. It merely causes some swelling and is painful for several hours, as I have found out myself. The color of the California scorpions is yellow-green, and some are as long as a finger, not counting the tail.

I do not know whether the centipede's bite is harmful. I have had no experience with that. But their mere appearance is enough to frighten anyone. In color they resemble the scorpions, but the centipedes are black on both ends. It is hard to tell which is the head and which the tail. They are flat, the large ones as wide as a finger, and are one span long. They have innumerable legs running the full length on both sides of the body, therefore the name centipedes. They are very lively and keep squirming and moving even when cut into pieces. I found one of the longest in my bed just as I was about to get into it, and another one, not much shorter, between my coat and my shirt.

To these treasures of California must be added a type of spider which the Spaniards in America call *tarántula*; I do not know why. There is no proof that their sting has the same effect as that of the tarantulas found in the Kingdom of Naples. One of these spiders is preserved in the Chamber of Natural History of the Elector in Mannheim, and there it is called "mortal sin." I find this name more appropriate. These spiders are hairy, more so than caterpillars, all black, but with a little yellow on the back. The body is as large as a big walnut, but with the big, heavy legs folded against the body it is no smaller than a hen's egg. When the legs are spread and the spider is moving, it looks much larger and much more impressive. It does not waste its time with spinning and weaving because it knows well that the weight of its body would ruin its work. Also, a mosquito or a little insect would be a poor meal for such a beast, which could easily fight a swallow or a sparrow. They live in the field, but some of them kept me busy in my home and workroom. I also observed two other spiders, all dark yellow, almost as large as the black

Of California Itself

ones. I do not know whether they too were hairy; I only saw them a few nights, scampering over my books and bookshelves, but I did not dare to examine them too closely.

Toads are present throughout the year, and can be expected to visit the house every day. During the summertime and the rainy season, they appear in larger numbers and more frequently. One morning after it had rained the previous night, half a dozen of them were jumping around in my bedroom. That was three months after I had moved into my new house. I had purposely raised the entrance five steps above the ground as a protection against such vermin.

The bats have free entry everywhere in California. Because of the heat, doors and windows are open all day until bedtime almost throughout the year. In the churches and homes (if they have straw roofs, as most of them do) they are found by the hundreds, especially if the mission lies near the mountains. In the old coat of one missionary, for instance, twenty-five pounds of bats had found a resting place.

There are many kinds of wasps, and each variety builds its nest differently of mud, some in houses or churches, but even chests and crates are plastered with their nests—on the inside, if the wasps find an entrance. Some are steel-blue, others gold or sulphur-yellow and half black. The largest, almost as thick as a thumb, are blackish with great, fiery-red wings, somewhat resembling the painted images of Satan. All of them are archenemies of the grapes, and all possible care and labor must be used for the protection of the crop or the wasps will finish the harvest before fall. Nothing will be left on the vines but the stems with the emptied skins of the berries hanging like a thief on the gallows. There is one kind of wasp whose sting is incomparably painful, just as though one had suddenly and with great force been pierced with a red-hot needle.

The ants (and everything seems to be alive with them—black ones, red ones, some with wings, and some crawling, short- and long-legged) are at times also rather trying because they fill the house and nothing edible is safe from them. Sometimes they attack while their victim is fast asleep, and no matter how many are killed, there is no relief unless he changes quarters and finds another place to sleep. While watching them, I had an opportunity of observing their industry and care, their brotherly and sisterly love, praised in the Scriptures. When a dozen of them were unable to move a fishbone, another dozen would immediately come to the aid of the tired and suffering ones to help them with their work.

Finally, California is often overrun by swarms of locusts. They are copper-colored and very large, but are yellow in their last stage. They always come from the southern part of the peninsula (where they seem to breed eternally) and take their course toward the north. They inundate the land, and the noise of their passing flight sounds like a strong wind. They cast a shadow on the sun, and of the little green they find in their path, they leave even less behind. When the young ones (left behind by their parents in the invasion) begin to move, they march like an army, straight forward, and nothing can make them deviate from their chosen course. They scale the walls of churches and houses if such stand in their way, or come through doors and windows by the thousands if they find a small crack or opening. How many bushels of wheat and corn could have been harvested in California if this plague of locusts did not exist! Father Ignatz Tirs,[16] of Komotau in Bohemia, who wrote some neat verses about them, could write a whole book about the devastation and damage done to his mission, Santiago, and also San José del Cabo, and about the terror and worries which the locusts caused him every year.

CHAPTER NINE : *Of the Pearl Fisheries and the Mines of California*

ALL THOSE who have written to any extent about California have made much noise about the pearl fishing. The book I mentioned in the introduction, published in Paris in 1767, states right on the first page: "Description exacte de ... et de la fameuse pêcherie de perles," although it is hardly worth while to speak about it or about the California mines.

Of California Itself

The whole California pearl fishing amounts to this. Every year in the summertime, eight, six, or twelve poor Spaniards (who, the whole lot of them, own nothing but whatever they earn by hard labor), as for instance, discharged soldiers and a few others like them, come from Sonora, Sinaloa, and other places on the Mexican mainland opposite the shore of California. They come in little boats or skiffs, hoping to make a small fortune, and bring with them a supply of corn, several hundred pounds of stone-dry beef, and some Mexican Indians who are willing to dive for pearls, for the California natives have shown up to now no desire to risk their lives for a few yards of cloth.

The divers are tied to a rope and lowered into the ocean. They pick up the shells and mother-of-pearl, or pry them loose from the bottom or the rocks, throw them into a sack, and when they can no longer hold their breath, they emerge and dump the trash or treasure brought up from limbo. The shells are then counted, but not opened, and one out of five is for the king. Most of the shells are empty, in others are black pearls, in some white ones, but mostly small and poorly shaped. If a Spaniard, after six or eight weeks of fear and hope, sweat and misery, has a net profit or one hundred American pesos, he esteems this a rare fortune which does not come to all of them, or every year. (One hundred pesos are equal to five hundred French *livres*, or a little more than two hundred Rhenish guilders, which in America is a very small and insignificant amount.) The Lord only knows whether this one-fifth share of all the pearls fished out of the California ocean netted the Catholic King one hundred and fifty or two hundred pesos year after year, even if everything was done without cheating. I have only heard it said of two men, whom I also know, that they had something worth while after more than twenty years of pearl fishing. The others were just as poor after their pearl fishing as they had been before.

The same holds true of the California mines, although as far as I know, neither the geographers nor the encyclopedists have so far made any mention of them, perhaps because they were discovered only a little more than twenty years ago. As soon as these writers hear about that, they will make a new Potosí * out of it.

---

* The *Frankfurter Reichspost-Zeitung* of November 26, 1771, reported among other assorted news items the following. The two Spanish provinces in California, Senora and Einaloa (it should read Sonora and Sinaloa), which

Observations in Lower California

Santa Ana and San Antonio, only three hours apart, are the two *reales de minas*, as the Spaniards call the places where they settle to dig for silver. Both are in the south not far from Cabo San Lucas, and therefore at the terminus of the peninsula. The founders of both places are still alive, unless they died just recently. One of them became so rich digging for silver that he begged for money to pay his passage to Spain (in 1767), so he could, as was rumored, apply at the Court of Madrid for a pension, because he was an offspring of the first Spanish-California captain. It is certain that he brought neither six pennies nor a Spanish real from his California silver mine to Madrid. The other man, born in Andalusia and a blacksmith by trade, owns some money, and a year ago he bought a wife in Guadalajara for his only son and heir for twenty thousand guilders.* But his wealth is derived more from pearl fishing (he has been doing that for more than thirty years and is one of the two men I mentioned before who profited by it), his butcher shop, his general store, and his unbelievable thrift than from his mine. He alone sells all the meat to his fellow men and their helpers, and also all the cloth, linen, tobacco, rags, and so on, which they and their families wear and which they use to pay their workers. He is the only man who is in a position to buy merchandise and to bring it from Guadalajara over land and sea; also he was the first man to take possession of the land over which his cows were grazing.

Aside from this mineowner, there are perhaps four or six more in the districts of Santa Ana and San Antonio, either discharged soldiers or former mission cowherds who scratched in the ground here and there or dug a tunnel in rock, trying to catch a piece of silver. Of these, one quits one day, the other the next, to move on and to find bread instead of silver in some other place, because he sees that he has to lay out more than he can earn.

---

make up New Andalusia are regions very rich in gold and silver mines. The treasures discovered there this year are immeasurable, etc., etc.

Those two provinces, Sonora and Sinaloa, or New Andalusia, are as much in California as Dalmatia and Macedonia are in Italy. They are on the Mexican mainland, on the other side of the California Sea, as anyone can tell by looking at the map. That both provinces are rich in silver and gold veins is a fact well known for more than a hundred years.

* The son was born and raised in California and received his cavalier-like training and education among his father's cowherds until his marriage to a highly respected person, the daughter of a merchant and business associate of his father, in the above-mentioned episcopal city.

Of California Itself

The inhabitants of these mining settlements, adults and children, black and white, all told, are about four hundred souls. They are partly Spaniards born in America, partly Indians from the other side of the California Sea. Just as the native Californian sees no point in going into the water because of a few pearls, he cannot understand why he should bury himself alive because of silver. The poverty and misery is much greater than the number of miners. The soil produces no more than in other regions of California, except perhaps a little more fodder for the animals. The little money they have is not enough to import bread from across the sea. The majority of the California miners consider themselves lucky if they get a corn pancake a few times a year to eat with their meat. Some Spanish families found themselves forced to go in search of food in the open fields, like the native Californians. It is the same with clothing; again like the natives, many grown children of the Spaniards run around the mines less than half-dressed.

It was often suggested to these miners that they demand of the Bishop of Guadalajara,[17] to whose diocese California belongs, that he should send a priest to them. On the one hand, it is very difficult for the missionary of Todos Santos, which lies thirteen hours away, to take care of a parish at such a distance; on the other hand, it is not wholesome for the miners to be so widely separated from their pastor. But they never cared to listen to these suggestions. The missionary carried out this charitable work without any compensation; he brought his own food, yes, and even the sacramental wine, when he was called to take care of the sick or when he made the journey voluntarily to read Mass or to preach to the miners. In contrast to this, they would have to pay a priest, aside from his parochial rights, the sum of six hundred, eight hundred, or even one thousand guilders per year, a sum which the whole group together would be unable to raise (unless the aforementioned pearl-fisher-grocer-butcher-silver-miner paid most or all of it). As of the pearls, so also of the silver, one fifth goes to the king; and those two "fifths" represent the whole income the Court of Madrid derives from California.

Whether or not in the whole widespread country more gold and silver lies hidden under the ground, outside of the two places mentioned, I do not know. Some people are inclined to believe so, especially in a district between the twenty-eighth and the twenty-ninth degree latitude, north, called Rosario. What I know is that wherever there may be gold and

Observations in Lower California

silver in California (especially in the northern regions) it will be impossible or at least extremely difficult to bring it to the daylight from the deep, dark earth because of the lack of food for man and beast, the lack of wood, the lack of water, and the shortage of labor. The few native Californians will never let themselves be used, nor can they be persuaded in any way if they do not want to do so.

In the region of San Ignacio sulphur is found, and so I was told, also veins of iron ore. On the island called El Carmen, very near the coast of Loreto, as also on the island of San José, and in various other places on both shores, there is much pure white salt. So much then for the character and the fruits of California, and especially of the disreputable pearl fishing and the mines.

From what I have written in the first part of the reports from California, the reader can easily conclude that:

First, it is of all the countries of the globe one of the poorest, whose poverty and misery will stand out even more sharply in contrast with the fertility and abundance of Germany. This observation should easily fill us with gratitude to the Creator of all things. It is true that it does not make much difference in what part of the world a man first saw the light of the sun, or whether he has spent the short span of life's pilgrimage in a fertile or poor land, whether he had it easy, or lived in poverty. The opulent European can take no more with him from this world than can the poor California native. But it is no less true that poverty as well as overabundance leads to all kinds of disorder and opens the door and paves the road to eternal damnation. This observation must have influenced King Solomon to despise the one as much as the other, wealth as well as poverty, and made him ask the Lord to protect him from both, saying: "Mendicitatem et divitias ne dederis mihi" (Proverbs, xxx: 8).

The aridity of California and the consequent lack of agriculture, trades, and work bring with them the constant idleness, the continuous roving about of the native Californians, and their lack of clothing and housing. This idleness and roving is the cause of innumerable misdeeds and much wickedness, even among the very young, from which the European, according to my guess, would not have been able to protect himself either had it been his lot to be born in such a land.

Second, it is easy to conclude that it is possible for only three classes

Of California Itself

of people to live in California. They are: one, a few priests who are willing to leave their fatherland and, for the love of God and their fellow men, to live amidst dangers and difficulties in the lonely wilderness of California. Thank God that until now there has never been a shortage of such men among certain Catholic orders, nor will there be, with God's help, a lack of such men in days to come. Two, a few poor Spaniards born in America, who are unable to earn their daily bread in any other place and come to California to serve as soldiers or cowherds. Three, the native Californians themselves, who seem to thrive on anything and for whom it is the most delightful place on the face of the earth, either because they do not know better, or because of the innate love all men feel for the land of their birth.

Although judging from what I have already said and what I shall say in the following Second Part, one could consider the California native as the poorest and most pitiable among Adam's children; yet, I wish to state with full assurance and without fear of contradiction that, as far as this earthly life is concerned, they are incomparably happier than those who live in Europe and upon the blessed soil of Germany, even those who appear to be living on the very pinnacle of temporal bliss. It is a fact that habit makes everything bearable and easy, and thus the California native sleeps as gently and as well on the hard soil under the open sky as a wealthy European spendthrift in his soft featherbed behind a rich curtain in his gilded room. In all his life the California native never has, or learns, anything to worry or distress him or to destroy his joy in life and make death desirable. Furthermore, there is no one, neither inside California, nor outside, to plague or persecute him, or to throw a lawsuit around his neck; no hail or army to lay waste his land, no fire or lightning to burn his barn or his farm. There is no envy, no jealousy, no defamation or slander to injure him. He has no fear of losing his property, no ambition to increase it. There is no moneylender to collect debts, no official to demand tribute, duties, head, road, and a hundred other kinds of taxes. There is no wife to hang more on her body than the income warrants, no husband who spends on gambling or wine the money which should feed and clothe his family. There is no worry about the education of the children, no daughter to marry off, no depraved son to bring disgrace and ruin upon his house. In one word, in

Observations in Lower California

California and among the native Californians there is no "mine and thine," which two words, as St. Gregory says, fill the few days of our lives with untold bitterness and evil.

The California natives seem to have nothing, and yet they have at all times whatever they need and as much as they need of it. That is because they do not care to shoot the arrow of their ambition farther than after whatever their poor country produces, and that they are always able to reach. Therefore it is no miracle that hardly one among them has gray hair, and then only very late in life, that they always are in good spirits, and that they joke and laugh continually. This perpetual gaiety is a clear proof that they are always contented, always joyful, which without doubt makes for real happiness. That is what everyone in this world strives and sighs for, each according to his position and ability, but only very few achieve it. If only the California natives, who really enjoy this temporal happiness, would also give a thought (now that the light of the true Faith shines upon them) to the bliss of the other world and the future life, and try to gain it by a more Christian conduct.

Those who live in Europe can envy the happiness of the California natives, but they will never achieve it except by a complete indifference toward worldly possessions, great or small, and through a full acceptance of the Will of God in all hazards of life.

PART TWO : OF THE INHABITANTS
OF CALIFORNIA

CHAPTER ONE : *Of the Physical Appearance of the Californians, Their Color and Number, When and How They Might Have Come to California*

THE CALIFORNIANS, whose physical appearance is quite similar to that of the Mexicans and other aboriginal inhabitants of America, differ from Europeans in the following: their skin from head to foot is of a dark chestnut or clove-brown color, shading almost to black in some and to a swarthy or copper-red complexion in others. This color, however, is not, so to speak, inherent, because when they are presented for baptism, there is hardly a noticeable difference between the native children and those born of white parents. The dark color appears soon after birth and attains its perfection in a short time. The hair is pitch-black and straight. All are beardless and have scanty eyebrows. Instead of being born with scales, they have hair almost half a finger in length. Their teeth are as white as ivory though never cleaned, nor their mouths rinsed. The angles of the eyes toward the nose are not pointed, but arched like a bow. The Indians are a well-shaped and well-proportioned people, very nimble and supple. They can lift stones, bones, and other objects from the ground with the big and second toe. With very few exceptions, they all walk perfectly upright, even when they are far advanced in age. Their children stand on their feet and walk before they are a year old. Some are tall and stately, others small of stature, as elsewhere, but none among them is conspicuously fat, the cause of which may be that they do much running and walking and therefore have no time in which to fatten.

In a country as poor and infertile as California, the number of inhabitants naturally cannot be great. Almost all of them would certainly die of hunger in a few days if their country was as densely populated as most of the provinces of Europe. There are consequently very few Californians, and in proportion to the size of the country their size is negligible; yet they decrease annually. The world misses little thereby and loses nothing of its splendor. A man may travel in different parts of the land for three,

Observations in Lower California

four or more days without seeing a single human being, and I do not believe that the number of Californians from the promontory of San Lucas to the Río Colorado ever amounted to more than forty or fifty thousand souls before the arrival of the Spaniards. It is certain that in 1767 in all fifteen missions, from the twenty-second to the thirty-first degree latitude, north, only twelve thousand have been counted.[18] This insignificant number and its annual diminution, however, are not characteristic of or peculiar to California. Both are common to all America. During my journey overland from Guadalajara to the Río Yaqui in Mexican territory and along the east side of the Gulf of California, that is, on a stretch of land of more than four hundred hours, I did not encounter more than thirteen little Indian villages, and on most days not one living soul. Father Charlevoix, in his first letter addressed to the Duchesse de Lesdiguières, writes that on his projected voyage through Canada or New France he would often have to cover fifty miles (a hundred or more leagues) without meeting a human being except his traveling companions.*

Compared with Germany and France, America (Mexico and some other countries excepted) was comparatively uninhabited even at the time of the discovery, but today it is still more so. Whoever has read the history of New France by the above-mentioned historian and has traveled six or seven hundred hours through Mexican territory and, besides, has obtained reliable information about other provinces, from people who for many years have been living therein, can safely reckon the number of brown inhabitants of North America. If, therefore, the southern part of the New World, or South America, is not one hundred times as densely populated as North America (which I am far from believing because of what I have read and what I have heard from trustworthy men who have lived there for many years and have traveled widely in that country), I should very much like to send these scribblers on global matters to America in order to have them look for and inspect the three hundred million Americans about which we read in their books. Who knows whether they would find fifteen or twenty million of them.†

---

* "L'on m'envoye dans un pays, ou je ferai souvent cent lieues et d'avantages, sans rencontrer un homme, et sans voir autres choses, que des bois etc." (Charlevoix, *Histoire de la Nouvelle France*, tome 5, p. 66.)

† In the *Frankfurter Reichspost-Zeitung*, of November 12, 1771, we

Of the Inhabitants

If the New World were as populated as these writers profess, the Negroes from Guinea and other countries would not find so much space here, and their transfer from one continent to the other could well be spared. Also, the so-called Portuguese mamelukes of São Paulo, in Brazil, and the Dutch from Surinam would not necessarily be engaged in slave trade, the former in Paraguay, the latter up the entire Orinoco River, and certain other people up the Marañón or Amazon River. They would find incomparably more human beings in their neighborhood and in their own colonies than they would need for their sugar, tobacco, indigo, and other plantations and factories. The many hundred languages which alone are spoken in South America are also sure evidence of its small population, although at first glance, this, as well as the existence of polygamy, might warrant the opposite conclusion. If there were more people, closer contact between them would naturally follow, and as a result, the use of fewer languages would be quite probable. My Ikas in California spoke a language different from the rest of the people in my mission, but I am quite sure the whole nation of the Ikas never numbered five hundred persons.

The reasons for this scanty population can be easily comprehended if the manner of living of the natives and their continual wars among themselves are considered. But I leave to others to divine why, after the discovery of the fourth continent, its inhabitants have decreased and daily continue to decrease. This is even true in those provinces where the Europeans have not ruled and are not yet masters and where the Americans have not been hurt and have retained their liberty, as the often-mentioned Father Charlevoix reports, referring to Canada and Louisiana (i.e., a country lying on both sides of the Mississippi), and as I did in regard to California. I content myself with what is written in Psalm xi, verse 9, namely, that the increase and decline of the human race in different countries is an inscrutable mystery. "Secundum altitudinem tuam multiplicasti filios hominum." I hope the reader will not take amiss this brief digression which was occasioned by the small number of natives

---

read as follows: *Niederrhein*, Nov. 6. "In the first three parts of the excellent work, etc., just coming off the press in Berlin, we find that among other curiosities and incomparable essays the number of living inhabitants in America is given at one hundred and fifty millions." Neither this statement nor the reputation which the author of this praised work may have shall make me change my mind concerning the population of America.

and which I considered necessary so that nobody would be too surprised about a phenomenon which is common to all of America.

However small the number of California Indians and though they represent only an infinitesimal part of the total number of the inhabitants of the earth, they are nevertheless divided into a great many nations, tribes, and tongues. A mission may consist of a thousand souls only, yet it may easily have among its parishioners as many different little nations as Switzerland has cantons, allies, associates, and dependencies. I counted among my own: *Paurus, Atschémes, Mitschirikutamáis, Mitschirikuteurus, Mitschirikutaruanajéres, Teackwàs, Teenguábebes, Utschis, Ikas, Anjukwáres, Utschipujes,* all being different tribes but hardly amounting in all to five hundred souls.

At this point someone might ask why there existed fifteen of these missions, for it would seem that twelve thousand and more Indians could very well be instructed, taken care of, and supplied with the Holy Sacraments by three or four priests. The answer is that this might be feasible in Germany as well as in one hundred places outside Europe wherever circumstances permit it, but it would be hardly possible in California for the following reasons. First, if three or four thousand California Indians were to live together in a small district and belong to one mission, the scanty amount of food available would soon be insufficient to feed them. Second, each native, each tribe, and each people have a fatherland, of which each is as much enamored as is any other people, yes, even more so, for, quite unreasonably, no one would under any circumstances allow himself to be transplanted fifty or more hours away from his birthplace. Third, these tribes and peoples, whose respective fatherlands are rather distant from one another, foster constant animosity, which would bring evil results if they were stabled together, nor would they let themselves be easily driven into the same corral. Fourth, in times of the plague and of general contagious diseases, which occur not infrequently, a single priest could not perform his duties to their full extent. He could not visit the many sick parishioners so widely scattered for many miles over the country and administer to their spiritual and temporal wants. The number of my parishioners did not amount to a thousand souls, yet their camps were often thirty hours apart. There are also not a few languages and dialects in this country, and a missionary is glad if he has mastered one of them.

Of the Inhabitants

It remains now to state my opinion concerning the problem wherefrom and how the natives might have come into this noble land. They may have started from different localities, and it may have happened in different ways, either voluntarily, by accident, or because of dire necessity. But that people should have migrated into California without being forced and pushed seems to me difficult, indeed, impossible to believe. America is large enough and could support fifty times more inhabitants on better land and soil than that of California. How then is it credible that someone should have decided of his own free will to establish himself amid such sterile and arid rocks? It is not impossible that accidently the first inhabitants succeeded in getting to California by crossing the Gulf from the opposite side of the California Sea, namely, from Sinaloa and Sonora. As far as I know, however, navigation never has been practiced by the Indians of this coast, nor is it in use among them at the present time. Said place also lacks for many miles inland the kind of timber suitable for building even the smallest boat. From the Pimería, which is the northernmost country opposite California, a passage might have been easier either by land, after crossing the Río Colorado, or by water, the sea being in this place rather narrow and full of islands. The latter might have been done, if not in little boats, then at least in *balsas*, or in little rafts made of reeds. Balsas are also used by those of my natives who live near the sea either for catching fish or turtles, or for crossing over to an island two hours distant from the shore. I believe, however, that if those Pimerians, induced by curiosity, ever had crossed over to California or had been driven there by a storm, after having surveyed its dreary conditions, they would have searched for and found soon again the way to return. Therefore there remains as the only possibility compulsion through distress. This could have easily occurred with the first California Indians, as well as with hundreds of other small American tribes, in the following manner. Nearly all neighboring tribes of America which are not subject to European rule are incessantly fighting with each other, and often there is no end to these wars as long as one party is capable of resistance. Such wars, even between different groups of the same nation and of the same language, may be caused by the most trivial reasons. Whenever the forces of one party are thoroughly weakened, they take to their heels and settle somewhere else at a sufficient distance from the enemy. I believe, therefore, that the first California Indians, pursued by their enemies, entered this peninsula on foot from the north in search of a safe refuge. The California annals, or at least the traditions handed down from father to son, could give us the best information in this respect. But these annals have not yet seen the light of day, and concerning traditions, no Californian knows what has happened in his fatherland before he was born. Nobody would even try to reveal to him who or what kind of people his parents were, should he have lost them during his childhood.

Before the Indians had seen the Spaniards for the first time, almost three and a half hundred years ago, they, to all appearances, believed that California was the whole world and they themselves its only inhabitants, for they visited nobody and nobody visited them. Each little people kept itself within its own small district. Some of my parishioners believed themselves to be descendants of a bird, others of a stone which was lying not far from my house, while others dreamed of something different along these same lines. Each dream in turn was more absurd and more foolish than the other.

CHAPTER TWO : *Of the Habitations and Shelters of the Californians*

SINCE returning to my fatherland from California, many questions have been put to me concerning the California cities, villages, and the College of the Jesuits, because nobody can imagine a settled country without these, nor a monk without a monastery. The oft-mentioned French translator [19] also uses not infrequently the words *villes, villages,* which mean cities, villages, and even the expression *métropole,* which, if I understand it correctly, means a principal city or the seat of an archbishop, although there is no bishop or archbishop residing in California

Of the Inhabitants

and none has ever set foot in it nor, in all likelihood, will ever do so in the future. The field chaplain [20] of Señor Portolá, at present Royal Governor of California, imagined, however, that there would be no dearth of goldsmiths in the California city of Loreto to repair a silver reliquary which had been damaged on his journey. He found himself in this, as in many other respects, miserably mistaken.

Except for the churches and the dwellings of the missionaries (which the padres built as well as they could, and as time and other circumstances permitted, some of stone and lime, others of stone and mud, of huge unburned bricks, or of other materials), and except for some barracks built by those few Indians employed in the fifteen missions for daily house and church services and by a few soldiers, sailors, cowherdsmen, and miners—except for these, I say—there is nothing to be seen in California which bears a resemblance to a town, a village, a human dwelling, a shack, or a doghouse.

The Indians therefore dwell, eat, sleep, and live all the time under the free sky, in open fields, and on the bare ground. Yet, by using brushwood, they construct in winter, when the wind blows somewhat sharply, a kind of wall in the shape of a half-moon, two spans high. They erect it only toward the side whence the cold is coming, revealing thus, in contrast to their usual stupidity, that they understand "how to trim one's sails to the wind." Nothing else is possible, and no more can be asked from them, unless they were forced to carry their houses consistently on their backs like snails and turtles or transport them on carts like Tartars, for which methods this land, as has been mentioned above, is admirably suited, of course. They spend all their lives wandering about unendingly, driven to it by the necessity of collecting food. They cannot start every morning from the same place and return to it in the evening, because a small stretch of land is not sufficient to provide them with provisions for the whole year. This is true in spite of the small size of the tribes. Today water may fail them here, tomorrow at another place seeds which they collect for food may be getting scarce. Thus they fulfill to the letter what is written about all of us, that we have no abiding place on this earth.

God alone, who has numbered our steps even before we were born, knows how many thousands of miles a native eighty years of age has wandered about until he has found his grave, from which he was all his life separated only by a finger's length. I am certainly not greatly mistaken

Observations in Lower California

when I say that many of them change their sleeping quarters more than a hundred times a year. They hardly ever sleep in the same place and in the same territory more than three successive nights, except when they are staying at the mission. They lie down wherever night overtakes them without worrying about harmful vermin or the uncleanliness of the ground.

The Indians do not live under the shade of trees (as some authors state, who do not credit them with towns and villages) because there are no trees in California which would serve that purpose. Nor do they live in holes dug in the ground (as other writers would make us believe), but rather in cleft rocks and caves, and that only when it actually rains and if such places are close at hand. However, there are not many of these caves, and they cannot be found everywhere.

If the Indians make a shelter for a sick person as a protection against heat or cold, the entrance to this shelter is, as a rule, so low that it is necessary to crawl into it on hands and knees. The whole structure is so small that a man can neither stand up nor find room to sit on the ground in order to hear confession or comfort the sick. Similar huts are built by those Indians who live permanently at a mission because of their work or for other reasons. These huts are often so small, so narrow and low that a man and his wife can barely sit or lie down in them. The reason for this is that the California Indians know nothing about standing together in discussion or conversation or about the habit of walking back and forth inside or outside their dwelling. Also, their belongings do not take up much space in their houses.

Those who are not occupied spend their time sitting or lying down. When they call on the missionary, they sit down on the floor as soon as they have stated the reason for their visit, without waiting until they are asked to do so. The women sit with legs stretched out, the men cross them in the Asiatic manner. They follow this custom in church as well as in all other places. They care so little about having a house or a roof overhead that I would often find a sick, old man lying out in the open when I had had a shelter made for him only the day before. So powerful is the force of habit.

CHAPTER THREE : *Of the Manner of Dress and Decoration of the Californians*

Those authors who wrote about the capital cities and the residences of the archbishops of California should also have told us about the luxury stores, the weavers of velvets and silks, and the makers of lace, because artists, merchants, and craftsmen are usually found in such places, and the inhabitants like to adorn themselves with their products. But there is nothing of all that in California. As it is with the houses, so it is also with the clothes of the California natives, not because of their laziness, but because of their poverty and the lack of material and means to acquire them.

Just as the open air serves the Indian as his dwelling, so his dark skin replaces coat and overcoat, trousers and doublets, sleeping fur and shirt, summer and winter clothes, holiday attire and everyday garments, and all finery. On the other hand, this has its compensations. They never have to fear the loss of their homes by fire. Their clothes and wardrobes will neither be damaged by moths nor stolen by thieves. Their topcoats will not fit too tightly or their overcoats be too short. They cannot gamble away their shirts. And finally, they are ready, harnessed and fully dressed, at any hour of the day. Many a vain woman has irresponsibly squandered precious hours for this "important" business, a loss she may one day regret without being able to repair.

Notwithstanding what I have just reported, and in spite of the fact that entirely undressed females have been found in the northern part of California, among the other California tribes the women (but they alone) have always tried to cover themselves at least a little. The general custom among them was, and still is, to pull white threads out of the branches of a plant known in Germany as aloe and to make little cords out of this wild "hemp" or "flax." On these they string hundreds of short-cut pieces of a water reed, like beads of a rosary. A great many of those strings are fastened to a belt, closely and thickly together, about a span in width, and hang down in back and below the stomach. The length varies. Women of some tribes wear them to the knee, others even to the calf or to the feet. The sides, however, as well as the rest of the body, are and remain covered with nothing else but the bare skin. Some of them, in order to save labor, wear a piece of untanned deerskin in the back (miner's fashion) instead of the aforementioned strings, or any rag of woolen or linen which they can get nowadays.

Out of two such pieces of deerskin, if available, they also make their shoes or sandals, without ligament or upper leather. They fasten them to the foot by passing coarse strings of the above-mentioned aloe between the big and small toes and around the ankles.

Whether there is wind, fog, rain, or sunshine, men and women, big or small, always keep their heads uncovered, even those of a certain mission who know how to make fairly good hats out of palm leaves for other people. Because of their lightness these hats were frequently worn by the missionaries on their trips. On certain occasions and on festive days, the Indians paint their entire bodies with red and yellow colors, which they obtain by burning stones.

Such then are the costumes and finery, the mourning and wedding, the summer and winter attire of the unbaptized California natives. After baptism, both sexes move about more decently and honorably, since once or twice a year the missionary gives each of the men a piece of blue cloth, six spans long and two wide, with which to cover the lower part of his body. He also presents them, if his resources permit, with a blue woolen short skirt. The women and girls, however, are provided with a roughly woven, thick, white veil of wool, which covers the head and all of the body down to the feet. In some missions the women also receive skirts and jackets made of blue flannel or woven cotton shirts, and the men, trousers of coarse cloth and long coats, Polish style.

However, as soon as they leave the church, the women throw off their veils and the men their long coats because these coverings are too cumbersome and an awful impediment to their wanderings, especially in summer.

Almost all of these textiles come from the city of Mexico, since it would have been impossible to clothe the natives with that which California produced. The number of sheep that can be kept there is very small, and most of their wool remains on the thorny bushes they pass by or march through.

Of the Inhabitants

The clothes which the baptized male or female California Indian wears would certainly not contradict Christian humility, either for the materials used or for the artistry applied in fashioning them. They could neither be less expensive nor more simple. Yet, as far as I know, their bodies will not decay more rapidly after they have died than if they had wrapped themselves in silks and velvets all through life or had glittered with gold and silver resplendent with pearls fished from the sea, like gods or goddesses. You may be strutting about, dressed the way you like, but remember, very soon the grave awaits you, putrefaction will be your bed, and the worms your clothes (Isaiah, xiv:11).

CHAPTER FOUR : *Of Property and Utensils, of Labor and Occupations of the Californians*

THE MOVABLE goods of the California Indians are nothing but rocks, bare mountains, and sandy, bone-dry soil; the movable goods consist of piles of stones, thorny bushes, and everything which runs and creeps on top and below the earth. Their household utensils—if I may call them that—consist of bows, arrows, a stone instead of a knife, a bone or a pointed piece of wood for digging roots, a turtle shell used as basket or cradle, a large gut or the bladder of an animal for fetching water or carrying it on trips, and finally, if luck is with them, a little knitted sack, like a fish net, made of the above-mentioned aloe fibers or the skin of a wildcat, in which they keep and carry their provisions, sandals, and all kinds of filthy old rags. To be more specific, the implements and possessions of the California Indians will reveal that the earth is their eating and gambling table, their club chair, couch, and bed, their drawing room, study, bedroom, kitchen, and dining hall; the rugged mountains and cliffs are their curtains and wallpaper; a landscape full of green or dry briars and horrible thorny bushes serves as their park, their pleasure ground of walks and avenues; water puddles and swamps, always stagnant, are their enormous mirrors or crystal rooms. These are the riches and pleasures of the California natives, with which, however, they spend the days of their lives in health and in greater peace of mind, serenity, and joyfulness than thousands upon thousands of human beings in Europe who know no end to their possessions and are hardly able to count their old and new coins. To be sure, California has its thorns, but they do not hurt and wound the feet of the Indians as often or as deeply as do those which are stored up in the money chests of Europe, stingingly worrying the hearts of their owners, according to what is written in St. Luke, chapter VIII, verse 14—not to forget the many mortal wounds which such wealth, when abused, inflicts upon its owners. Thus, the extreme poverty of the Indians and their total lack of those goods which seem indispensable is a fair proof that nature is not complicated and life can be maintained with very little. Consequently, it is not want but immoderate luxury and excessive lust which led to the invention of thousands of small items, the value of which would be enough to feed and clothe so many poor people.

Whatever crafts and arts their ancestors might have known and exercised, whatever the tools they had once known how to use, in time they must have fallen into disuse and complete oblivion. This fact is found among all the American Indians, and therefore among the California natives also. Bows and arrows are the only things which have survived and have been retained by all the California Indians because they need these weapons for their protection and to obtain their food. The bows of the natives are more than six feet high, slightly curved, and are commonly made from the root of the wild willow. They are round, about five fingers thick in the center, and become gradually thinner and pointed at both ends. The bowstring or cord is made of strips of animal gut. The arrows are of common reed straightened by the heat of fire and are more than six spans long. At the lower end, they have a notch to catch the string, and three or four feathers as long as a finger, which do not project very much and are let into slits made for that purpose. At the other end of the shaft, a pointed piece of heavy wood is inserted, a span and a half long, bearing at its tip a piece of flint, triangular in shape, almost

Of the Inhabitants

resembling a snake's tongue, and serrated at the edge like a saw. They practice with bow and arrow from early childhood. Consequently, many good marksmen are found among them. All science, work, and occupation of the male Indian, therefore, consists of making bows and arrows. The men always carry these weapons with them wherever they go. The womenfolk, on the other hand, know nothing else but to make for themselves and their own the above-mentioned little aprons. Concerning the kitchen, each person is his own cook, and all, men and women, young and old, concentrate on cooking as soon as they are able to move about and to stir a fire. When the above-mentioned things (bows, arrows, and aprons) are made, all natives, big and small of both sexes, do nothing else all year long but search for food, consume it, sleep, chatter, and be idle. In fact, they are not able to do anything else except when occupied in the now established missions.

CHAPTER FIVE : *Of Food and Drink, of Cooking and the Voracity of the Californians*

IN SPITE OF the barrenness of California, no native ever dies of hunger, unless perhaps one of them is taken ill in the field and far from the mission (for the healthy ones care little for the sick and hardly trouble themselves about them, even if these should happen to be husbands, wives, or other close relations), or unless perhaps a little child has lost its mother, because nobody else is to be found, not even its own father, who would take care of it and give it the smallest service of love.

He who preserves the birds in the air (of which five may be bought for a penny and which till the earth as little as the California Indians do) burdens Himself also with the worries of many thousands of these poor

Observations in Lower California

people. He who with His blood has purchased heaven for them knows how to feed them in the midst of thorns and stones. Their food is poor, but it is very cheap, and it keeps the Indians healthy. They grow strong on it and live to a very old age.

Four different varieties of food and California delicacies growing unaided by human effort can be distinguished. To the first variety belong some roots, one of which, called *yucca*, provides the daily bread for many American Indians and not a few Spaniards on the island of Cuba. But in California the yucca is not plentiful, and although in other places a kind of bread or cake is made from the ground roots of the yucca, the natives of California find this process much too slow and tedious and prefer to roast them in a fire as if they were potatoes. I have also seen them devour the raw roots of common water reed, just as they were pulled out of the water. To the first variety belongs, as well, the root, or better, the head of the aloe plant, of which there are many kinds in California, although not all of them are edible. They do not grow, however, as abundantly as the Indians might wish. Since drinking water is rarely to be found at the places where the aloes grow, they often have to be brought from another place two or three hours away. It also requires much time and effort to prepare this plant for eating, as will be explained later.

All kinds of small seeds belong to the second variety of food. The natives even scrape together the tiny seeds of dry hay, although much smaller than mustard seeds. They gather all sorts of pods growing on shrubs and small trees, of which, according to Father Píccolo,[21] there may be more than sixteen different kinds. All of this variety, however, would hardly fill the California granary. The seeds and pods which a man can collect with much toil during a whole year may scarcely amount to twelve bushels.

The third variety includes all meat, or all that which is alive and has some resemblance to meat. There are the quadrupeds and the birds already mentioned in Part One, and nowadays dogs, cats, horses, asses, and mules, also night owls, mice, rats, lizards, snakes, and bats. There are also grasshoppers and crickets, a kind of green caterpillar without hair, about a finger long, and an abominable white worm as long and as thick as the thumb, which occasionally is found in old, rotten wood, and tastes like pure bacon, so they claim.

The fourth variety consists of all kinds of unclean things. It includes

Of the Inhabitants

almost everything teeth can chew and stomach digest. The natives will eat, for instance, the leaves of the Indian fig tree, a certain kind of tender wood and shoots, tanned and untanned leather, old straps of rawhide with which a fence or something else was tied together for years. They will eat what another person has chewed for a while and then spat out. They will devour bones of small poultry, sheep, goats, and calves, also rotten meat or fish, green with decay, smelling abominably and alive with maggots, raw and moldy wheat or corn, or any other such neat little morsel, if available. They make use of everything, and it is their medicine against black hunger.

I believe that anything which in Europe would be thrown to the pigs could be offered to California natives, and they would neither be offended nor consider themselves badly treated. For this reason, nobody would think of first cleaning the wheat or corn, which is cooked in a large kettle, of the black worms and the little bugs, even if there might be just as many vermin as there are little kernels of grain.

I met one day a seventy-year-old blind man who was pounding an old shoe made of raw deerskin between two stones and stuffing his mouth and stomach with the dry and hard pieces, yet he had a grown daughter and a twenty-year-old granddaughter. With about a hundred and fifty bushels of bran daily (which they also eat dry and raw), I could have induced my whole tribe to settle in the mission, except during the time of the pitahayas. Hardly is an ox or a cow slaughtered and the hide spread upon the ground to dry than half a dozen boys or men rush upon it, scratch, scrape, and tear pieces from it with knives, stones, and teeth, trying to get as much as they are able. They stuff the pieces at once into their mouths, and they continue to do this as long as the hide is either in the open or until it is full of holes.

In Mission San Ignacio and in others farther to the north, there are persons who will attach a piece of meat to a string, swallow it, and then pull it out again, like pearl fishers pulled out of the water, repeating the performance a dozen or more times in succession for the sake of prolonging the taste and enjoyment of the meat.

At this point I ask permission of the patient reader to mention something of an exceedingly inhuman and repulsive nature, the like of which has probably never been told of any other people in the world. It discloses better than anything else the poverty of the California Indians,

Observations in Lower California

their voracity and uncleanliness. In Part One of this book (chapter six) I mentioned that the pitahayas contain a great many small seeds, resembling grains of powder, which for reasons unknown to me are not consumed in the stomach but passed in an undigested state. In order to use these small grains, the Indians collect all excrement during the season of the pitahayas, pick out these seeds from it, roast, grind, and eat them with much joking. This procedure is called by the Spaniards the after or second harvest! Whether all this happens because of want, voracity, or out of love for the pitahayas, I leave undecided. All three surmises are plausible and any one of them might cause them to indulge in such filthiness. It was difficult for me, indeed, to give credit to such a report until I had repeatedly witnessed this procedure. It is useless to try to persuade them to abandon this old practice. They will not give it up, neither this nor other similar habits. Yet, they have always abstained from eating human flesh, in contrast to the barbaric usage of many other American natives who would find it much easier to abstain from cannibalism because they suffer much less from the lack of food than the California Indians.

It could easily be imagined how these people would fight for the crumbs falling from the tables of so many rich people in Europe. I would not, however, advise anyone to send these "crumbs" to California. It would be a little too distant. Besides, there is no lack of paupers in Europe who offer well-to-do people daily opportunities to be as charitable as they should be. It does not matter which one of the needy receives our alms, for it is Christ himself who receives them in the person of one or the other, according to His word in Matthew, chapter xxv: "Amen Dico vobis, quam diu fecistis uni ex his fratribus meis minimis mihi fecistis." (Verily I say unto you whatever you have done unto the least of my brothers, you have done unto me.)

At this point, I have nothing to report about the beverages of the California natives. In chapter three of Part One, the reader already was introduced to their precious "wines and cellars." Yet, God be praised, they know of no other drink but water, and in this poverty-stricken land they have no opportunities to produce drinks from the Indian corn, aloe, and other plants, as in so many other provinces of America, for American natives like to drink such things solely for the purpose of getting drunk.

Now that I have given an account of the different articles used and

Of the Inhabitants

found in a California kitchen and pantry, it seems to be appropriate to describe how Indians prepare their food. They know nothing about cooking, boiling, or roasting as it is understood in Europe, partly because they do not possess the necessary tools and knowledge, partly because they would not have the patience to wait for three or four hours until a piece of meat was well cooked or thoroughly roasted. They simply burn, singe, or roast in or on a fire everything which is not eaten raw. Meat, fish, birds, snakes, field mice, and bats are simply thrown in the middle of the fire or flames or on the glowing embers like a piece of wood, then left there to smoke and sweat for about a quarter of an hour. Then the roast, which is charred on the outside, but raw and bloody within, is thrown on the ground or on the sand. After it is sufficiently cooled off, they shake it a little in order to remove the sand and dirt, and the banquet is ready. Everything which, according to the definition given above, might be called meat is prepared after this recipe. It must be added that, before roasting the meat, they do not skin the mice or disembowel the rats, nor do they deem it necessary to clean the half-emptied entrails of larger animals or to wash the meat which has lain in the dirt.

They eat everything unsalted, though they could easily get salt. Since, however, they cannot eat roast meat every day, and since they change their quarters almost daily, it cannot be denied that they would find it cumbersome to carry a salt store with them wherever they go in the event that they were fortunate enough to find something to roast.

The preparation of the aloe or *mescale*, as the Mexicans and Spaniards call it, requires more time and labor. After cutting off the branches, the heads must be roasted in a strong fire for several hours. Thereafter, twelve to twenty of them are buried in the ground, covered well with heated stones, hot ashes, and earth. Finally, after twelve to fourteen hours, the "dead" are dug out again. The aloe heads, which were white inside before, now appear golden yellow and are quite tender. They do not taste badly. Many times I have eaten them either because of necessity or as a dessert in lieu of fruit. However, those who are not accustomed to them might easily suffer from diarrhea and will have a somewhat rough mouth for a few hours afterward.

In California all the things which are not roasted in the manner described above are fried on hot embers in a turtle shell or a kind of frying pan woven out of a certain plant. The contents are first mixed by shaking the pans, then tossing the contents into the air and catching them on the way down. The roasted product is then ground to powder between two stones and eaten dry as it is. The Indians would not think of a drink either after the meal or during half a day afterward. All the seeds, podded grains, and meat of insects, like that of grasshoppers, green caterpillars, wood worms, and others as mentioned above, in short all the small things which would be lost in the embers or in the fire are prepared in such a manner. Bones are likewise roasted on hot coals and then pulverized. Fire, necessary in the kitchen and for warmth, is not lighted with the use of steel or stone. It is obtained by rubbing two pieces of dry wood together. One of them is round and pointed on the one end. The point fits into a round cavity in the other piece, and by twirling the pointed stick with great rapidity between the hands, the lower piece is ignited.

The California Indians have no fixed time for any of their activities. They eat whenever they have food or whenever they feel the urge to eat, an urge which is rarely absent. I never asked one of them whether he was hungry without receiving an affirmative reply, although I noticed that his belly (as they call it) appeared rather tight. The noonday meal is least customary among them, because they all set out early in the morning on foraging expeditions and do not return to the place of departure before evening, provided they want to return and do not decide to pass the night at some other place. Thus they spend their time in going and coming, in searching for food. They save nothing for the coming day, and should by any chance anything be left over in the evening, they certainly will eat it up during the night if they awaken, or on the following morning before leaving.

They can endure hunger much more easily and longer than other people. On the other hand, they are also more capable of feasting than others, when they have the opportunity. I often asked one of them for a piece of venison while the deerskin was still fresh. I offered to pay for it, but I always received the answer that nothing was left. I knew well the hunter needed no helpers to eat it. Twenty-five pounds of meat in twenty-four hours per person is not too unusual. To see anything edible is a temptation for an Indian which he cannot easily resist. Not to eat up all the food before night would be a victory he is very seldom able to achieve.

One of them requested a number of goats from his missionary in order

Of the Inhabitants

to live, as he put it, like a human being, that is, to keep house, to pasture the goats, and partly to support himself and his family with the goat's milk and the flesh of the kids. Yet, after a few days not a single goat of the twelve presented to him by the missionary was still alive. A trustworthy priest who had lived more than thirty years in California assured me repeatedly that he had known a native Californian who had gorged seventeen watermelons * at one sitting, and another one who, having received from a soldier six pounds of refined sugar as payment for a certain debt, sat in front of the door where the sweets had been given to him and did not rest until, eating one piece after another, the six pounds had disappeared. This one paid with his life for his voracity within a few hours. The former, however, was saved by taking a certain curative. I myself was urgently called one evening to three or four persons who thought they were dying and wanted to confess. I learned, however, after arriving at the place where they were lying, that their sickness consisted merely in belly-aches and vomiting. Then I remembered that early the same morning three bulls had been distributed among twenty-six men (with their wives and children amounting to about sixty persons) in compensation for some labor. I immediately recognized the nature of their illness, and after properly reprimanding them for their gluttony, I returned home.

---

* The watermelons are as big as the common melon, thoroughly green on the outside, round or oval shaped. They have a pink-colored flesh which is nothing but juice and pitch-black broad seeds. They are, however, not half empty from within as other melons.

CHAPTER SIX : *Of Marriage and the Education of Children in California*

As soon as a young Indian finds a companion, he marries without delay. Yes, sometimes young natives impetuously demand a partner from the missionary. This is particularly true of the girls, even before they have reached the legal age of twelve. I purposely said when they find a partner, for there was common complaint that in all but one mission the number of males was considerably greater than that of the females.

Few questions are asked about the mate, and hardly any attention is paid to the morals and qualities of a person about to be married. To tell the truth, there are few differences among the natives concerning their intellectual and spiritual gifts. I do not know if anyone was ever married in California, be it bride or groom, who would have revealed something of the first, second, fourth, or fifth of the five qualities of the well-known Latin verse *sit pia*, etc. Contemplated marriages very frequently become impossible because of the *impedimentum affinitatis* unless a dispensation can be secured. Aside from this they may marry whomever they like. They are always sure to marry their equals as far as wit, virtue, mores, and riches are concerned, following thus the old rule: "Si vis nubere, nube pari."

Not many of them enter the state of matrimony as God intended it. They simply want to have a partner. Besides, the husband wants a servant whom he can command, although his authority does not reach far; the women are not particularly anxious to obey.

They know nothing of solemn promises and engagements, even less of parental arrangements or marriage contracts. Without further ado, that is, without a public announcement, they want to be married as soon

---

[*Impedimentum affinitatis*, canon law forbids marriage between persons already connected by marriage; that is, a man cannot marry his wife's blood relations, and *vice versa*. The relationship constitutes an obstacle to marriage.]

Of the Inhabitants

as they have informed the missionary of their intention. Frankly, such public announcement would be wholly superfluous, for nobody would raise any objections. Of course they are joined in matrimony according to the rites of the Catholic Church, but on their part they add nothing to the ceremony. Neither parents nor friends are present; no evidences of joy, like a wedding feast, are shown unless the missionary presents the newly-wedded pair with a piece of meat or some Indian corn instead of receiving himself the *jura stolae*.

Whenever I joined a couple in matrimony, it took considerable time before the bridegroom understood how to put the wedding ring on the correct finger of his wife, and much more time till he actually succeeded. As soon as the ceremony is over, the husband will go in one direction, the wife in another, each for himself, in search of something to eat. They act as though one was of no more importance to the other today than he or she was yesterday; they will not see each other again that day. The reasons for this behavior are easy to guess for one who knows the Indian!

Just as they acted on their wedding day, so they will act on the following and every day in the future. Husband and wife will wander wherever it pleases the one or the other. For many weeks they will not live together without previous understanding or mutual permission. As far as food for their support is concerned, the husband does not provide for his wife, nor the wife for her husband, nor either for their children beyond infancy. Both parents eat whatever they have or find, each one for himself, without being concerned about the other or about their offspring.

Before they were baptized, each man took as many wives as he liked and wished. They paid little attention to friendship or affinity in marriage. A few years ago there was one man who counted his own daughter among his wives, at least so he believed. At that time they joined without ceremony. They did not even have a word for "to marry," which now is expressed quite ingeniously in their language by the words *tikére undiri*, that is, to touch each other's arms or hands.

The word "husband," which they had and still use, is, according to its meaning and etymology, applicable to any man abusing a woman. Nobody lived at that time who did not daily commit adultery without fear or shame; thus their living together resembled anything but a true

---

[*Jura stolae*, canonically the fee given to a priest officiating at baptism, marriage, death, etc.]

Observations in Lower California

matrimonial state. Basically, it was a common affair of all with all, although jealousy remained an unknown beast to them. This went so far that different neighboring tribes visited one another with the sole intent of spending some days in common debauchery, and on such occasions general prostitution prevailed. Would to God that such abuses (after having baptized and wedded two people according to divine law and Christian custom) could have been weeded out by sermons and Christian instruction, by admonitions and persuasion, thus suppressing such raw practices. Yet it is better to have pity for them than to feel incensed, for temptations are many and ever present, and it is very difficult, if not impossible, for the natives to escape them or for us to eliminate them.

In the first chapter of this part, I mentioned some essential facts about the small number of natives in California. Should the reader like to know whether this small number is the result of the natives' sterility or is due to their disorderly way of life, he may consult M. Pluche's *Spectacle de la Nature*.[22] It is certain that many native women never bear any children; others, and not a few, bear only one; and only a few out of a hundred or two hundred will bring forth eight or ten. Should the latter ever happen, rarely more than one or two of the children will reach maturity. I baptized seven children for one woman, recently married. One by one I buried all seven of them before they were three years old. When I was about to leave the country, I advised her to dig a grave for the eighth, which she was expecting. The number of unmarried natives, adults and children of both sexes, is generally much smaller than that of the married and widowed ones.

The Indian women bear their children very easily, without assistance. Should the child be born as far away as two or more hours from the mission, they will carry it there themselves on the same day in order to have it baptized. It is not astonishing that many of their infants die; it would be a wonder if many survived, for (in addition to M. Pluche's remarks in his book just cited concerning this matter) as soon as the infant first sees the light of day, there is no other cradle for it but the hard soil or still harder shell of a turtle, in which the mother drags the poorly wrapped infant with her wherever she goes. Sometimes, in order to have a chance to wander about unburdened, she will leave her child in charge of some old woman, thus imposing upon it a fast lasting ten or

Of the Inhabitants

more hours. As soon as the child is a few months old, the mother carries it, quite naked, astride her shoulders, its legs hanging down in front over her chest; consequently it has to learn how to ride before it can stand on its feet. The mother roves about all day in such fashion, in heat or frost, in the burning sun or chilly winds. The food of the child, till it cuts its teeth, is only the mother's milk. If that is lacking or insufficient, there is hardly another woman to be found who would want to do the charitable work of feeding the starving child. Also, many women would not be able to help under these circumstances. Thus these women care rather little for the lives of their children. Indeed, a mother might even be glad if she is early relieved of the burden, especially if she already has one or two children. Furthermore, she has no fear that family property will pass into strangers' hands. At least I have not seen many women who tore their hair when their children died, or who treated them with much love, although a kind of dry weeping is not wanting on such occasions. The father, or the woman's husband, is even less sensitive and does not even look at his wife's child so long as it is an infant.

Nothing causes the California Indians less trouble and worry than the education of their children. All schooling is restricted merely to feeding them while they are incapable of searching for their own nourishment, that is, digging out roots, catching mice, and killing snakes. Once they are strong enough and have learned to help themselves, it is all the same to the young ones whether or not they have parents. Neither have they to hope for instruction or care, nor need they fear admonitions, punishments, orders, prohibitions, a sour face, or a good example. They may do as they please and behave as they wish. If the parents, instead of growing angry, felt pleased or at least exercised some patience whenever their little ones are slightly chastised by order of the missionary, even for gross crimes committed by them, it would be of great help. Just the opposite happens. The mother begins to lament whenever her son or daughter is facing such punishment. She screams like a fury from hell; she tears out her hair, beats her naked breasts with a stone, and pricks her head with a pointed bone or piece of wood until blood flows, as I have witnessed more than once.

As a consequence, the children do everything they wish. They learn to imitate very early all evils committed by others of equal age or by their elders. If they are caught by one of their parents in the act of committing

Observations in Lower California

some misdeed, they do not have to fear any rebuke. Children who live in the mission roam about all day long after Mass and the hour of religious instruction is over. Those who live in the open fields will go wherever and with whomsoever they choose and not see their parents for many days. Their parents in turn do not manifest the slightest anxiety about them or even inquire after their whereabouts. In view of such conditions, which a missionary cannot remedy, it is not hard to imagine that there is little use in instructing, advising, or punishing such youngsters.

May God further enlighten the Indians and preserve Europe, and especially Germany, from rearing children in the Indian manner, which in part corresponds to the plan outlined by that base-minded zealot J. J. Rousseau in his *Emile*, and also to the moral teachings of some modern philosophers belonging to the same fraternity of dogs. They would like to have temptations and instincts run their course freely. They think that education, so far as Faith and the fear of God are concerned, should not be taught before the eighteenth or twentieth year, which is to say, if viewed in the proper light, that all such education should be omitted. Such a plan would entirely conform to the admirable methods of the California Indians.

CHAPTER SEVEN : *Of Diseases and Medicines, of Death and the Burial Customs of the Californians*

IN SPITE OF their bad diet and many hardships, the California Indians are seldom sick.[23] They are, as already mentioned, generally strong and hardy, much healthier people than many thousands who are served abundantly every day with whatever their hearts desire, even with what Parisian cooks prepare. It is very probable that most of them, after

Of the Inhabitants

having overcome the dangers of childhood, would reach a very old age if they were not at times so immoderate in eating, running, bathing, and certain other matters, and did not indulge in excesses. Except for consumption and that *particular disease* which was brought from America to Spain and Naples and thence spread over various countries, they are little subject to the epidemics common in Europe. Cases of podagra, apoplexy, dropsy, cold and petechial fever are neither heard of nor seen.

Their language has no word for "sickness," nor has it expressions with which to designate specific diseases. "To be sick," *atembà-tíe*, when literally translated, means "to lie" or "to be on the ground," though all healthy natives may be seen lying or loafing on the ground throughout the day unless they are eating or searching for food. When a sick man is asked what ails him, the usual reply is, "I have a pain in my chest"; that is all.

For smallpox [24] the California Indians, like all other Americans, are indebted to the Europeans. This disease is as contagious as the worst kind of plague. In 1763 a traveling Spaniard who had just recently recovered from smallpox presented a shred of cloth to a native. Within three months this gift caused the death of more than a hundred people at a small mission, without mentioning those who were cured thanks to the untiring efforts and care of the missionaries. Not one of them would have escaped unharmed had not the majority run far away from the hospital as soon as they realized the contagious nature of the disease.

In April of the same year, 1763, a young, healthy, and strong woman of my mission suffered from eructations from the stomach through her throat. The eructations followed one another after an interval of a few minutes. The noise was heard at a distance of forty or more paces and resembled a thunder arising out of the body, each time lasting about half a minute. The appetite of the patient was good, and she complained of nothing else. A week later, however, she collapsed. and I thought she would forget to rise again. Yet these eructations, this thunder, these fits of falling and rising continued for almost three years until she was so weakened that on the twentieth of July, 1766, she was buried. A few days after the outbreak of her malady, her husband was taken ill with the same sickness. On my departure in 1768, I left him behind without hope for a longer life. Subsequently the woman's brother and his wife suffered in

---
[Syphilis.]

Observations in Lower California

like manner, and finally, after these, several other Indians, principally of the female sex. Neither the oldest of the natives nor missionaries with thirty years of experience in California had hitherto been acquainted with this extraordinary and apparently contagious malady.

The patience of sick Californians is really unusual. Hardly a sigh is heaved, though a patient may lie on the ground, a pitiful sight, and suffer torturing pains. They look without fear upon their boils and wounds and submit to being burned and cut. Yes, they even make incisions in their own flesh whenever they are stung by a thorn, as if they were without feeling or as if the operation were performed on someone else. It is, however, a symptom of approaching death when they lose their appetite.

Their surgeons and doctors finish their studies quickly, and their drugstores are permanently empty. The art of medicine is limited to one device. No matter what the disease, the ailing part of the patient's body, be it his chest, abdomen, foot, or arm, is bound tightly, if possible, with a cord or a coarse rope. At times a kind of bloodletting is practiced; that is, the patient is given several small cuts with a sharp stone in the middle of the face and in the center of infection in order to draw some blood from these wounds and thus force out the disease. Nowadays in nearly all cases of illness, they beg for tallow, with which they rub themselves, and for Spanish snuff as a cure for headaches and sore eyes. Except for the remedies just mentioned, they know of none, neither for snake bites, boils, wounds, and other external injuries, nor for internal disorders. Though they may repeatedly have seen the missionary using this or that kind of simple remedy according to circumstances, they will never, either from forgetfulness or from indifference, make use of it for themselves or their fellow men or their closest relatives. They will always prefer to trouble the missionary again.

Aside from the two natural and general remedies mentioned, they also resort to supernatural means against their diseases, although these quite certainly have not helped anyone. The fact is that many among them pose as healers although they are nothing but stupid impostors. Yet the simple Indians have such great faith in them that for any disorder they send for one, two, or more of these rascals. These quacks wash and lick the patient, or with a small tube they blow at him for a while. They make various grimaces and mumble something which they do not understand themselves. Finally, after much panting and laboring,

Of the Inhabitants

they show the patient a flint or something similar previously hidden about their person and announce, "The cause of the evil, which was this stone, has been eliminated, and the root of the pain torn out of the body." One day twelve of these impostors received their merited reward from me, and the whole people had to promise to keep away from them, or else— this was my threat—I would not preach to them any more. But as soon as one of the workers at the mission was taken ill a few weeks later, the blower was immediately called in to do his work. The sick man had been one of the first to swear off the devil in the presence of everyone!

It is to be feared that some of those who fall ill far away from the mission and who cannot be carried thither are buried alive, especially old people or those who have only a few relatives. The natives are in the habit of preparing the grave two or three days before the patient dies; and it seems tedious to them to sit with an old person, waiting for his end, a person who had meant nothing to them for a long time, who was a burden now, and who would not live much longer anyway. I know of a case where a girl was revived with a good dose of chocolate. She was already wrapped up in a deerskin, according to custom, and about to be buried. She lived many years afterwards. Some natives broke the neck of an old blind and sick woman on their way to the mission in order to be spared the trouble of carrying her a few miles further. Another was suffocated because the natives, in order to protect him from the many gnats, covered him up in such a manner that he could not breathe. To transport a sick person from one place to another, they bind him to a ladder made of crooked pieces of wood, and two carriers bear this stretcher on their heads. This is truly a bed of torture for any person who lacks Indian bones.

As far as I know, the natives, while sick, remain perfectly quiet, untroubled by their conscience or the thought of eternity, and they die as though they would not miss heaven. As soon as they give up their spirit, a terrible howling and crying is raised by the women present and by all the others when they hear about it. No one, however, sheds tears, excepting perhaps the nearest relatives, for all this is mere ceremony.

But who would believe that some of them show aversion and disgust toward a burial in the Catholic-Christian manner? I observed myself how some, still strong enough, though dangerously ill, refused to be led or carried to the mission in order to obtain there both spiritual and material care. I demanded an explanation and was told that they considered it a mocking of the dead to bury them with the ringing of bells, chanting, and other Catholic-Christian customs.

CHAPTER EIGHT : *Of the Character, Nature, and Customs of the Californians*

As a general rule, it may be said that the California Indians are stupid, awkward, rude, unclean, insolent, ungrateful, mendacious, thievish, abominably lazy, great talkers to their end, and naïve and childlike so far as intelligence and actions are concerned. They are an unreflecting people, without worries, unconcerned, a people who possess no self-control but follow, like animals in every respect, their natural instincts.

Nevertheless, the California Indians and all other American natives are human beings, true children of Adam, as we are. They have not grown out of the earth or stones, like moss and other plants, as a shameless freethinker and a greater liar than all the Indians combined will have us believe. At least I never saw one growing like that or ever heard of any of them who originated in that particular manner. They are endowed with reason and understanding like other people, and I think that, if in their early childhood they were sent to Europe, the boys to seminaries and colleges, and the girls to convents, they would go as far as any European in mores, virtues, in all arts and sciences. Many good examples of that can be found in different American provinces. Their animal-like stupidity is not inborn but grows slowly, just as intelligence does with others, and becomes more pronounced with the years.

I have known several of them who learned some mechanical trades

Of the Inhabitants

in a short time, sometimes by mere observation. Others, on the contrary, seemed to be more stupid after twelve or more years than at the time when I first became acquainted with them on my arrival in their homeland. They, therefore, received their gifts and talents from God and nature, like others, but they are likely to rust and become rustier and rustier with every day for lack of experience. A contributing factor, aside from their bestial way of life, may also be the habit of keeping their heads uncovered from earliest childhood on, regardless of nightly frosts or the cruel heat of the day. For these reasons, it is only too true that they are very awkward, clumsy, and of slow intelligence. It is only at the expense of much pain, patience, and time that the Christian doctrines can be poured into them. After reciting a sentence of only a few words twelve or more times, they still are not able to repeat it.

It is appropriate to mention here what Father Charlevoix [25] writes about the Canadian natives. One should not imagine that an Indian is convinced of something he is told, simply because he seems to approve of it. He always says, "Yes," and assents to anything, even though he has not understood its meaning, still less reflected upon his answer. He does so either because of self-interest, or to please the missionary, or out of pure unsusceptibility or indolence.

Their art of counting and arithmetic does not go beyond the number six, with some only to the number three; therefore, no native knows or can tell how many fingers he has. The reason for this is that they have nothing to count which would be of any value to them. It matters little to them whether the year has six or twelve months, and the month three or thirty days. Every day is a holiday, a blue Monday, for them. Neither do they care whether they have one or none, two or twelve children, since twelve do not cost more, nor do they cause more trouble than two, and the inheritance will not be lessened by a plurality of heirs. And thus it is with all other things. Should they be interested in the "more" or "less" of something, they would not consider it important to know or to express exactly how much more or less it is, because they cannot calculate and do not need to give an account of anything. Whatever goes beyond the number six is expressed in their language by "much," regardless of whether this "much" be seven, seventy, or seven hundred. The father confessor, or anyone else who wishes to, may guess the correct number.

They do not readily confess a crime unless caught in the act, because

Observations in Lower California

they fail to comprehend the force of evidence and how one event is the consequence of another. Also, they are not at all ashamed of lying. For this reason, a certain bread carrier did not admit his second theft because, while eating two loaves, he carefully hid under a stone a letter which was sent with the bread, thus "binding its eyes." He believed that this letter had seen him the first time and had betrayed him to the other missionary, to whom he was to deliver four loaves.

The priest at Mission San Borja ordered his Indians to strew the way with some greenery, because he wanted to bring the Holy Sacrament to a sick person. The Indians zealously tore up all the cabbages, greens, and whatever vegetables they could find in the missionary's little garden and threw them on the path.

Notwithstanding their incapacity and little intelligence, they are, nevertheless, sly, and on many occasions give good evidence of thorough craftiness. They will sell all of their poultry to the missionary at the beginning of a sickness, and afterwards they do not want to eat anything else but chicken meat so long as there is a chicken in the missionary's coop. A prisoner will pretend to be deathly ill and ask for the Last Sacrament, in order that, out of mere pity, he may be relieved of his fetters and may later find a chance to escape. They steal in a hundred different ways. In order to divert suspicion when the cupboard is found open, an Indian will confess for the purpose of giving another thief time to close the door. They invent a falsehood, relate it sincerely to the missionary with the one purpose in mind of preventing a marriage and playing the bride into the hands of another. These tricks, and many hundreds like them, only prove that the California natives are not animals, that they are capable of reasoning when selfish interests or necessity demand it.

They are daring and at the same time extremely fainthearted and timid. They will climb to the top of a frail and trembling cardón without hesitation or will mount a badly tamed horse and, without bridle and saddle, ride on it at night upon roads which I was afraid to use in the daytime. They walk on the most miserable scaffolds of a high building with the ease of cats, or they venture one or two hours into the open sea on a bundle of brushwood or on the thin stem of a palm tree without thinking of any danger. Yet a gunshot makes them forget their bows

Of the Inhabitants

and arrows, and half a dozen soldiers are capable of keeping several hundred Indians in check.

Gratitude toward benefactors, respect for superiors, reverence toward parents, friends, or relatives, politeness with fellow men are unknown to them, and words for these attributes are not in their dictionary. They speak freely and do not pay compliments, regardless of who stands before them. An Indian accepts a gift, turns his back upon the donor, and walks off. That is his procedure unless the Spanish phrase "Dios te lo pague" (God reward you), together with a slight bow, has been enforced upon his memory.

Where there is no honor, thus the saying goes, there is no shame. I always wondered how the little word *ié*, which is "to be ashamed," happened to become a part of their language, for among themselves none would ever blush because of any vice they indulge in. If a man had killed his father or mother, robbed churches, or committed other infamous crimes, and had been whipped and pilloried, he would, nevertheless, walk into a house with open countenance, a cheerful expression, and head held high. He would not lose the previous esteem, favors, and love of his fellow men.

Laziness, lying, and stealing are their three hereditary vices, their three original sins. They are not a people upon whose words one can rely. In one breath they will say "yes" six times and just as many times "no" without being ashamed or without at times even realizing that they contradict themselves. They never work, never bother about anything except when it is absolutely necessary to still the pangs of hunger as it overtakes them or as they feel it approaching. Consequently, if work has to be done in the mission, nothing is accomplished unless one drives the natives on every turn. During such periods there are sick Indians every day until the week is passed and it is Sunday, the day of miracles, as I called it because all those who had been sick the whole week were unfailingly well on that day. They could easily improve their living conditions at least a little if they were more industrious and more willing to work. Here and there they could sow a handful of corn, plant pumpkins, and cotton. They could keep small herds of goats and sheep, yes, even of cattle. They could make jerkins and coats out of deerskins, which they have now learned to prepare, but nothing of this kind must be expected of them. They do not care to eat pigeons unless they fly roasted into their mouths. To work today in order to gather the fruit of their labor a quarter or half a year later seems unbearable to them. In short, the brown Californian would rather turn white than to change his customs and his mode of life.

Books could be filled with accounts of their thefts. Gold and silver are out of danger; but anything that can be chewed, be it raw or cooked, above the ground or below, ripe or unripe, is just as safe from them as a mouse from a cat unless the eye of the owner is on it. The sheep or goat herdsman will not even spare the dog given to him as a safeguard for the herd. One day I secretly observed my cook reach with his hand into a kettle which stood over the fire and take out one piece of meat after another, chew off part of each, and throw the rest back into the kettle. An excellent horse, indispensable to a missionary, and for which he had recently refused twice the price of the original cost, was shot in the stomach by an arrow during broad daylight only a quarter of an hour away from where the missionary had dismounted for a few minutes. In the bodies of nineteen head of cattle which were slaughtered one day at the mission were found, after the removal of the hides, more than eight flint arrow points. The shafts had been broken off against the rocks and bushes, and lost by the wounded animals. The noonday meal or the supper of a missionary, be it in the kitchen or on the table, is not safe when he is hurriedly called away. The robes of the acolytes might be stolen. Even the supply of holy wafers in the sacristy is not safe from them. It is rather strange when at times they make off with things which are of no use to them, as for instance, soap, for they have nothing to wash. This shows how strong the habit of stealing can become.

The Indians admire nothing, and nothing is repulsive to them. The most beautiful and richest ecclesiastic garment of silver and gold arouses no interest; they will hardly look at it or reveal any surprise; they act as if it were made of wool and the galloons of common flax. They would rather see a piece of meat than the rarest piece of textile from Milan or Lyon. Therefore, a certain Canadian, after returning from the Old to the New France, remarked that nothing in Paris pleased him better than the butcher shops.

On the other hand, they will put on a piece of rag, though it may be as filthy and repulsive as possible, and they will wear it, if the weather

Of the Inhabitants

permits, till it rots on the body. They waste little time in decorating and attiring themselves. A chimney sweep would find enough dung on their chests, backs, hands, and faces to manure a field of turnips. They touch any filth without showing disgust, rather handling it as though it were a rose. They kill spiders with their bare hands, and with the same hands they throw aside a toad which comes too close. Many times I heard from reliable priests that these natives eat a certain kind of long-legged spider, also known in Germany, if they find many of them in one place; likewise, that they eat lice off one another's heads; that mothers lick the running substance off the noses of their little ones and swallow that. All this I have heard but never observed myself. I have seen, though, how at noon they fetch Indian corn in a half-washed turtle shell which they had used all morning to carry dung from the folds of the goats or sheep.

The California Indians are exceedingly good runners. I would gladly have given them my three horses to eat had I been able to march as well as they did. Whenever I traveled, I became incomparably more tired from riding than they from walking. They will walk twenty hours today and return tomorrow to the place they started from without showing much fatigue. A boy offered to accompany me on a trip, but I told him that the way was very long, my horse very brisk, and that I had to hurry. Whereupon he answered quickly, "Your horse will tire, but I will not." At another time—it was the end of December at sunrise (that is around seven o'clock in California)—I sent a fourteen-year-old boy to the neighboring mission, situated six hours from mine. About one and a half hour's distance from his place of destination, the boy met the missionary to whom he was to deliver a letter and who was just then on his way to pay me a visit. At once the boy turned around and at about noon arrived at my house with the missionary, who was riding a good mule. He had covered on foot within five hours a distance of more than nine hours.

Continuing the description of the morals and behavior of the native Californian with regard to the Christian religion, I am unable to praise those among whom I lived for seventeen years and, consequently, had enough time to become thoroughly acquainted with them. I must, rather, admit with great sorrow that, although I have used many means to educate them, together with the seed of the Divine Word, which was preached to them so many times, my labor has borne little fruit. This

Observations in Lower California

seed fell into hearts hardened by evil from tender youth by bad example and seduction. No human zeal on the part of the missionaries would ever be enough to guard the Indians from temptation. The opportunities for doing evil are numberless and offer themselves daily to young and old. The parents, the Spanish soldiers, cowherds, and a few others who come to the country or pass through it for the purpose of pearl fishing or mining add not a little to increase the evil. On the other hand, there are none of those human motives existent among them, nor natural and temporal ones, which, as in other places, keep so many people within the bounds of decency. These factors clear the way, so to speak, for the freer entrance of supernatural thoughts and of Divine grace into the human heart. The natives behave in certain matters in such an indescribable manner that it is better to recall the advice of the Apostle to the Ephesians, chapter v, verse 3, and to keep silent.

In all bad habits and vices the women are no better than the men and perhaps even surpass them in impudence and lack of devotion, in contrast to the habit of the women in all the rest of the world. From all the remarks made and still to be made about the ill-behaved California natives, the reader must not draw any general conclusions, applying them to the other baptized Americans. Just as among other objects, there are marked differences here and there among human beings in Europe, so it is in this world of the savages. It is difficult and unusual to find many good Christians in a country which offers no opportunities for work or community life. So much more remarkable is Catherine Tekakovíta (not to mention many other examples), whose grave with its many miracles shines brightly in Canada, and likewise the fortitude of so many others, women among them, who faced the cruel torture of fire among the inhuman Iroquois Indians. They are proof enough that the seed of the Divine Word and the sweat of the evangelical laborers not only bears fruit in the most barren fields of America but also bears hundredfold fruit in many other and different places.

CHAPTER NINE : *Of Certain Mores and Manners of Living of the Californians*

SINCE THE California Indians never had a police force, any form of government, or anything which resembled a religion, as I shall explain later in this chapter, but on the contrary, lead a completely animal-like existence, nothing extraordinary about their customs will be related here. The reader, therefore, has to be satisfied with the description of some trifles and of some customs of a varied nature which I observed among my natives.

In earlier times, both ear lobes of newly born male children were pierced with a pointed piece of wood; later on, the openings were extended by inserting bones and pieces of wood, so that the ears of some old natives almost touched their shoulders. Nowadays they omit this custom, not, however, the filthy habit of washing themselves with urine. The effect of this practice is now and then quite noticeable when they approach one or appear in the confessional. Lack of water or mere indolence accounts for this, for they are too lazy to fetch water from a near-by place, or sometimes the cold is too much for them.

The Indians do not know what a year really is, when it begins or ends. For instance, when they wish to say "a year ago" or "in this year," members of the Guaicura tribe, among whom I lived, use the following expressions: "An *ambía* is already past" or "this *ambía*." Ambía in their language means pitahaya, a fruit which has been spoken of in Part One, chapter six. "Three pitahayas" therefore means as much as three years, although they seldom make use of such a phrase because they hardly ever speak of a year or years among themselves but merely say "a little while ago" or "long ago," which might indicate one or twenty years—it makes no difference to them. For the same reason, they do not speak of months; they have not even a word expressing this idea. A week, however, is called *ambúja*, that is, "a house" or a place where someone lives, which name they have now, *per antonomafiam*, bestowed upon

Observations in Lower California

the church. Since they have to spend one week of every month at the mission and have to attend church services, they call the week "house" or "church."

The men let their hair grow to their shoulders, the women, in some places, wear it much shorter, like the Anabaptists. During periods of mourning for a deceased, both men and women cut it off almost completely. Formerly, all cut hair had to be given to their medicine men and exorcists, with which the latter manufactured horrible wigs or garments used in rituals. With their knives and shears, which are sharp stones, they cut reeds, sticks, aloe, disembowel and strip animals, yes, even use these same instruments to cut their own hair close to the skin. With this "lancet" they practice bleeding and cupping, and extract thorns or splinters from their hands and feet.

The men carry all burdens on their heads, but the women let the load hang down their backs, suspended by ropes that pass around their foreheads. To prevent the rope from cutting into the skin, they place between the rope and the forehead a piece of untanned deerskin, which reaches considerably above the head and resembles from afar a helmet or the high headdress worn by many ladies.

When they visit someone for any purpose, they practice the unpleasant custom of not uttering a word. When asked about the reason for their visit and what they want, their first reply will always be *vára*, which means "nothing." They do not greet anyone, for that would smell of civility, of which they have none; neither do they have a word for "to greet" or "greeting." When they are told something or face something which they do not like, they spit out sideways and scrape and scratch the ground with the left foot as a sign of their displeasure.

As long as polygamy was prevalent among them, the men used to marry all the sisters in a family (if there were several). The son-in-law was not allowed to look into the face of his mother-in-law or his wife's next female relations for a certain period of time. Whenever these women were present, he had to step aside and hide himself.

One of them told me that his people had formerly broken the spine of the deceased before burying them, and had thrown them into the grave, rolled up like a ball, insisting that they would rise up again if not treated in this barbaric manner. I observed several times, however, that they put shoes on the feet of the dead before burying them, which rather seems to

Of the Inhabitants

indicate that they were preparing them for a journey. Whenever I asked them why they followed this probably old custom, they had no answer.

Those who want to show, after a death, their love and tenderness for the deceased, or for the widow or widower, for father or mother, brother or sister of the dead, will hide in a place near the seat of the mourner or where the latter has to pass; and at his approach they creep out from their hiding place, half sitting, half standing, and intone a gloomy, mournful "hu, hu, hu," resembling a kind of dry weeping; then they beat their heads with pointed, sharp stones until the blood flows down their shoulders. They will not give up this barbaric custom in spite of the many prohibiting edicts which have been issued. A few years ago I learned that some had done this again after the funeral of a certain woman. I left the offenders the choice of either submitting to a fixed punishment or of repeating the ceremony in my presence. They chose the latter. I thought that this ritual was nothing but bluff, but soon I saw the blood trickling down from their lacerated heads.

With boys and girls who have arrived at the age of puberty, with pregnant women, new-born children, and women in childbed, they observed, and secretly still observe, all kinds of absurd and superstitious rites, which, for reasons of decency, cannot be described here.

They also cling to a song which they call *ambéra didi* and a dance called *agénari*. The first is an inarticulate, meaningless whispering and shouting with which they express their joy and pleasure and which varies according to each one's mood. Their language and their intelligence does not allow for a better form of rhymed poetry. The dance, which always accompanies their singing, is nothing else but a foolish, preposterous kind of gesticulating, jumping, and hopping, of walking in a circle, and of silly advances and retreats. Yet they enjoy this so greatly that they spend half or even whole nights with such singing and dancing, in which respect they resemble Europeans, among whom more have killed themselves dancing during the carnival season and at other times than have died from fasting or praying.

I have pointed out that the natives will not give up this singing and dancing, although both kinds of entertainment, innocent in themselves, have been rigidly forbidden because they are always accompanied by much disorder, viciousness, and infamy.

There have always been and still are sorcerers and conjurers among them, but much is wanting to deserve such titles. There are male and female exorcisers who never saw the devil; there are others who exorcise diseases, which they never cure, or they promise to make pitahayas, though they could only fetch and eat them. All these miracle men and clairvoyant women are in reality, like the rest of them, nothing but a stupid and clumsy group of people who at times go into a cave and by changing their voices try to give the impression to the people that they are conversing with some mysterious being. They threaten their fellows with diseases and famine or promise to drive the smallpox or another plague away. When these charlatans and windbags appeared in their gala ceremonial apparel they were enveloped in long capes or mantles made entirely of human hair. The missionaries burn a great number of these garments at all the newly established missions. The aim of these native swindlers is to get their food for nothing, without the work of gathering it in the fields. The foolish people bring them as much as they can and the best of what they are able to find in order to curry their favor and keep them in good humor. Their prestige is not very great today, yet the sick will not cease to place their confidence in them, as I have already remarked elsewhere.

Their talent for feigning a sudden and severe illness and letting themselves be carried over many miles to the mission could almost be called a custom. A good whipping, however, would quickly restore most of them to health. Of the many cases, I remember two men who were so good in pretending to be near death that I did not hesitate to give them Extreme Unction. Another frightened me terribly by insisting that he had smallpox, which actually raged in the neighboring mission, causing the priest there indescribable trouble and daily worry for three months and keeping him almost constantly on horseback. A fourth man, called Clemente, also appeared ready to give up the ghost. Since, however, he had never seen a dying person (he had not even witnessed the death of his wife, whom I buried, for he was never at home when I visited her), but had observed many cows and oxen which his arrow had brought down, he imitated such dying cattle so naturally, lolling his tongue and licking his lips, that he was called "Clemente Vaca," which is Clemente the cow, a name which still sticks to him.

The reason for such make-believe and disgusting lies is either to escape work, which they hate so much, though it is sometimes for their

Of the Inhabitants

own good, or to escape punishment which they may incur for their villainous actions.

Punishment for extraordinary crime is fixed by the royal officer who at the same time is captain of the California squadron, but common misdemeanors fall within the jurisdiction of the corporal of the soldiers stationed at each mission. Murder alone is punished by death (shooting). For all other misdeeds the culprit is either given a number of lashes with a leather whip on his bare skin, or his feet are put into irons for some days, weeks, or months. There are no ecclesiastical penalties because the Roman popes did not consider it wise to apply them to the American Indians. Concerning money fines, the German saying might be in order: "Where there is nothing, even the emperor loses his rights."

Here would be the time and place to tell about the California form of government and religion before the natives were converted to Christianity. Yet there is nothing to say about these two subjects except that not a trace of either can be found. Consequently, they had no magistrates, no police, no laws, no idols, temples, no religious worship, no rites, or anything comparable. They neither prayed to the true and only God, nor did they believe in false deities. What kind of a magistrate, what kind of government could there be in a country where all are equal, where no one owns more nor would be able to own more than another, where no one possesses anything but his own body, his soul, and black-brown skin? Where a child, as soon as he is able to walk, refuses to obey his parents and does not consider it his duty to obey?

Each native did as he pleased, asking nobody, caring for nobody, and all vices and misdeeds (provided they thought in such terms) remained unpunished unless an offended private person or his relatives took the law in his own hands and sought revenge. The different tribes did not represent communities or a commonwealth; they rather resembled a herd of wild pigs, each one going his own way and grunting wherever and whenever he pleased, together today, scattered tomorrow, and another day accidentally meeting again, without order or leadership, without any head or any obedience. In one word, the California natives lived, with all due respect, as though they had been freethinkers and materialists.

It seems that where there is no authority religion cannot exist, for the latter requires laws and their enforcement. Probably for this reason, our

Observations in Lower California

present-day illusionists and atheists freely confess that they are no less enemies of all rulers and authorities than of all religion. They rail as much against the sovereign as they scoff at all services of worship, and they would like to see Europe reach the state where all people, as in California, are socially of the same estate and California republics would replace monarchies. Well, no honest man will envy these gentlemen their fraternal and blood relationship with such a noble nation as the nonbaptized Californians were and still are. So far as religion is concerned, there is a wide difference between the two. It is one thing to be ignorant and not to think of a supreme being because of negligence and lack of reflection, and another thing to deny out of pure wickedness the existence of a supreme and eternal being by zealously seeking to contrive deceptive arguments.

I diligently inquired and investigated among those with whom I lived to ascertain whether they had had any conception of God, a future life, and a soul, but I never could discover the slightest trace of such knowledge. Their language has no words which would signify one or the other; therefore, the Spanish words *Dios* and *alma* have to be used in sermons and in the teaching of the catechism. It could hardly be otherwise among people who think only of eating and amusing themselves but do not care to reflect on or think about anything, people who look at the sun, the moon, the stars, and everything else with as much interest as do animals. If something not connected with eating and amusement catches their attention, they dismiss it with the phrase *aipekériri*, that is, "Who knows that?" When I asked them, for instance, whether they never wondered who might have created the sun and the moon or who preserves and directs them, I was sent home with a *vára*, which means "no" in their language.

The daily pattern of life of unbaptized California Indians always runs like this. In the evening, when their bellies are filled, they lie down or sit together, talking until they are tired of it or cannot think of anything more to say. In the morning, they sleep till hunger or the lust for food makes them get up. As soon as they are awake, they start to eat, if anything edible is around, and immediately the laughing, chatting, and joking is resumed. After this kind of morning prayer, when the sun is already fairly high, the men reach for their bows and arrows, and the women tie their yokes or turtle shells around their foreheads. Some go to the

Of the Inhabitants

right, others to the left, here six, there four, over there eight or two, or sometimes just one alone. The chattering, laughing, and joking continue all the way. They watch for a mouse, lizard, snake, hare, or a deer to appear. One of them tears up a yucca or some other root, another cuts off half a dozen aloe heads. They rest a little, sitting together or lying down in the rare shade if any can be found; all the while their tongues keep wagging. At length they rise again, play or wrestle to find out who is the strongest man or woman among them and who can throw his opponent to the ground. Finally they start on their way back or walk for another few hours. At the nearest water place they stop and begin singeing, burning, roasting, and grinding the food they found during the day. Constantly chattering, they eat as long as something is left and there is still space in their stomachs. After more childish or indecent prattling, they go to rest again, as they did the night before. In this manner they spend the day, month, the whole year. Their talks or chatterings are about eating, childish nonsense, and all kinds of mischievous tricks. They still adhere to almost the same manner of living if they are not or cannot be put to some useful work at the missions, which is in many ways to their advantage.

Who would, under these circumstances, expect to find even a little spark of religion among such people? They discuss the course taken by a wounded deer that escaped at nightfall, with an arrow in its side, and how they are going to pursue it the next morning, but they never think about the course of the sun and the other heavenly bodies. They talk about pitahayas long before they are ripe, but never bother to discuss or dream about the origin and the creator of the pitahayas and all other things. They never take pains to reflect.

I know well that someone wrote of at least one tribe in California which had been found with some knowledge of the incarnation of the Son of God and the Holy Trinity. Since, however, the knowledge of these mysteries could only have been imparted by preaching the Gospel to them, there can be no doubt that this is an exaggeration and a lie conceived by some California natives recently instructed in Christianity and baptized, who do this in order to flatter a missionary. They are masters in bragging and lying and not at all scrupulous. It is quite human to let oneself be deceived and duped, especially if a man is inexperienced and unfamiliar with the tricks of the natives. In all probability there has never been anyone who lived among them who would not have a hundred similar experiences under various conditions. If it were necessary, I myself could recite many examples to substantiate this.

It is, moreover, a tremendous task to draw some clear and definite statement out of the natives in answer to questions and inquiries. Besides their shameless lies, deceptions, and all kinds of roundabout talk, from inborn awkwardness and negligence they either tangle up the subject in question so frightfully or contradict themselves so often that a white man's patience almost gives out. A missionary once begged me to find out whether a certain N. had been married to the sister of another N. before his baptism, which he received when he was a grown man. A simple "yes" or "no" would have decided the matter, but more than three quarters of an hour was spent with questions and answers without ever getting to the bottom of the case or finding out the truth. I put the whole conversation down on paper and sent the protocol to the missionary, who was no more successful than I in finding out whether N. had been married to the sister or not. That is how dark and confused the attic of these California Hottentots seems to be.

CHAPTER TEN : *Of the Language and the Manner of Speech of the Californians*

I PURPOSELY postponed the treatment of this subject so that the reader might get a foretaste of what this language may be after having acquired some knowledge of the character, mores, and other peculiarities of this people from the previous pages. My readers will be less surprised and it will be easier for them to comprehend why the Indians speak as they do, after knowing in advance something of their manner of living.

Of the Inhabitants

A people without government, police, religion and laws, without honor and shame, without clothing and dwellings; a people which occupies itself with nothing, speaks of nothing, thinks and meditates about nothing, cares for nothing except for food and other things which they have in common with animals; a nation which cultivates no friendships with other nations, has no common interests and no trade with others, never moves out of its own small district inhabited by a few hundred souls, and where nothing is seen but thorns, stones, wild animals, and vermin—of such a nation, I say, it is easy to imagine what kind of graceful language, rich in words and beautiful expressions, it must have.

A man about sixty years old ran away from my mission with his son, a boy of about six. After they had spent five years all alone in the California desert lands, they were found and brought back again to the mission. It is easy to imagine how and on what noble subjects these two hermits may have conversed in their daily association. The boy, then almost twelve years old, could hardly utter three words in succession. Except for "water," "wood," "fire," "snake," "mouse," and the like, he could name nothing. His own countrymen called him the stupid and dumb Pablo, or Paul (for that was his name). It is not difficult to apply the story of this boy to the whole people.

Disregarding a great many dialects and the five entirely different languages spoken in California,* as it is known today, I shall deal only with the Guaicura language, which I, with God's help and so far as it was necessary, have learned. I can say that it is savage and barbaric in the highest degree. When I use the terms "savage and barbaric," I do not mean a hard pronunciation or a succession of many consonants, for these things are not essential and innate characteristics of a language but are, it would seem, purely accidental and superficial. They are imagined by those who do not understand the so-called savage language. As everyone knows, the Italians and the French accuse the Germans, and the Germans the Bohemians or the Poles, of speaking a barbaric tongue; but they do so only until they are able to converse with each other. Keeping this remark in mind and adding that the Guaicura alphabet

---

* These are the Laymóna in the district of the mission of Loreto, the Cochimí in Mission San Xavier, and other languages toward the north, the Uchities and the Pericúes in the south, and the still unknown language spoken by the tribe which Father Linck visited on his trip.

Observations in Lower California

does not have the letters "O," "F," "G," "L," "X," "Z," nor "S" (except for a "tsh"), the barbarism of this language consists of the following.

1. A surprising and pitiful lack of a great number of words, without which, I believe, it is hardly possible for reasoning creatures to converse with each other, still less to preach to them or teach them the Christian doctrine. There are no words to express whatever is not material and not perceptible by the senses and can neither be seen nor touched, no words to express virtues and vices or qualities of feeling (i.e., no substantives or nouns of that type and only three or four adjectives which can be read in the face, namely, merry, sad, tired, and angry). There are no terms which relate to social, human, or rational and civil life, and no words for a multitude of other objects. It would be futile to look in a Guaicura dictionary, for instance, for the following words: Life, death, weather, time, cold, heat, world, rain, reason, memory, knowledge, honor, decency, consolation, peace, quarrel, member, joy, grace, feeling, friend, friendship, truth, shame, enmity, faith, love, hope, wish, desire, hate, anger, gratitude, patience, meekness, envy, industry, virtue, vice, beauty, form, sickness, danger, fear, occasion, thing, diversity, punishment, doubt, servant, master, virgin, judgment, suspicion, happiness, happy, reasonable, bashful, honorable, intelligent, moderate, pious, obedient, rich, poor, young, old, agreeable, lovely, friendly, half, quick, profound, round, contented, to greet, to thank, to punish, to be silent, to walk, to complain, to worship, to doubt, to buy, to flatter, to caress, to persecute, to dwell, to breathe, to imagine, to idle, to insult, to comfort, to live, and thousands of words like these (in general all German nouns ending in -heit, -keit, -niss, -ung, and -schaft).

The word "life" as a noun or as a verb in a natural or a moral sense is lacking, but not the adjective "alive." They have no words to indicate bad, narrow, short, distant, little, and so on, except by adding the negation *ja* or *ra* to words like "good," "wide," "long," "near," and "much." They have particular words for "old man," "old woman," "young man," "young woman," and so forth, but the terms "old" or "young" do not exist in their language. They possess only four words for denoting all the different colors and do not distinguish yellow from red, blue from green, black from brown, white from ash-colored, and so on.

Now let anyone try to speak to them about European affairs or to

Of the Inhabitants

translate for them some article from a Madrid newspaper, a copy of which was occasionally seen in California a year or a year and a half after publication; or try to deliver a beautiful sermon in praise of the saints, explaining how they crushed all vanity under their feet, forsook princely domains and entire kingdoms, distributed all their belongings and possessions among the poor, voluntarily chose poverty, subjected themselves for years to the severest penances, conquered their inclinations, subdued their passions, spent eight and more hours daily in prayer and divine meditation, hated the world and their own lives, how they were chaste and humble, slept on the bare ground, ate no meat, drank no wine, and so on. Concerning European affairs, the preacher simply has to put his finger to his mouth for want of words; and concerning the life of the saints, a California Indian will tell him that he never slept in a bed in all his life, that he does not even know what bread is, much less how beer and wine would taste, that he hardly ever ate meat, except that of rats and mice.

The California natives do not have the above-mentioned words, as well as many others in their "dictionary." Since they never talk about such things and their manner of life is so close to that of animals, the use of such terms is unnecessary. Heat and cold, rain or sickness, are described by saying "it is warm," "it rains," "this" or "that person is sick," nothing else. For instance, such common phrases as "the sickness has much weakened this or that person," "cold is less bearable than heat," "after rain follows sunshine" are certainly very simple in themselves and current among all European peasants; yet they are far above the level of thinking and talking of California Indians. Whoever wishes to determine whether certain words or phrases might be found in the Indians' dictionary should consider whether such words or manners of speech could possibly be in accord with their way of life, daily occupations, childhood, and education as described above.

They have no names for the separate parts of the human body, no terms like "father," "mother," "son," "brother," or words referring to other relatives, or expressions like "word," "language," "breath," "pain," "comrade," and many other things. They will always prefix these words with the possessive adjectives "my," "thy," "our," etc. They say, therefore, only *bedáre, edáre, tiáre, kepedáre,* etc. (i.e., my, thy, his, our father) when thinking of men, and *bécue, écue, tícue, kepécue* when speaking of women. So also *mapá, etapá, tapá* (i.e., my, your, his forehead); *minamú, einamú, tinamú* (for my, thy, his nose); *betanía, etanía, tishanía* (my, thy, his word); *menembeû, enembeû, tenembeû* (my, thy, his pain); etc. There is not a single Californian of the Guaicura speech who could understand and answer if I asked the meaning of *are, cue, tania, apá, namú,* and *nembeû* (for the terms: father, forehead, speech, pain), since words of an abstract nature are not known to them. They could never dream, think, or speak, for instance, of the obligations of a father, of a gloomy, a serene, a narrow, or a large forehead, of a long, a flat, or an aquiline nose.

2. The barbarism of the Guaicura language is also apparent in the deficiency and lack of prepositions, conjunctions, and relative pronouns, except for the prepositions *déve* or *tipítsheû*, which is "on account of," and *tína*, which means "on" or "upon." Instead of all the other prepositions, like: out, in, before, through, with, for, against, by, etc., they manage with *me, pe, te*, which have the same meaning, or they simply omit them entirely. Little words like: that, therewith, but, while, because, therefore, thus, neither, yet, however, as, though, etc., are missing in their language, as is the *relativum* "which" ("who") so necessary and so frequently used in other languages.

3. They lack the comparatives and superlatives, the words "more" and "less," and nearly all adverbs, including those derived from adjectives, like: lately, early, entirely, almost, etc. Instead of saying "Peter is taller and has more than Paul," they say "Peter is tall and has much; Paul is not tall and has not much."

4. They have no conjunctive, imperative, and almost no optative mood. There is no passive verb form and no reciprocal verb as alternative, which the Spaniards and French use so much. There are no declensions, no articles. Their verbs have only one mood and three tenses. The latter are formed by affixing certain endings to the verb; namely, *re* or *reke* (in the present); *rikíri, rujére, ráupe,* or *ráupere* (in the preterit); *me* or *meje* or *éneme* (in the future). These are equal for all persons and both numbers. Sometimes the plural is formed by prefixing the syllable *ku*, or *k* alone, to the verb, or by changing the verb's first syllable or letter into *ku*; for instance, the verbs *piabakè* (to fight), *umutù* (to remember), *jake* (to chat) change to *kupiábake, kumutú,* and *kuáke* when there are several fighters, thinkers, and talkers. A few of their verbs have also a

Of the Inhabitants

preterit passive participle, for instance, *tshípake* (to beat), *tshipitshürre* (a beaten one, i.e., a person who has been beaten), plural *kutipaû*. Some nouns and adjectives are likewise subject to changes in the plural, as for instance, *ánaï* (woman), *kánaï* (women), *entuditú* (ugly or bad), and *entuditámma* (bad or ugly women). *Be* stands for "I," "to me," "me," and "my"; *ei* means "thou," "to thee," "thee," "thy," and so on through all the possessive pronouns. Yet *becún* or *beticún* also signifies "my"; and *écun* or *eiticún*, "thy." They always place the conjunction "and" at the end of a sentence. They know nothing about metaphors; therefore, the phrase "blessed is the fruit of thy womb" in the "Hail Mary" has simply been replaced by "thy child." On the other hand, they are very shrewd in inventing names for things they have never seen before; for instance, they call a door, "mouth"; bread, "light" (weight); iron, "heavy"; wine, "bad water"; a gun, "bow"; the officials, "bearers of canes"; the Spanish captain, "wild or cruel"; oxen and cows, "deer"; horse and mule, *titshénu-tshà*, that is, "child of a wise mother"; and the missionary, in speaking of or to him, *tiá-pa-tù*, that is, "one who has his house in the north" or in short "man from the north."

In order to speak such a wild, poor, primitive, and clumsy language, a European has to make many adjustments and almost become one of the natives. To teach the Christian truth, which they need so badly, to the natives in their own tongue, one must use all kinds of paraphrases which, when literally translated into German or any other European language, would often sound odd and even ridiculous to European ears. And since the curious reader may be pleased to see a sample of this admirable language, I shall give an illustration from the California Guaicura catechism, the "Lord's Prayer" and the "Creed," each with a double translation, and also the whole conjugation of the verb *amukíri*.

The Lord's Prayer
in the California Guaicura Language
and Literal English Translation

Kepè - dáre	tekerekádatembà	daï	eï - rì	akátuikè
Our father	arched earth	thou art	Thee O, that	acknowledge

pu - me	tshakárrake	pu - me	ti	tshie:	ecùn	gracia - ri
all will	praise	all will	people	and:	Thy	grace O, that

Observations in Lower California

atúme	catè	tekerekádatembà	tshie:	eï	ri		jebarrakéme
have	we	arched earth	and:	Thee	O, that		obey
ti	pù	jaûpe	datembà	páe	eï	jebarrakére,	aëna kéa:
people	all	here	earth,	as	Thee	obey,	above are:
kepecùn	búe	kepe	kên	jatúpe	untâiri:	catè	kuitsharrakè
our	food	us	give	this	day:	us	forgive
têi	tshie	kepecùn	atacámara,	páe	kuitsharrakère	catè	tshie
you	and	our	evil,	as	forgive	we	also
cávape	atukiàra	kepetujakè:	catè	tikakambà	têi		tshie,
they	evil	us do:	us	help	Thou		and,
cuvumerà	catè	uë	atukiàra:	kepe	kakunjà	pe	atacára
will wish	no we	anything	evil:	us	protect	from	evil
tshie.	Amen.						
and.	Amen.						

Translation

Our Father, Thou art in Heaven; O, that all people may acknowledge and praise Thee! O, that we may have Thy grace and Heaven! O, that all men may obey Thee here in this world, as those who are above obey Thee! Our food give us this day and forgive us our sins, as we also forgive those who do evil to us; and help us that we may not desire anything evil and protect us from evil. Amen.

The Twelve Articles of the Creed
and Its Literal Translation into English

Irimánjure	pè	Diòs	Tíare	uretì -	pu -	puduéne,	tâupe	me
I believe	in	God	Father	make	all	can,	this	of
buarà	uretírikíri	tekerekádatembà	atembà	tshie.	Irimánjure			
nothing	has made	arched earth	earth	and.	I believe			
tshie	pe	Jesu	Christo	titshánu	íbe	te	tiáre,	éte
also	in	Jesus	Christ	his son	alone	of	his father,	man
punjére	pe	Espiritu	Santo,	pedára	tshie	me	Santa	Maria
made	by	Holy	Ghost,	born	and	of	Saint	Mary

Of the Inhabitants

virgen.	Irimánjure	tshie	tåu	vérepe	Jesu	Christo	híbitsherikíri
virgin.	I believe	also	this	same	Jesus	Christ	has suffered

tenembeû	apánne	ïebitshéne	témme	pe	Judea	Pontio
his pain	great	commanding	being	in	Judea	Pontius

Pilato;	kutikürre	rikíri	tína	cruz,	pibikíri	kejenjùta
Pilate;	stretched out	was	on	cross,	has died	under earth

rikíri	tshie;	keritshéü	atembà	búnju;	me akúnju	untâîri
is buried	also	gone down	earth	below;	three	days

tipè - tshetshutipè	rikíri;	tshukíti	tekerecadátembà,	penekà	tshie
alive again	was;	gone to	arched earth,	sits	also

me	titshuketà	te	Dios	tiáre	uretì - pu - puduéne.
his	right hand	of	God	his father	make all can.

Aipúreve	tenkíe	uteürì - ku - méje	atacámma	atacámmara	
From thence	reward	give will come	good	evil	

ti	tshie.	Irimánjure	pe	Espiritu Santo;	Irimánjure epì
people	also.	I believe	in	Holy Ghost;	I believe there is

santa	Iglesia catholica,	communion	te	kunjukaráü ti	tshie,
Holy	Catholic Church,	communion	of	washed people	also,

Irimánjure	kuitsharakéme	Dios	kumbáte - didì-re,	kutéve - didì-re
I believe	will forgive	God	hate well,	confess well

ti	tshie	kicùn	atacámmara	pánne	pù.	Irimánjure tshie
men	and	their	evil	great	all.	I believe and

tipè	tshetshutipé	me	tibikíu	ti	pù;	enjéme típe dêi
alive	again		be dead	people	all;	then alive ever

méje	tucáva	tshie.	Amen.
will be	the same	and.	Amen.

Translation

I believe in God the Father, Who can make everything; He has made Heaven and earth of nothing. I believe also in Jesus Christ, the only Son of his Father, Who was made by the Holy Ghost, Who was born of the Virgin Mary. I believe also this same Jesus Christ suffered great pain while Pontius Pilate reigned in Judea: He was stretched out on the cross; He died and was buried; He descended below the earth; He came to life again in three days; He went up to Heaven; He sits at the right hand of God his Father, Who can make everything; He will come from there to give payment to the good and the bad. I believe in the Holy Ghost; I believe there is a Holy Catholic Church, communion of the baptized. I believe God will forgive those men who thoroughly hate and completely confess all their great sins. I believe also all dead men will come to life again and then they will live forever. Amen.

Concerning this "Lord's Prayer" and "Creed" and its translation, the following remarks should be kept in mind.

1. That the first version is translated immediately under the Guaicura text, word for word, almost syllable by syllable. This may sound awkward and absurd to the European ear. The other translation is more pleasing. The Indian text conveys an idea of how a native hears and imagines it. This applies also to those who understand the Guaicura language and have become accustomed from childhood on or by long practice to the weird and unreasonable composition of words and the omission of relative pronouns and of prepositions.

2. Because the California Indians do not have any expressions for the following words: holy, church, God, Ghost, communion, grace, will, cross, virgin, name, hell, kingdom, bread, guilt, temptation, creator, indulgence, or forgiveness, life, resurrection, happen, daily, Lord, almighty, third, etc., Spanish words were used in order to avoid too lengthy and not easily understood circumlocutions. Sometimes the word was replaced by paraphrasing it, if this proved easier and less awkward, or some words were even omitted when it was possible to do so without changing the meaning or when no equivalent could be found, as for instance, the word "daily" in the "Lord's Prayer" and the word "Lord" in the "Creed."

3. I could not use "He shall come to judge the living and the dead," for an Indian would not understand the ethical or theological meaning of these and similar words. Neither was it permissible to say "the flesh will live again," for "flesh" is to them the meat of deer or cattle; they would laugh if they were told that a human being was also "flesh" or has "flesh." Consequently, they would come to believe that deer and cows

Of the Inhabitants

would rise on judgment day if they were told of the resurrection of the "flesh."

4. In general, the Guaicura Californian calls "Heaven" usually *aëna,* that is, "above," or also, but less frequently, *tekerekádatembà,* which means curved or arched earth or land, because the firmament resembles a vault or an arch. "Hell," on the other hand, they were told to call "the fire that never expires," but this expression could not be used in the sixth article of the "Creed" unless they were Calvinists in accordance with the blasphemy which Calvin wrote Book II, chap. x, 10.

Complete Conjugation
of the verb *Amukíri,* to play

Present

Singular	bè	I			
	eï	thou	amukírire		play
	tutâu	he			
Plural	catè	we			
	petè	you	amukírire		play
	tucáva	they			

Preterit

Singular	bè	I	amukiririkíri		
	eï	thou	vel	rujére	have played
	tutau	he	vel	râupe	
			vel	râúpere	
Plural	catè	we	amukiriríkiri		
	petè	you	vel	rujére	have played
	tucáva	they	vel	râupe	
			vel	râúpere	

Future

Singular	bè	I	amukírime		
	eï	thou	vel méje		shall play
	tutau	he	vel éneme		

Observations in Lower California

Plural	catè	we	amukirimè	
	petè	you	vel méje	shall play
	tucáva	they	vel enneme	

Imperative

| Singular | amukiri tei | play |
| Plural | amukiri tu | play |

Optative

Singular	be - ri		
	eï - ri		
	tutau - ri	amukiririki	Would to God,
		rikára vel	I, thou, he,
Plural	catè - ri	amukirirujerára!	we, you, they
	petè - ri		had not played
	tucava - ri		

PART THREE : OF THE ARRIVAL OF
THE SPANIARDS, INTRODUCTION
OF THE CHRISTIAN FAITH,
AND OF THE MISSIONS

CHAPTER ONE : *Futile Expeditions of the Spaniards to California. Father Salvatierra Gains a Firm Footing and Establishes Mission Loreto*

T HE ONLY purpose of Divine Providence in the discovery of the route to the East Indies around the Cape of Good Hope and in the finding of the fourth continent seems beyond a doubt to have been the expansion of the Christian Faith and the eternal salvation of the many heathen who live in the East and the West. Aside from this, as Saint Theresa has said, these discoveries have brought to Europe and Europeans more harm than good. Many white men go to eternal perdition in India who could have found salvation in Europe. Men could have lived very well, just as in former times, without the goods, without the gold and silver which are brought from the New World and which only serve to increase pomp and voluptuousness. These things, however, were the little decoy whistles, or the bait, which lured foreign nations into the New World, and their explorers certainly did not spare any effort—particularly in America—to find treasure. There was no ocean they did not cross, no river they did not ford, no corner they did not search in the first century of their occupation.

As a consequence of this untiring zeal to search for and to discover new treasures in these new lands, poor California could not very long remain hidden. The conqueror of the land and city of Mexico, Hernán Cortés himself, wanted also to become the conqueror of California. In the 'twenties of the sixteenth century he had sent several people to California, but all of them had poor success. Cortés' luck was better than that of the previous explorers; he at least saved his skin and got away to Acapulco! After Cortés, more than ten other Spaniards attempted to conquer California for the Crown of Spain, partly at the king's expense, partly at their own; but until the end of the century all their efforts and expenses were in vain. Their enterprises remained fruitless more because of the barrenness and aridity of the soil, as

Observations in Lower California

described in Part One of these reports, than because of the resistance of the inhabitants which the Spaniards encountered. Although there were bloody heads at times, because the California Indians felt bitter toward the whole Spanish nation, thanks to the evil behavior and infamous practices of the many pearl fishers who had enraged the natives.

The Spaniards thought they would find rich gold and silver veins in California, as well as rich and productive soil. Since they found neither and were forced to live off the provisions they had brought along on their ships, all of them soon lost courage and turned back. It went so far that the Royal Council in Mexico proclaimed California an unconquerable land, and with this decision, California was forgotten. During the reign of Charles II, a certain Francisco Luzenilla [26] wanted to risk one more expedition to California—at his own expense and without assistance from the royal treasury—but his request was rejected.

A member of the Spanish expeditions to California undertaken in the 1680's was Father Eusebius Kino,[27] then a Jesuit missionary in Sonora and formerly professor of mathematics at Ingolstadt. It did not seem impossible to him, or even very difficult, to conquer this land, provided the sole purpose was the eternal salvation of the natives, and if one brought with him a good supply of patience, generosity, and fortitude.

One of Father Kino's contemporaries was Father Juan María Salvatierra, a Jesuit from Milan, of noble ancestry, formerly missionary in Tarahumára, Superior of all the missions, and later Provincial of the New Spain or Mexican Jesuit province. He was known to be a man of great religious zeal, gentle disposition, humility, patience, and kindness. At the same time he also possessed a healthy, strong, and powerful constitution. He gave many proofs of his qualities, as can be read in the history of his life, which has appeared in print. Father Kino discussed California at length with Father Salvatierra when the latter visited the missions of Sonora in his official capacity. Both men longed to go there; both felt a great desire to start the missionary work and the conversion of the Indians in California; however, God reserved this honor for Father Salvatierra alone. He finally received permission to sail to California after overcoming many objections from his superiors, as well as from the High Council and the Viceroy of Mexico, and after many presentations, much pleading, and loss of time. The Viceroy, however, stated that the undertaking must be carried out at the expense of Father

Of the Arrival of the Spaniards

Salvatierra, that the Father could not hope for help from the royal treasury, and would have no right to demand such help. Father Salvatierra had nothing except a few good friends, his gentle disposition, and his faith in God. And God did not forsake him, but provided him with a number of benefactors who desired to participate in such a holy work. Among others, a secular priest from Querétaro, Juan Cavallero y Ozio, donated no less than twenty thousand pesos; that is, forty thousand Rhenish guilders. He added to this gift his pledge to honor and pay promptly all notes drawn by Salvatierra on Juan Cavallero's name. A rich gentleman from Acapulco, Gil de la Sierpe, lent him a small galleot, gave him some alms, and made him a present of another vessel.

Thereupon Salvatierra enlisted five soldiers, hired several others who could be of use, and loaded the ship with a small cannon and enough corn, dried beef, and other necessities to supply the group, as well as the California Indians, for several months. In October, 1697, Father Salvatierra ordered the anchors to be lifted and set sail from the province of Sinaloa under Divine guidance and the mighty protection of Our Lady of Loreto. Happily he landed nine days later, on a Saturday, in the Bay of San Dionisio, which is now named after Our Lady of Loreto.

The California natives soon noticed the difference between these foreigners and new guests and those others whom they had seen previously in their land from time to time. After a few days, they laid aside their mistrust and sought to make friends with the newcomers. Father Salvatierra increased this friendship day by day with the help of small gifts and his own kind and gentle manner. Yet at times minor frictions did occur, but were settled without bloodshed. It was impossible to let the Indians have their will in all things, or to satisfy completely their voracity, because they sought to acquire by force what was not given to them voluntarily.

A tent was set up to serve as a chapel, several huts were built of the poor California lumber, and all was enclosed by a parapet and a low bulwark. Everything which was necessary or customary under such circumstances was done as well as possible as a safeguard against unexpected or sudden attack from the barbarians.

No time could be lost. There were too many mouths to feed, few provisions available, and absolutely nothing could be drawn from the land. For these reasons it was considered wise, after a few weeks had passed, to send one of the two ships back to Sinaloa in order to fetch more provisions for California. In the meantime, Salvatierra began to learn the native language and to instruct his new parishioners. For this purpose he taught Spanish to a few young Californians. Thus he laid the foundations for the first mission, which he wished to be called Loreto in honor of the Mother of God.

After a few months, the little ship which was sent to fetch provisions returned well loaded, just as want was beginning to make itself felt. It also brought some new soldiers and Father Píccolo, a Jesuit from Sicily. Before a year had passed, Father Salvatierra had learned the essentials of the native language, and he undertook a trip into the surrounding territories to visit neighboring tribes. Father Píccolo, however, laid the foundations for a second mission, eight hours from Loreto, in the year 1699. He named it for the Apostle of the Indies, St. Francis Xavier.

CHAPTER TWO : *Of the Progress of the Established Missions and of the Founding of New Ones*

THE YEAR WAS 1700. Heretofore the enterprises of Father Salvatierra had brought no expense to the Catholic King. With the growth of the new mission, however, and with the preparations to penetrate farther into the land to found additional missions, expenses increased considerably. Salvatierra submitted a complete account and report to the Viceroy of Mexico, informing him of all that had occurred up to that time. He put before the Royal Council in Guadalajara an account not only of past expenditures, but stressed particularly the poverty of the mission. He mentioned the shipwreck of one of the vessels, the poor condition of the other, and emphasized the necessity of putting the

Of the Arrival of the Spaniards

soldiers' pay on a stable basis. He pointed out that the casual alms which he received might cease any day, and might suddenly force him to abandon the enterprise. The Royal Council referred Father Salvatierra's case to the Viceroy. The latter reminded Salvatierra that he had been granted permission to go to California only if he could cover his own expenses. The Viceroy, however, did not consider the fact that taking possession of land is one thing, while holding it for the future is another. Salvatierra had already accomplished the first. The latter, however, he could not promise to do. After many remonstrances and a lengthy correspondence, the whole case was submitted for the king's judgment. Owing to His Majesty's sickness and subsequent death, however, as little was achieved and gained in Madrid as in Mexico.

To these complications must be added the false rumors and the jealousy of those Spaniards who did not believe that the Jesuits should have ventured to penetrate into the California world of rocks, thorns, and barbarians, to live there solely and exclusively for the glory of God and the salvation of California Indians. Many Spaniards had sailed to California before the Jesuits; yet they could not and would not remain there. These rumors had already caused a decline in the generosity of some donors. Furthermore, in reports sent to Mexico, the captain of the soldiers then in California violently slandered the padres, sarcastically referring to their enterprise as an impossibility, as an insane whim. He did this because he was not permitted to employ the natives for pearl fishing as he wished. According to a royal decree, he owed obedience to Father Salvatierra, and the latter forbade him to use the Indians for such purposes. Besides, the great amount of work and hardship, of which there was no lack in such a country and at the beginning of such an enterprise, had already tired and irritated him.

In view of so many negative answers and delays, and in view of the dangers and difficulties in securing quickly and safely the necessary provisions from across the sea, Salvatierra conceived the idea of opening a land route to California. At that time it was still uncertain whether California was a real island or only a peninsula. Missions had been established along the coast, on the Mexican side of the Gulf of California, from the twenty-fifth to the thirty-first degree. Salvatierra believed, if California were not an island, that it would not be difficult to establish communication by land between these missions and others to be founded

Observations in Lower California

in California in the future. This would be an advantage to the new missions. He did not know, nor could he imagine at that time, that seventy and more years would pass before the missions on either side of the gulf would meet at the Río Colorado. He begged his old and good friend Father Kino to undertake a trip from Sonora to the above-mentioned river to determine whether California was part of the mainland of North America, or was cut off by an arm of the sea and therefore an island. The journey was made not once but several times, although not along the seashore because of lack of water and the sandy coast, which is rather wide and almost thirty hours in length. By long, though necessary detours, the Río Gila was reached, and finally the Río Colorado. The expedition sailed down the river for several miles, crossed it, and marched many miles inland on the other shore. For the first time, although not with absolute certainty, California was declared a peninsula, much to the pleasure of Father Salvatierra. Nevertheless, much was lacking and still is to this day to bring about communication by land and to make possible the transport of provisions from the Pimería to California, as conceived by Father Salvatierra. Although by now the missions in California extend to the thirty-first degree, there still lies a considerable stretch of apparently bad land across from the point where California meets the Pimería. In the Pimería, Caborca is still the last mission to the north, just as it has been for more than seventy years. The many revolts and incursions, not only by the Pima and Seri Indians, but above all by the cruel Apaches, have kept these territories in constant fear for the last sixty years. These savages have plundered the land, destroyed the missions, and with their lances and arrows sent many a Spaniard to his grave.

Meanwhile, not only had the two original missions of Loreto and San Xavier become more and more firmly established, but one by one eighteen others had been erected. The entire work was accomplished by missionaries themselves, although their efforts, worries, and troubles were more than once about to be abandoned and destroyed, since hundreds of dangers had to be faced, hunger, numerous shipwrecks, and native wars and uprisings.

Philip V, of glorious memory, contributed not a little to this growth, for hardly had he ascended the throne than he ordered his regent in Mexico to pay annually to all the missionaries of California as much as to all the other missionaries, that is, six hundred Rhenish guilders for

Of the Arrival of the Spaniards

their support. Furthermore, the California churches were to be equipped with bells, appointments for the celebration of Mass, and other necessities. In addition, a company of twenty-five soldiers was established, and a ship with a pilot and eight sailors was provided to serve the missions. For the permanent support of the entire undertaking, the treasury of Guadalajara was instructed to pay thirteen thousand pesos, or twenty-six thousand florins, annually. These were the royal orders. Many years passed, however, before they were carried out. Since no news from Mexico was received in Madrid announcing the execution of these decrees, they were reissued in 1705, 1708, and 1716, and, finally, in 1716 actual payments were made for the first time.

Before that time, that is, from 1697 to 1716, more than three hundred thousand Spanish *pesos duros*, which is more than six hundred thousand guilders, had been spent on poor California. This sum, not so impressive in the New as in the Old World, yet not small or insignificant anywhere, had been collected by Father Salvatierra and his padres, and magnanimously donated by private persons eager to help in the work of saving souls. This may illustrate the generosity of rich Spaniards born or residing in America in instances where God's honor was concerned. These benefactors of the California missions were not left without just reward. For instance, money almost seemed to rain into the house of His Excellency, the high and well-born Marqués de la Villa-Puente, whose money chests were at all times at the disposal of the California and China missions, as well as other spiritual and worldly charitable organizations. He could equip and deliver several regiments of soldiers to his king during the protracted War of the Spanish Succession. When his good friend Don Gil de la Sierpe died in Mexico, Father Salvatierra envisioned his entrance into heaven, guided by fifty innocent and beautifully clothed children, at the exact hour of his death. The Father told those who were about him of this vision, and soon thereafter news from Mexico arrived verifying and ascertaining the truth of his statements as to the day, hour, and passing of Don Gil. All of these fifty children were baptized California Indians, and just that many and not more had died up to that time. Would similar rewards be lacking elsewhere if examples such as Don Gil's were followed? There is no virtue, according to Holy Scripture, which promises more rewards than charity. Yet even without any advantages it would be recompense enough for a

Observations in Lower California

Christian heart to have done good, to have helped the soul or body of a person in need, and thus to have offered a helping hand to Jesus our Lord Himself.

Meanwhile, in 1704, the first church was consecrated to Our Most Blessed Mother of Loreto. Shortly thereafter the sacrament of baptism was administered to a large number of adult California natives for the first time. It was considered prudent, yes, necessary, to test the perseverance of the newly converted for six years.

About this time, Father Salvatierra had to leave California for a time. In spite of his refusals, he had been forced to take upon himself the office of Provincial in the Mexican province. His absence, however, was not of long duration. Even during the first year of holding his new office, he crossed the sea, spent two months in California, and worked like any other misssionary. In 1706, he received permission from Rome to resign his post, and returned to California in the following year, firmly resolved to spend the rest of his days among the natives. In 1717, however, he had to obey the orders of His Excellency, the Viceroy of Mexico, who called him to that city in order to confer with him about California. Father Salvatierra undertook this trip in spite of his advanced age and feeble health. He did not get farther than Guadalajara, the residence of the bishop, about a hundred and fifty hours distant from Mexico. He fell ill, and in the college, amid his brethren, Father Salvatierra died. It is to be believed that he soon reached the shores of eternal bliss after having crossed the California Sea more than twenty times and having exposed his life to many dangers by helping others solely for the love of God and his fellow men. The glory he acquired through his heroic virtues and his pains and labor for the salvation of the natives is everlasting. For this reason the whole city mourned, and he was interred there in the Lauretan chapel with all signal honors rendered to him by the cathedral chapter as well as by the Royal Council.

I have already reported that, all in all, eighteen missions had been established in California. Of these, some were later transferred to other places and given different names. Two were combined into one, so that at the beginning of 1768 fifteen missions were counted. I want to enumerate them, not in chronological order, but according to their geographic location from the south to the north.

The first is called San José del Cabo because it is situated very close

Of the Arrival of the Spaniards

to the *cabo* or promontory of San Lucas on the California Sea. It was founded in 1720. The next, Santiago, or St. James, is twelve hours distant from the first named and four hours from the California Sea. It was established in 1721. The third, Todos Santos (All Saints), is situated across the peninsula from the aforementioned mission, almost on the shores of the Pacific Ocean. It was established in 1720. A missionary could make the trip between the two missions in one day were it not for an almost insurmountable mountain range, the furthermost point of which is called San Lucas, running between the two. A detour of three days is necessary should one of the two missionaries wish to visit the other. The one living at Santiago also administered Mission San José del Cabo. The fourth is called Nuestra Señora Dolorosa (Our Lady of Sorrow). It is about seventy or more hours distant from Todos Santos and six hours from the California Sea, and was founded in 1721. The fifth, San Luis Gonzaga, is situated between the two seas, seven hours from Mission Dolores, and was established in 1731. The sixth, San Xavier, is thirty hours distant from the aforementioned mission and eight hours from the California Sea. It was founded in 1699. The seventh, Loreto, was started in 1697. It is eight hours northeast of San Xavier, within a stone's throw of the California Sea. The eighth, San José Comondú, is situated closer to the Pacific than to the California Sea, a day's journey from San Xavier toward the northeast. It was established in 1708. The ninth, Purísima Concepción (Immaculate Conception), is a hard day's journey from San José del Cabo, going northwest, and not far from the Pacific. It was established about 1715. The tenth, Santa Rosalía, lies half an hour from the California Sea, a long day's journey from Purísima Concepción in a northeasterly direction, and was founded in 1705. The eleventh, Guadalupe, and the twelfth, San Ignacio, were founded in 1720 and 1728, respectively. Mission Guadalupe is a two-day journey from Purísima Concepción toward the north, not far from the Pacific Ocean, and San Ignacio is situated almost in the middle of the country, a one-day trip from Guadalupe and Purísima Concepción. The thirteenth, Santa Gertrudis, a two-day journey northwest of San Ignacio, was established in 1751. The fourteenth, San Borja, is a hard two-day journey from Santa Gertrudis in a northeasterly direction. It was founded in 1762. The fifteenth and last, Nuestra Señora de Columna (Our Blessed Lady of Columna), is a three-day journey from San Borja toward the California

Observations in Lower California

Sea, and below the thirty-first degree, north. It was established in 1766.

Each one of these fifteen missions had in my time its own priest, except the first two, which were both administered by the same missionary. All of them are built along an *arroyo* or rain-water course. Nearly all of them stand between high, forbidding, almost barren rocks which are difficult to climb. They are situated in places, which, after much searching and counseling, were considered the most favorable. A permanent store of drinking water was of foremost importance in choosing each location.

Of these fifteen missions, six were endowed by the Marqués de la Villa-Puente; two by the Duquesa de Béjar and Gandia, of the house of Borgia; two by the secular priest Don Juan Cavallero y Ozio; one by Don Arteága; one (from his inheritance) by Father Luyando, a Jesuit from Mexico and a missionary in California; one by the Marquesa de la Peña; another by the Marqués Luis de Velasco; and finally, one by a certain congregation in Mexico. Out of gratitude and to their eternal glory, these honored founders and benefactors are mentioned here.

Many hardships were checked by the payments received from King Philip V and by the aforementioned endowments to the missions (to which all the California natives belonged who lived between Cabo San Lucas and the thirty-first degree, north). Although it required great effort, almost all the missions had found some land for sowing and planting and for breeding large and small animals, horses and mules. Thus help could be given not only to the sick and needy Indians, but also to soldiers and sailors. Notwithstanding these efforts, many thousands of bushels of Indian corn, dried vegetables, many horses and mules, fats, and sometimes also meat had to be brought from places across the sea. The supplies were at times so meager in California that a soldier received only half his grain ration, or had to eat his meat without bread, as one missionary had to do for six weeks.

After enumerating the missions, their location, and their benefactors, it might be agreeable to the reader if he were introduced to the foremost of these missions, the one of Loreto, the capital city, and at that time the residence of the California Governor and Viceroy. From this description, the reader may draw his own conclusions about what to think of the rest of those California cities and places to be found on maps, in histories, and other books, but which are not actually in California. Loreto is, as I have already remarked, situated only a stone's throw from

Of the Arrival of the Spaniards

the California Sea. It lies in the center of a stretch of sand which reaches for almost half an hour's distance up to the mountains. This land is without grass, without a tree, a bush, or any shade. Loreto bears as little resemblance to a city, a fortified place, or a fortress, as a whale to a night owl. The dwelling of the missionary, who was also the administrator and who had a lay brother to assist him, is a small, square, flat-roofed, one-story structure of adobe brick thinly coated with lime. One wing of the building is the church, and only this one is, in part, constructed of stone and mortar. The other three wings contain six small rooms each, approximately six yards wide and as many yards long, with a light hole toward the sand or the sea. The vestry and the kitchen are found here, also a small general store, where the soldiers, sailors, their wives and children buy buckles, belts, ribbons, combs, tobacco, sugar, linen, shoes, stockings, hats, and similar things, for no Italian or any other trader ever thought of making a fortune in California.

Next to this quadrangle are four other walls, within which dried steer and beef meat, tallow, fat, soap, unrefined sugar, chocolate, cloth, leather, wheat, Indian corn, several millions of small black bugs which thrive on the grain, lumber, and other things are stored.

Beyond these imposing buildings, a gunshot's distance away, a shed may be seen which serves simultaneously as guardhouse and barracks for unmarried soldiers. The entire soldiery and garrison of Loreto, their captain and his lieutenant included, consists occasionally of six or eight, but never more than twelve or fourteen men.

In addition, there are toward the west two rows of huts made of dirt, in which dwell about a hundred and twenty natives, young and old, men and women. About two to three and a half dozen mud huts are scattered over the sand, without order, looking more like cowsheds of the poorest little village than homes, and usually containing but one single room. These are occupied by the married soldiers, the few sailors, the one and a half carpenters and equally numerous blacksmiths, and their wives and children, and serve as lodging, living room, storeroom, and bedroom. Finally, a few poles thatched with brush make up the armory, or the shipyard. All this is Loreto, the capital city of California! He who has seen the Moscovite realm, Poland, or Lapland will know whether there is any small village in these countries or whether there is a milking shed in Switzerland more dilapidated than Loreto and its huts. Moreover,

Observations in Lower California

the heat in summer is incredibly intense, and there is no other relief from it save a bath in the sea. There is neither running nor standing water on the surface, although it can be found by digging down into the sand to a certain depth. On the other hand, there is no scarcity of mosquitoes!

May God be gracious to the honorable gentleman Don Gaspar Portolá, a Catalonian, captain of dragoons, and first Governor of California from 1767. The office was conferred upon him as an honor and a reward, because of false reports about the good quality and wealth of the land. His punishment, however, could not have been more severe (except death, the gallows, or prison for life) had he sworn a false oath to the king or proved a traitor to his country. Of all the physical and mental pleasures which people of his character usually seek, none is to be found in California. He is practically forced to remain within his four little walls, day in and day out, throughout the year. Where could he go? With what and with whom could he entertain and enjoy himself or pass the time? In the environment of Loreto and in all of California, there is no hunting, except for the natives, no place to walk, no games to be played; there are no conversations possible, and no visits paid. In a word, there is nothing, literally nothing, for such a man to do. The amount of business, or the dispatching of couriers will not shorten the time for him. All that a viceroy of California can do in the course of a year is to mediate a few minor quarrels and brawls between the hungry miners, or to mete out punishment if necessary. There may be a few letters for the secretary, whom he brought along, to write ordering some Indian corn from overseas for his dragoons and miquelets.[28]

There is, however, one advantage he can draw from this governorship if he were money mad or wished to save. He receives a yearly salary of six thousand Rhenish guilders. Since there is absolutely no opportunity in California to be extravagant or to squander money, he can probably lay aside five thousand nine hundred guilders every year without being accused of penny-pinching or miserliness. His field chaplain, Don Fernandez, a secular priest, wanted to leave the country as soon as he saw that there was no one to speak to all day long and nothing to do but to sit in his hermitage, to gaze at the blue sky and the green sea, or to play a piece on his guitar.

CHAPTER THREE : *Of the Revenues and the Administration of the Missions*

Some of the revenues, which provided the missionaries and many of the Indians with food and clothing and helped to maintain the churches, were certain (except for the dangers of the sea), others accidental. To the latter group belonged everything which soil and the animals produced in return for much effort and work. More will be told about these in chapters five and six. The first mentioned were one thousand Rhenish guilders designated for each mission by the respective founder and benefactor. This sum could be spent at the missionaries' discretion.

According to the will and command of Philip V, each missionary in California was supposed to receive six hundred guilders annually from the royal treasury; that is, he was to receive as much as any other missionary who worked in the vineyard of the Lord in the Spanish possessions in the Americas. Such a decree was, however, not acceptable for three reasons. In the first place, the income was not secure, since the royal officials, using all sorts of pretexts, would at times omit payments for several years in succession. Then, too, the income did not seem sufficient, considering the infertility of the land and the necessity of importing everything which this money could buy from Mexico, which is such a great distance away. And finally, there was no lack of generous people who offered a thousand guilders. Perhaps it was foreseen that California would bring very little to the royal treasury and that the expenses for ships and soldiers, already large enough, would be likely to increase in the future.

Consequently, from 1697 to 1768 all the missionaries in California were supported by private persons and not by the Catholic King. These benefactors donated either twenty thousand guilders in cash for every new mission or enough property to guarantee an income of about one thousand guilders per year. These properties and others bought with donated money and dedicated to the support of California missionaries specialized largely in raising livestock. These were scattered all over

Observations in Lower California

Mexico, some of them as far as two hundred hours away from the capital city, Mexico, the home of the administrator, who had to take care of everything. His task was not easy, and his office caused him much travel and much sweat. Every year, in March, he had to send to each missionary the equivalent of a thousand guilders in goods. Each consignment depended upon the individual missionary's needs. These goods were moved overland by mules a distance of two hundred and fifty hours from Mexico to Matanchel on the California gulf. There they were loaded on ships and sent across the sea to Loreto, another three hundred hours' journey. On sea, everything was duty free; the sea transport itself did not cost the missionary anything, but the freight on land was more than one hundred guilders for only four bales of goods, even though the mules, after being relieved of their burdens, could graze freely, without any cost, on the pastures of America.

These bales contained all the precious things which a missionary in the course of a year needed for himself and for his church. They might include a coat, a few yards of linen, a few pairs of shoes, twenty or more pounds of white wax, some chocolate (which in America is like daily bread and which any common laborer thinks he is entitled to drink), and again, some linen or cotton goods with which other possible necessities, especially Indian corn for the natives in the event the harvest at the mission was insufficient, were to be bought in Loreto during the year. One year a surplice might be ordered, or some other priestly vestment; the next, a stole; the third, a choir cope, a bell, a carved or painted picture, an altar or something else for the church. The remainder, which usually made up about three quarters of the entire consignment, consisted of all kinds of blue and white, coarse and rough cloth to cover the naked Californians.

Of these naked ones who had to be clad, as many as could be fed and employed by the missionary were, so to speak, permanent residents at the mission. They worked at agriculture; they knitted and wove. Some were needed in the service of the mission as a sexton, goat herdsman, attendant for the sick, catechist, magistrate, fiscal, or cook (there were two and they were dirty, one for the missionary and one for the natives). Only four of all the missions, and small ones at that, were able to clothe and support all of their parishioners and therefore keep them in the mission throughout the year. In all the others, the natives were divided into

Of the Arrival of the Spaniards

three or four groups, and each in turn had to come to the mission once a month. There they had to encamp for a whole week.

Every day at sunrise all the natives attended Mass. During the service they recited the Rosary. Before and after the service they were taught Christian doctrine by being asked questions in their own language. After this, the missionary gave them instruction, also in their native tongue, for a half or three quarters of an hour. Then, after having received breakfast, each one went either to work or, if he pleased, to wherever he wished; if the missionary was unable to provide him with food, he searched in the field for his daily bread. Toward sunset, at the call of ringing bells, they all assembled again to recite the Rosary and the Lauretan litany in the church or, on Sundays and holidays, to sing. Customarily the bells were rung three times a day, but they were also rung at three o'clock in the afternoon in remembrance of the mortal agony of our Lord and, according to Spanish custom, at eight o'clock in the evening to remind everyone to pray for the dead. After the week had passed, the natives returned to their native land, some three, others six, others fifteen and twenty hours from the mission. I mean by "native land" those districts in the open where each little tribe is accustomed to live, although each of them has at least a half dozen such districts. One of these territories gives its name to many tribes.

On the highest holidays of the year and during Passion Week, the whole congregation assembled. In addition to the usual fare, they received the meat of several head of cattle and a few bushels of Indian corn. Dried figs and grapes were generously distributed, provided these things were available. Similar foods or some pieces of clothing were also distributed as prizes in games or shooting contests.

To safeguard order in and outside of the mission, fiscals and magistrates were chosen from each group. Their duties were to bring those present at the mission into the church at a given signal and, at the proper time, to round up those who had been roaming the fields for three weeks and to lead them to the mission. Furthermore, they were supposed to prevent all disorders and public misconduct, to review the catechism in the morning before the natives left the mission and in the evening after they had returned, to persuade them to recite the Rosary in the fields, to punish culprits for minor offenses, to report serious crimes to the proper authority, to see that the natives preserved silence and

Observations in Lower California

were reverent during religious services, to attend the sick in the field and bring them to the mission, and similar duties. As insignia of the office and the power vested in them, each carried a staff, sometimes one with a silver knob. Most of them were proud of their position, but only a few did justice to their functions, for quite frequently they received the beating and pushing around which they should have delivered to others. In addition to these officials, there were catechists who recited the Christian doctrine to the natives and instructed those who were especially ignorant.

To prevent disorder when there was not enough food for all the natives, the missionary or someone in his place distributed every day, after Mass and Christian instruction, cooked wheat and Indian corn among the blind, the aged, the weak, and the pregnant women. This was repeated at noon and in the evening after the Rosary. For those who were ill, special food was prepared, and the sick received meat at least once a day. When there was work to do, the laborers were offered three meals a day if they attended to their duty. The work was not hard. Would to God there had been enough of it to make all California natives labor and toil industriously all day as the poor peasants and craftsmen do in Germany. How many vices and misdeeds could have been prevented every day! The working hours began very late and ceased even before the sun had set. At noon the workers took a two-hour rest. Without doubt six common laborers in Germany achieve more in six days than twelve of these natives do in twelve days. Moreover, all their labor was exclusively for their own and their fellow men's advantage and benefit. The missionary gained nothing by it except worry and annoyance, and he could easily have procured somewhere else the twelve bushels of wheat or Indian corn he consumed during a year.

However, this missionary was the only refuge of young or old, the sick or the healthy. Upon him alone lay the responsibility for everything which had to be done. From him the natives solicited food and medicine, clothing and shoes, tobacco for smoking and snuffing, and tools if one of them wanted to do some work for himself. He alone had to mediate quarrels, look after small children who had lost their parents, care for the sick, and find someone to watch over a dying person. I knew of more than one missionary who could rarely begin his breviary by the light of the sun, such was his drudgery throughout the whole day. I could relate at length how, for instance, Father Ugarte [29] and Father Druet,[30] mud and water well over their knees, worked harder in the

Of the Arrival of the Spaniards

stifling field than the poorest peasant and day laborer. Or, how others labored for their church and house, did tailoring and carpentering, or practiced the professions of masonry, cabinet-, harness-, brick-, and tile-making, or were physicians and surgeons, choirmasters and teachers, managers, guardians, hospital attendants, or beadles. The intelligent reader will easily understand all this when he recalls what was said in Parts One and Two of this book about the character of the land and its inhabitants. For the same reason, he will be able to conclude which were the revenues and incomes of the missionaries in California as well as in hundreds of other sections of the New World.

To the "revenues" the reader may also add the hearing of confession and the visiting of the sick out in the field and far away from the mission. At all times, day or night, the missionary might suddenly be called to a distant place, three, six, twelve, or twenty hours away, to administer the sacrament to a sick person. Sometimes he arrived too late despite his zeal and speed; at other times, however, the sick man himself walked part of the way to meet him. Or perhaps the missionary, after a long and exhausting march, would find the patient at the indicated place, but with nothing more serious than a slight swelling or the colic. Of one thing the missionary was certain. He would find no roof or bed on the whole journey but the sky and earth, and no food but what he carried with him. This caused difficulties and hardships for some missions, for often there was nothing to take along on such occasions. Under such conditions the missionary had to rely upon chocolate while traveling to and fro.

On one such occasion, I had to spend three consecutive nights in the open field. Because of a particularly bad stretch of way which I did not care to traverse in the dark, I had not been able to reach my house on the third day, as I expected. For my evening meal I had not even four ounces of bread (or more correctly speaking, corn pancakes) and not quite a cupful of water, and this was to be distributed among three people! The humorous part of the situation was that, shortly before opening my "cellar" and "bread basket," I had read in my breviary the following passage from Isaiah: "Dabit vobis Dominus panem arctum; et potum brevem." The patient in this case had nothing but two swollen cheeks. This happened in 1758. He was still alive and well in 1768.

To hear confession was in every respect a very disconsolate, highly annoying, and melancholic task (particularly after I came to know the

Observations in Lower California

natives very well and learned to see behind their trickiness, hypocrisy, and their wicked way of life). This was not only because of the coercion or the fictitious devotion which was for many the only reason to go to confession, but also because of their stupidity and limited intelligence and the surprising ignorance they revealed in spite of repeated instruction. There were also the many temptations which they did not care very much to avoid, and the father confessor was unable to do anything about it. And finally, most annoying was the lack of preparation for confession and the continuous return to sin of all or most of them. I once asked a native woman who understood Spanish (it must have been during the pitahaya season) why she had not done the penance imposed on her after previous confession (and which may have consisted of reciting one or several rosaries). In good Spanish she replied, "De puro comer," "Because I was eating." I asked another woman, a rather intelligent person, what she had done or thought before my arrival at the church. The blunt answer was, "Nothing." She did not have to swear an oath; I believed it. My experience of many years with many such cases proved to me only too well that nothing is less important to the natives than to prepare for confession. One reason among others is that preparation for confession is an exertion engaging head, heart, and soul. Such efforts a California Indian dislikes even more than manual labor.

CHAPTER FOUR : *Of the Churches in California, Their Furnishings and Ornaments*

THE MISERY and poverty of California was least apparent in the churches. Although the homes of the missionaries were poorly furnished and the kitchens badly equipped, the churches were richly decorated

Of the Arrival of the Spaniards

and the vestries well supplied with everything. The missionary's kitchen contained a copper pan, a small copper vessel in which to prepare the chocolate, both tinned for the first and last time when they were bought in Mexico; two or three pots made of clay and goat manure, unglazed and only half baked on charcoal in the open air; a small spit, which often remained unused for half a year; and some cow bladders filled with fat. In the rest of the house were to be found a crucifix, some paper pictures on the wall, an adequate library, two or three hard chairs, an equally hard bed without curtains, or in its place, a cattle skin on the bare ground. These items comprised the complete furnishings of kitchen and house. In the churches, however, it was quite different.

As a rule, the churches were built before any thought was given to housing comfortably its servants. The churches were well and as beautifully constructed as possible. Lime was carried from a distance of many miles, and lacking other material, the hard wacke stones were hewn into cornerstones and frames for doors and windows. The church of Loreto is very large, yet consists only of four artless walls and a flat roof made of well-joined beams of cedar wood. However, no other church could compete with its paintings or in the costliness of its clerical vestments. The vaults of three other churches were made of bricks or tufa stone. A fourth, which in size and artistic beauty was to surpass all others, was about to receive a vault when the architect, a native-born Mexican missionary and builder, was expelled and forced to depart for Europe. From the New World, his native land, he was sent to the Old World and into misery. He was not even told whether the construction of the church or something else was responsible for his banishment. The church of Todos Santos is vaulted, but with wood which was brought to the mission with the help of a great many teams of oxen over many miles from a very steep and high mountain range. It is large, richly and amply decorated. The church of the mission of San Xavier was built like a cross, with three imposing doors and three completely gilded altars, a high tower, a graceful cupola, and large windows, which were the first and only glass windows to be seen in California during those last few years.

No church had less than three bells; but at Loreto, at San Xavier, and at San José Comondú from seven to nine bells can be counted. They do not sound badly when they are rung, or to speak more correctly, when they are struck, according to Spanish custom. Two churches had organs; a third expected to receive an organ from Mexico. Most of the altars were completely gilded, and the walls were covered with pictures in golden frames.

Aside from a few which were rarely ever used, I never saw in California a clerical vestment or choir cope which was not silk lined and bordered with good galloons. The material of which they were made was usually very rich and costly, and thirty to forty guilders were paid for a Spanish ell (four spans). Chasuble and antipendia were matched and made of the same cloth.

In all the churches, the steps leading to the altar were covered with carpets (different ones were used on work days, Sundays and high holidays). In one church there was also a carpet for the choir, covering the entire, and not very small, floor; it was used only on the highest holidays.

All chalices, of which each mission had more than two, the ciboria, the monstrances, the little wine and water vessels, the censers, and sometimes the holy water fonts which hang near the entrance, the little altar bells, the two big lamps, the various crucifixes used on the altar and in processions, and more than two dozen big candlesticks for the altar were made of solid silver. A big tabernacle, an antipendium of hammered silver, and a chalice of solid gold can be seen in Loreto, unless they have recently been melted down.

The surplices, humerales, choir robes, and altar cloths were of the finest linen, and many of them were adorned with beautiful white embroidery. None of the surplices, choir robes, and altar covers were without lace, some of it very wide and shot through with threads of gold.

Creditable singing, like beautiful Lauretan litanies, could be heard in some churches. Father Xavier Bischoff,[31] from the county of Glatz in Bohemia, and Father Pietro Nascimben,[32] of Venice, Italy, were particularly responsible for introducing choral singing to California. They had trained the Californians, both men and women, with incomparable effort and patience.

A few questions might now arise in the reader's mind, which, before I proceed further, I should like to answer. First: How is it possible to erect such churches in California? Answer: Building material, like workable stone, lime (and the necessary wood for burning it), is hard to find

Of the Arrival of the Spaniards

at most missions. It takes much effort to transport these and many other materials to the proper places. However, the zeal to serve the glory of God, as well as time, industry, hard work, patience, and a large number of donkeys or mules will overcome all difficulties. Many California natives learned stone masonry and brick laying. A missionary, a carpenter, or a competent soldier supervises the construction, or a master builder from another place is engaged for pay. The common labor is performed by the Indians. While the building is under construction, the natives do not have to roam the fields in search of food, and they are not missed in their household or business anyway. For scaffolding, any kind of rough lumber and poles will do. Should some pieces be too short, then two or more of them are tied together with strips of fresh leather; also the trunks of palm trees are used for scaffolding. When none are available nearby, they are sometimes brought from a distance as much as eighty or more hours away. Instead of constructing the framework for the vault with boards, all sorts of odd pieces of useless wood and the dry skeletons of thorn bushes (described in another place in this book) are used and coated over with clay or mud. Except for the three missions in the south, the land is full of common building stones. It is therefore possible to construct within a few years and with little expense such a respectable California church as would do credit to any European city.

Second: Where did all these treasures come from, such as silver vessels, altars and paintings, since there are no painters, goldsmiths or sculptors, and there is not even a skillful tailor in California? Answer: Everything is imported from the city of Mexico, five to six hundred hours away from California, where there is such a surplus of these artists, artisans, and craftsmen, white and dark, that at times they purposely produce poor work so they may soon get another order. The high altar of San Xavier was sent in thirty-two boxes, piecemeal, and already gilded. The cloth for the church vestments was also imported, but they were made in California. When I was forced to leave California, I was at work on a piece of cloth which cost forty guilders an ell, and hardly any of the silk could be seen in it.

Third: How is it possible to acquire such rich church ornaments in a country as poor as California? The answer to this question and the solution of this riddle I shall withhold until the end of the fifth and the sixth chapter. Meanwhile I will state, however, that such treasures could be and were purchased thanks to good management. The fervent aim was to induce reverence and respect for the house of God in the newly converted Indians, and also to create among them prestige for the Catholic religious services. It is to be desired that certain gentlemen in Europe—particularly those living in the country—take this as an example. Their houses are incomparably better decorated and equipped with necessary and ornamental fittings than their churches and sacristies, and these gentlemen appear better dressed in public than in front of the altar. Although churches of many villages are poorly endowed and have little or no income, those who attend the services of such a church or own the village get so much more. These gentlemen undoubtedly could win the love of their fellow parishioners and subjects and earn eternal gratitude if they donated some of their surplus to their church, either for the acquisition of a new, clean altar, a neat pulpit and benches, a fine alb, a respectable mass book, or a silver ciborium, or something similar. Thus they might make it possible to throw aside the age-old, worn out, badly torn, shrunk and half-decayed altar vestments, and coarse surplices which have served them and their ancestors long enough.

CHAPTER FIVE : *Of Agriculture in California*

IT SAYS IN the Holy Scriptures that the evangelical worker deserves his pay and that he shall eat that which is given to him by the people he instructs and to whom he preaches. But what can the California Indian, who has nothing and who is barely able to ward off starvation, give to his missionary? And how could the latter endure the California victuals for a long period of time without the aid of a miracle? At which market could he buy what he needs? It was, therefore, important that

Of the Arrival of the Spaniards

the first missionaries who lived on the grain and meat they had brought with them from Sonora and Sinaloa, across the sea, should be intent on agriculture and animal husbandry in order to feed themselves and their successors, as well as the soldiers and sailors, the sick Indians and catechumen. Thus, at all missions where conditions permitted, the land was cultivated and livestock was introduced. Concerning land, there is enough of it, even though the soil is hard and full of rocks. But there is not sufficient water. Consequently, water was taken wherever and however it was found. The site for a new mission was determined, if possible, by the availability of at least some water which could be used to irrigate the land, either at the mission, or in a place several miles away. No effort was spared. In some places, water was brought half an hour's distance over irregular terrain through narrow channels or troughs carved out of the rock. At other locations, water was collected from six or twelve places—a handful from each source—and conducted into a single basin. Some swamps were filled with twenty thousand loads of stones and as many loads of earth. And sometimes just as many stones had to be cleared away to make this or that piece of land tillable. Nearly everywhere it was necessary to surround the water as well as the soil with retaining walls or bulwarks, and to erect dams, partly to keep the small amount of water from leaking out, and partly to keep the soil from being washed away by the torrents of rain. Even so, all the work was often useless. At best one had to patch and to repair every year, and sometimes it was necessary to start all over again.

But in spite of all this, and even though not the smallest area of productive land was left to lie fallow, and though the corn ripened twice a year, there was never enough corn and wheat to feed twelve to fifteen hundred adult Californians, or to get along without bringing in several thousand bushels of grain and other requisites from some other place for the sustenance of the soldiers.

The plow of California—and, from what I have seen, also of other districts in America—consists of a piece of iron shaped like a hollow tile, with a long point or beak on one end. On the other end a wooden stick is inserted into the hollow iron, which permits the plowman to guide the plow. It has no wheels, and the oxen drag rather than pull it. After the soil is cut and turned over by the plow, deep furrows are hoed. With a pointed stick, small holes are made on the slanting sides of each

Observations in Lower California

furrow. The wheat is placed in these holes, which are closed by pushing in the dirt with the foot and tamping it down. This is slow work, and much help is required. As soon as the seed is in the ground, the crows arrive and march from one hole to the next. Unless a large number of sentinels are standing guard to ward them off, the birds dig up all the grain.

The mice are even worse than the crows because they work unseen and during the night like other thieves. Thus, many times after half the seed had sprouted, more days were required for a second and third seeding. When the planting was finished, water was run through the furrows once every week throughout the growing season until the kernels began to harden. Grain could be planted all year long, but it was generally done in November. In May the wheat was either cut or the spikes were broken off one by one.

The same system was used for planting corn, beans, and a variety of large Spanish peas called *garbanzos* (chick-peas), without which the Spaniards cannot live and which they cook together with many other vegetables. As a rule, they are hard when served at mealtime.

Other things grown in California were squash, pumpkins, watermelons, and other melons. In three missions even some rice was raised. Besides these various garden plants, figs, oranges, lemons, pomegranates, bananas, and some olive trees and date palms were grown. Of European and German fruits, there were none in California except a few peach trees. From them, two rather small and stale peaches were once sent to me from a place thirty hours away. At two missions there was sugar cane. At several others cotton was planted, from which summer clothes, stockings, caps, and other things were woven and knitted for the natives.

It was not necessary to buy sacramental wine elsewhere. The land produces it, and without doubt it could become an excellent and generous product if cool cellars, good barrels, and skilled vintners were available, because the grapes are honey-sweet and of superior flavor. Five missions have vineyards. The juice is merely pressed from the grapes by hand and stored in stone jars. These jars hold approximately fifteen measures (one measure is two quarts, approximately) and are left by the ship which makes a yearly visit to California on her way from the Philippine island of Luzón to Acapulco in Mexico. The storage cellar for the wine is an ordinary room on level ground and—in California—

Of the Arrival of the Spaniards

necessarily warm. Therefore usually half of the grape juice, or even more of it, turns to vinegar. Ten or fifteen jars full of sacramental wine were sent each year to the missions across the California Sea and to the four or six missions in California which had no vineyards. When it left the cellar, the wine was good, but it did not always arrive in the same condition because it had to be carried on muleback in the hot sun for fifty or more hours. As a result, the wine often turned sour, sometimes on the way, sometimes soon after it was delivered.

It was not permissible to give wine to the Indians. Some of the missionaries never tasted any except during Mass. One measure of it sold for six florins, so that neither soldier nor sailor could afford to get drunk frequently. Yet there was no aged or choice wine in California.

From these facts it can be seen that only a small quantity of wine was successfully produced. It was not surprising that many times I and my colleagues had no wine, even for the Holy Mass. Yet it has been claimed that the missionaries of California sold much wine and sent it to other lands. The grape vines, as well as the fig and other trees in California, have to be watered just like wheat and corn.

CHAPTER SIX : *Of the Livestock in California*

ANIMAL husbandry was the other temporal matter which required much care and thought at the California missions, and without which they could not have survived. For that reason, horses and donkeys, cows and oxen, goats and sheep were brought there in the very beginning. Had any of these animals known about California or how badly they and their offspring would fare in the new colony, they would surely have preferred a hundred times to run away as far as their legs could carry them rather than to let themselves be shipped to California.

Observations in Lower California

Cattle, sheep, and goats had to supply the meat for the healthy and the sick, but they were also needed because their tallow was used to make candles and soap, for ships and boats, and they furnished the fat to prepare the beans. In California as well as elsewhere in America, the beans are not prepared with butter churned from milk, but with the so-called lard or rendered fat and the marrow of the bones. For this purpose, every time a well-fed cow or ox was killed, which was a rare occurrence, every bit of fat was carefully cut from the meat, rendered, and conserved in skin bags and bladders. This fat was used for the preparation of food and for frying the very lean or dried meat. Some of the hides were tanned for shoes and saddles and for bags in which everything was carried from the field to the mission or anywhere else. Other skins were used raw to make sandals for the natives, or were cut into strips for ropes, cords, or thongs, which were used for tying, packing, and other similar tasks. The natives used the horns to scoop up water or to fetch food from the mission.

Without horses or mules it would also have been impossible to exist. They were needed for guarding the cattle and carrying burdens, and also as a means for traveling by the missionary or by the soldier. It would have been difficult to make much progress on foot in such a hot and uneven land.

Sheep too can serve a good purpose for people who have no clothes—if only the flocks had not been so small because of the lack of feed. Moreover, the sheep left a good part of their fleece on the thorns through which they passed. Wherever a flock could be maintained and increased to a good number, there were also spinning wheels and weaving looms, and the people received new outfits more frequently than at other missions. Of pigs, there were hardly a dozen in the whole land, perhaps because they cannot root up the dry, hard ground and have no mud holes to wallow in.

Wherever circumstances permitted it, no labor was spared to plant or seed the ground. Small or large herds of sheep and goats were maintained, as well as a "flying corps" of cows and oxen, and care was taken that horses and mules would not die out.

The goats and sheep returned every evening with full or empty stomachs to their folds. At times it was difficult to extract a pint of milk from six of the goats. The cattle had free passage and were per-

Of the Arrival of the Spaniards

mitted to wander fifteen and more hours in every direction to find their feed. They were brought in only once a year when their tails were trimmed to make halters from the hair. At the same time, the calves born during the last year had a piece clipped off their ears and were branded with a sign, so that they could be identified if they lost their way or strayed into other territory. The same thing was done to colts and young mules.

To keep the livestock from straying too far, or from disappearing entirely, five or six herders were necessary. It was their job to ride one week in one direction, the next week in another, in order to keep the animals closer together. When the herders rode forth, they always took half a legion of horses or mules with them. Then they would go at full gallop over mountains and valleys, over rocks and thorns. Since neither horse nor mule was shod and fodder was so scarce and poor, and since at times the galloping lasted for many days, often weeks in succession, the herders needed to change their mounts many times a day. To protect a few hundred cows, therefore, almost as may horses were required. Hunger alone did not make these animals run so far afield. They also suffered from persecution by the natives, who killed more of them in the open than were brought to the mission for slaughter; nor did the Indians spare horses or mules. They relished the meat of the one as much as that of the other.

All these animals were very small. Scarcely three or four hundred pounds of meat and bones could be obtained from a steer. The milk was only for the calves. I have already reported in another chapter that for nine months of the year the animals were as skinny as dogs and carried not a pound of fat on their bodies. They ate thorns, two inches long, together with stems, as though they were the tastiest of grasses. Thus, except to furnish poor and insufficient food for not too many people, three or four hundred head of such cattle barely paid enough to buy the bread that two Spanish cow herders and their helpers ate in one year. Yet the herders were as essential at some missions as was the livestock. To allow the animals to go unguarded in California was like sending them to the slaughtering bench, or like setting the wolf to guard the sheep.

The goats and sheep were no better off than the cattle, and the laziness of the native herders added a good deal to their hardships.

Observations in Lower California

More than once during these seventeen years have I seen a flock of sheep numbering four to five hundred head reduced by hunger to eighty or even fifty. More than half of this time I received very little from them, because after they were skinned, the carcasses were more fit to be used as lanterns at nighttime than as roasts in the kitchen.

Among the California horses there was one very good strain, agile and hardy. They were small, however, and increased in number very slowly, so that every year others had to be bought outside of California to keep the soldiers mounted. Only the donkey, who is not so fussy and always patient wherever it may be, was fairly well off in California. It worked little and ate the thorns and stalks as though eating the finest oats.

If what I have reported in this and in the preceding chapter about agriculture and animal husbandry in California should lead to the conclusion, or even suggest, that the missionaries sought or found profit in these activities, such would be an error. I knew not one among them who did not regard this work as a heavy burden which he would gladly have slipped from his shoulders. It was definitely a hardship—equal to the services of shiftless soldiers—which had to be endured in order to help the California Indians win the Kingdom of Heaven. Aside from this benefit, the natives derived another profit from the labors of the missionaries. Through small gifts the hearts of a poor, barbarian people could be won, and such gifts saved many of them from pernicious laziness and idle roving.

Furthermore, even if the mountains of California had been made of solid silver, I cannot see what temporal prestige or selfish gain the missionaries could have acquired from such labor and worry, to which they certainly were not accustomed. Voluntarily and irrevocably they left their country, parents, brothers and sisters, friends and acquaintances, and last but not least, an easy life, free from worries, to enter an existence full of a thousand dangers on water and on land. All this they endured so they could, in the New World, in a wilderness, among wild and inhuman people, among disgusting vermin and cruel beasts, live well and gather wealth for others! To judge, to speak, or to write in such a way is not just average stupidity. It is rather to brand as the world's biggest fools a number of intelligent men, of whom it is said and written that they are not lacking in knowledge and reason. In respect to "gathering wealth for others," Father Daniel has already said, a short time ago, that since

Automobile Club of Southern California

Father Baegert's Mission San Luis Gonzaga

Nuestro Padre San Ignacio de Kadakaamang

Santa Rosalía de Mulegé

Neal R. Harlow

San Francisco Xavier de Biaundó

Side Door of Mission San Francisco Xavier

Neal R. Harlow

Tower of Mission San Francisco Xavier

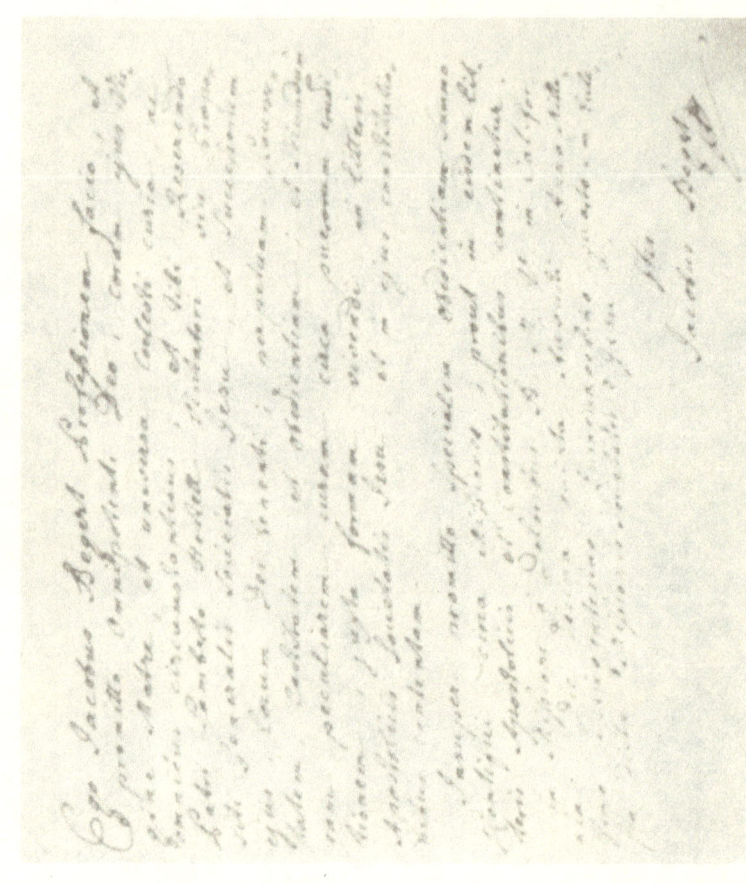

Father Baegert's Profession, August 15, 1754

Nuestra Señora de Loreto, Mother Mission of the Californias

Rivera Cambas, *Mexico Pintoresco*

Ruins of the Chapel of Mission San Juan Londó

Of the Arrival of the Spaniards

the beginning of the world, no one has ever heard of a band of thieves or robbers in which any of the group chose to live alone in the forests in constant danger of being broken on the wheel, so that the rest of the band might live in the city, well and at ease, and become wealthy from loot.

To tell the truth, for eight years I also had four to five hundred head of cattle and as many sheep and goats running around in California, until the thieving of the Indians from my own and another mission forced me to do away with them. For several years I had a small field of sugar cane in front of my house, until the Indians again went too far and pulled up nearly all of it before it was ripe. In six or seven years I gathered several thousand bushels of grain—corn and wheat—from the six or seven small pieces of land which I had caused to be planted here and there. Yet most of the time I had no bread in my house. And when I wished to honor a guest, I had to request a fowl from one of my soldiers—who kept a few chickens on his own corn rations—while I saved my wheat and corn for needy Indians. In my kitchen I also used suet, even on days of fasting, because I had no butter. In many years I hardly tasted meat other than that of lean bulls, which were killed every fourteen days. I never had veal. I seldom saw my roasting spit on the table, although more than once I saw maggots there. Finally, not to mention many other things, I often found myself forced to give up the evening meal entirely because I had nothing I cared to eat. For several years I fasted for forty days on dry vegetables and salted fish five or six times within twelve months. To let the fish swim in their element, my drink was precious, although not always the freshest, water.

Several times I could have changed my post and gone to another place where, I am sure, I would have found better food and many other things I did not have, but it was not very hard for me to resist the temptation. In California the missionary has small regard for temporal goods or personal advantages.

Now is the time to answer the third question in Part Three, chapter four, as I have promised to do. How then was it possible, in a poor land like California, to acquire such beautiful and rich church ornaments? Answer: It was possible to acquire them: first, from the thousand florins or more per year which represented the income from the endowed estates to each mission; second, from the sale of wheat and corn, wine and

Observations in Lower California

brandy (the latter was distilled from wine which was about to turn to vinegar), sugar, dried figs and grapes, cotton, meat, candles, soap, fat, leather, horses, and mules, all being products grown or made at the missions. These exceeded what the missionary needed for the support of the mission, and were sold to the soldiers, sailors, and miners. These sales could hardly have been refused, especially in cases of necessity, when crops had failed outside of California. Furthermore, whatever was of no value to the Indians was sold. Finally, everything a missionary could have but did not use for his own person, that is to say, what he denied himself, was also sold. Soldiers and other people often drank wine which the missionary could have enjoyed himself without drinking to excess. A good deal of this income was used to supply the Indians with clothes and provisions which they lacked and which had to be purchased. With the remainder the above-mentioned costly church ornaments were acquired little by little.

If anyone wishes to find fault with such expenditures or wishes to raise his voice against them—like the traitor Judas against the extravagance of Magdalene (John xii)—as someone has done in the Spanish language, although not about the California missions but about the churches of a certain religious order in general, and if he be a Christian, a Catholic Christian, I refer him to the words in Psalm xxv: "Domine, dilexi decorem domus tuæ." (Lord, I have striven for the beauty and adornment of thy house.) I wish also to advise him to look homeward concerning extravagance, and to criticize the silver dishes, tapestries, and the like found nowadays in private homes before he censures the ornaments in the houses of the Lord.

Leave to the Lutherans and Calvinists—until God will convert them—their austere altars, their bare walls and empty barns, and let us beautify our churches as true houses of God, as best we can. Those who do not care to contribute should leave other people who desire to do so unmolested.

It was impossible to use all the revenue from animal breeding or agriculture for the benefit of the Indians. They were poor, so poor that their poverty could not be greater, but their poverty is of a different nature and character from that prevalent among so many people in Europe. An Indian cannot be helped by paying his debts or by releasing him from prison, by giving money to a girl so that she might enter a con-

Of the Arrival of the Spaniards

vent or be married. It is not necessary to pay their rent or buy their freedom from servitude, pay their doctor or apothecary bill. For the California Indian, everything centers on food and clothing. With these two necessities the missions were well provided through agriculture and livestock breeding. They could, considering the standards of the native, give them all the help they needed. There was no other use for the surplus than to adorn the churches, to make the service of the Lord impressive and dignified, and to console the servants of the Church through the greater honor of their God and through the edification of their fellow men.

Finally, because I have spoken several times of "bread" in this little work, I must make it clear to the reader that I did not speak of bread made of wheat or corn flour, but of little pancakes made of corn meal. The corn is lightly boiled, then ground by hand between two stones. The meal is formed into thin, flat, little cakes, made warm over a hot iron plate. These pancakes are eaten by all the people in all America, and are served like warm bread with meat and other foods. I found them a healthful food and very pleasing to the taste after having eaten them for several weeks.

CHAPTER SEVEN : *Of the Soldiers, Sailors, Craftsmen, as well as of Buying and Selling in California*

THE ENTIRE Second Part of these reports dealt with the black-brown natives of the California peninsula, and in the First Part all that is essential about a handful of silver miners has been told. What remains is to report about some other white men who are living in California.

It would be foolhardy to go and preach the Gospel to these half-human Americans without taking along a bodyguard. It would even be daring to live without protection among those already baptized, because of their vacillating and changeable character. The only thing a missionary without protection could expect to find among these people is an untimely death and the loss of the expense of such a long journey. For this reason, the Catholic Kings have recently issued a decree forbidding a missionary to venture among these heathen without sufficient escort of armed guards. In all the new missions one or more soldiers have to be maintained at the expense of the king. Therefore Father Salvatierra supported as many soldiers as were deemed necessary to keep the newly converted natives and the neighboring heathen in check and to put down possible revolts; or, to state it correctly, he maintained as many soldiers as the alms he received permitted. This situation lasted until 1716, when for the first time the soldiers received their pay from the King of Spain. At that time there were twenty-five of them. However, owing to the serious revolts which broke out at different places, particularly in the southern part of California, and after two missionaries had been killed by the Pericúes, the number of soldiers, including the officers, was finally increased by royal order to sixty men.

These men are not regular soldiers. They know nothing of military exercises; they ask for and receive their discharge whenever they desire it. They are in every respect inexperienced, ignorant, and clumsy fellows born in America of Spanish parents.*

Their officers are a captain, a lieutenant, a sergeant, and an ensign. Their weapons are a sword, a musket, a shield, and an armor of four layers of tanned, white deerskin, which covers the entire body like a sleeveless coat. Otherwise they wear whatever they like; they have no uniforms. They serve on horseback or on mule, and because of the rugged trails, each man is obliged to keep five mounts. The soldiers have to buy these animals as well as their weapons, clothing, ammunition, and all their food. Their annual pay amounts to eight hundred and fifty guilders.

Their duties are these: to serve the missionary as a bodyguard, to

---

* One of them asked me, after reciting the Rosary, "What is an hour?" Another remarked, while we were riding through a territory full of great masses of stones in the plain and in the mountains, "God must have worked hard bringing so many stones to the surface."

Of the Arrival of the Spaniards

accompany him on all his travels, to keep watch during the night, to keep an eye on the Indians, and if a crime is committed, to carry out the punishment. They take turns riding out every day to see that their or the missionary's horses do not stray, for these animals roam freely in the field. And finally, the soldiers have to obey the missionary in everything which concerns good discipline and the affairs of the mission. Such were the wise and beneficial orders issued by the Catholic Kings, Philip V and Ferdinand VI. These orders keep the soldiers from roving through the land at will, using the Indians and their wives for pearl fishing and for other work, or abusing them in any other way.

A certain Viceroy of Mexico [33] changed these provisions, but after a short time of confusion, he found himself compelled to reëstablish the old order.

To increase the dependence of the soldiers and to make sure of their obedience to the missionary in matters mentioned before, the two kings also authorized the missionary to send all those who misbehaved and were more troublesome than useful back to their captain in Loreto without giving them any previous warning. It was also ordered that the soldiers were to receive their pay from the head of the missions or his representative at the place. All these precautions were not adequate, however, to keep such people within the limits of decent behavior. In the course of only a few years, I had to send at least two dozen of these men back to Loreto, though as a rule there were only three or four soldiers stationed at my mission. Yet these regulations were better than having none at all. Imagine what would happen if these soldiers possessed complete freedom at the missions and were permitted to do or go where they pleased or to visit anyone anywhere and at any time!

The same arrangement regarding the pay of the soldiers also applied to the sailors, of whom there were only about twenty. Every year in April these men sailed from California to Matanchel in two small sloops (these and three of four rowboats made up the entire California navy). They brought back Mexican goods and wood, so that the cabinet-makers and carpenters could repair the ships. Several times a year the ships went across the gulf to Sinaloa. They returned with Indian corn, dried vegetables, and also meat, fat, horses, and mules.

Once a year the royal officials in Mexico delivered the full sum for the payment of the sailors and soldiers to the Father-Administrator who managed all the foundation estates of the missions. Of course a few thousand pesos were always deducted. They remained glued to the fingers of the officials as a "present." The administrator did not send this money to California, and neither soldier nor sailor ever received any silver. It would be of no use to him, since there were no bakers, butchers, innkeepers, or merchants in California from whom he could have bought any necessities. The Father-Administrator, therefore, purchased with this pay everything, excluding food, which approximately eighty men and a number of wives and their children might need in the course of a year. He sent these commodities, together with the articles requested by each missionary (for his thousand guilders), to Loreto.

Another administrator resided in Loreto. He received all the goods sent from Mexico. During the year the soldiers and sailors were given on account whatever they requested within the limit of the amount of their salary. The administrator of Loreto was also obliged to report annually, under oath, to the Viceroy, stating that the number of soldiers was complete and that they had been duly paid. If one of them received his discharge and left, he was given linen or other goods for the amount of pay still due him.

Each commodity, such as cloth, linen, tobacco, sugar, soap, meat, chocolate, Indian corn, horses, and so on, had its set price according to a tariff fixed by royal officials. These prices were the same at all stations where the soldiers bought their supplies from the captain, whether it was in California or any place outside the peninsula. As a rule, this tariff set the prices at double what the goods sold for in Mexico, so that an article which cost one or two pesos in Mexico would sell for two or four in California. Once fixed, the prices of the tariff remained in force for all times, even if the purchasing price of a commodity, because of war or other circumstances, was higher in Mexico than the sale price in California.

Thus a few years ago, when the price of smoking tobacco was suddenly increased from five to thirteen *reales* in Mexico (because of the granting of a trade monopoly—the cause of many different rebellions in America), this commodity nevertheless had to be sold to the soldiers and sailors in California at the customary price of ten reales.

Everything was strictly accounted for. The administrator's office was periodically inspected by royal officials. Any surplus was used for the

Of the Arrival of the Spaniards

repair of ships or the building of new ones, to cover unusual expenses owing to new activities on land or water. At times it was also used for the support of the soldiers when the royal treasurer in Mexico did not make any payments, as happened during my time.

Aside from the soldiers and the few sailors, the other residents found in California (in Loreto, to be exact) were two so-called carpenters, two so-called cabinetmakers, and as many blacksmiths. At times another cabinetmaker of this type, carrying all his iron tools in his trouser pockets, roamed the country, trying to earn a little at the missions if there was no lack of wood. Except for these, there were no other craftsmen. As a rule, everyone was his own shoemaker, tailor, plasterer, harness maker, miller, baker, barber, apothecary, and physician. Up to this time nobody had the idea of inviting wig and card makers, fashion tailors, confectioners, pastry and Parisian cooks, lace merchants, coffeehouse keepers, rope dancers, and comedians to California. So long as California will exist, such people will get there much too soon. How many things can I do without, said the philosopher!

There is no money in circulation in California, and no silver in the land, except for the little which the miners dig out and that in the churches. Nothing is imported into California but horses and mules, dried vegetables and corn, fats, wood, and the annual pay for the soldiers and missionaries. And this last, as has been explained above, consisted only of goods. Nothing left the country except a few awms of wine for the missions of Sinaloa and Sonora, some deerskins sent by the soldiers, and some cotton and linen goods originally imported from Mexico. These things were used in the purchase, or to speak more correctly, the barter for the above-mentioned horses and victuals. This may convey an idea of the extent of trade between California and other nations.

Commerce on the peninsula was equally limited. Whatever a missionary advanced to his bodyguard in the form of provisions or other goods was refunded to him by the chief administrator in Loreto—and always in the form of provisions and clothing or other necessities for the Indians. Wine and fruit sent to Loreto by the missionaries for the use of the soldiers was paid for in the same manner. Sometimes the missionary would receive from the administrator in Loreto a draft for services rendered, payable by the chief administrator in Mexico. This draft would be honored the following year, not by cash payment, but in goods requested by the missionary for his church or his Indians.

Trading with the miners was on a different basis. They paid for their purchases in plain, uncoined silver, for they had nothing else. When short of silver, they bought on credit until they were rich again. Most of the silver vessels in the churches were made from such silver.

The missionaries understood one another's problems, and so long as one had something, he always gave brotherly help to the one who had nothing. This help was extended not only to the missionaries, but also to the Californians. I often experienced this, and I want to report it here in order once more to show my deep gratitude, particularly to Father Lambert Hostel,[34] from the Duchy of Jülich, and Father Franz Ináma,[35] from Vienna, Austria.

CHAPTER EIGHT : *Of the Death of the Two Jesuit Fathers, Támaral and Carranco*

Among people like the California Indians, and in a land like theirs, not many significant events occur which deserve to be recorded and made known to posterity. But God creates miracles wherever and whenever it pleases Him. Notwithstanding the small number of missionaries, it has been deemed wise to make known to the world some of those whose virtues deserve to be revealed. Even during these last years, there were those who abstained from wine, although they had the best that was grown in California, who rarely took off their *cilicium* and slept every night on the bare floor or on the altar steps, or those who for days and nights tended the sick in uncomfortable sick-houses, depriving themselves of their only bed and offering it to a sick person. Some even had

Of the Arrival of the Spaniards

scruples about acquiring the necessary clothing and food for themselves for fear they might thereby deprive the poor Californians. Others, who never had a kitchen of their own, ate as their chief meal a thin piece of bone-dry meat warmed a little in the community copper kettle used for preparing Indian corn for the Indians.

Among the Indians there were also some who, after their conversion, led an edifying life, although those giving a bad example were much more numerous, nearly excluding the good. It could well be said of them, "Beatur vir, qui inventus este sine macula." (Blessed is he who lives among them without acquiring coarse vices and committing crimes.) Where is such a one that we may praise him? Together with their other vices, the Indians show lust for revenge and cruelty. Human life means little to them and they will kill for insignificant reasons, as during my time several persons, including the master of a small boat, had to learn. Because of a severe tongue lashing which this master had addressed to the natives, his skull was crushed with a heavy stone when he was eating his evening meal on land. Then, his little boat, loaded with provisions for two poor missions, was set adrift. One boy about sixteen years old was stabbed in the abdomen and hit over the head with a heavy club by another boy of about the same age. This premeditated and treacherous attack occurred at two o'clock in the afternoon on Ascension Day of the the year 1760, in full view of the whole community, and only a stone's throw from the church and the missionary's house. The murderer hoped to escape on a horse he had previously selected, and to find refuge in a church thirty hours away. He almost succeeded.

Up to 1750 many uprisings occurred in different parts of the country. Several missionaries were forced to abandon their missions at one time or another and find safety elsewhere. One cause of these revolts was the decline of the power and prestige of the sorcerers and conjurers, another that the natives were admonished to fulfill their promises made at the time of their baptism.

The greatest and most dangerous revolt occurred in the southernmost part of the peninsula and began in 1733 among the tribes called the Pericúes and the Córas. Both have a very proud and unruly nature, even to this day, as their last missionary, Ignatz Tirs, has experienced. In this year of 1733, four missions comprising several thousand Indians, three priests, and not more than six soldiers were established in that territory.

Observations in Lower California

The missions were La Paz, or "Peace," with one soldier but no missionary in residence; Santa Rosa, with Father Sigismundo Táraval,[36] a Spaniard, but born in Italy, and three soldiers; Santiago with its missionary, Father Lorenzo Carranco,[37] a Mexican of Spanish parentage; and San José del Cabo, with just its missionary, Father Nicolás Támaral,[38] a Spaniard from Seville.

The causes of the uprising were, in part, as many Indians afterwards confessed without shyness, the unwillingness of the recently converted Californians to be married to only one woman, as was their obligation and as they had promised, and in part the dislike of being verbally reprimanded by the missionaries for transgressions they had committed.

The principal instigators and leaders who had secretly and quietly stirred up the people were named Boton and Chicóri. Their aim was to kill the three priests and to obliterate all signs and marks of Christianity, which the large majority of the natives had accepted ten years before. Thus they could return to a life of freedom and license without fear of opposition. The plot, however, was discovered before the fire burst forth into a blaze. To all appearances, it was smothered at the beginning of 1734 by a simulated peace offer on the part of the Indians. This peace, however, did not last long, for it lacked sincerity. Within a short time, the perjured rebel leaders tried anew to realize their aim at all costs; they carried out their plans the following October. Again they did not succeed completely, for Father Táraval found means to escape their hands.

The only obstacle which stood in their way was the force of six soldiers. When in October the natives found one of them of Mission Santa Rosa alone in the field, they treacherously murdered him. Then they sent a message to the mission, stating that the soldier was very ill and that either the priest should come and hear the sick man's confession or he should send the two remaining soldiers to carry their sick comrade back to the mission. Their intention was, of course, to murder the Father or the two others in the same manner. The messenger, however, executed his commission so badly that it was easy to guess what had already happened and what the rebels intended to do next. Consequently, neither the priest nor the soldiers did what was asked of them. A few days later the lone soldier who guarded Mission La Paz lost his life.

The news of the two murders and of further indubitable signs of an

Of the Arrival of the Spaniards

approaching mutiny and general uprising in the south spread and soon reached the ears of the prefect of all the missions, who was at that time at Mission Siete Dolores, almost ninety hours away. Immediately he sent orders to the three priests whose lives were in danger: they should save themselves as best they could. The letters, however, fell into the hands of the rebels; but even if they had reached their destination, they would have arrived too late.

The conspirators planned to deliver the first blow against Mission San José del Cabo and Father Támaral, but they discovered that Father Carranco had already heard of their intentions. They quickly decided to turn against him and Mission Santiago before the priest would be able to escape or take precautionary measures. On a Saturday, the second of October, the rebels arrived there. The Father had just read the Holy Mass and retired to his room in order to finish his prayers without interruption. Unluckily his bodyguard of two men had left on horseback to fetch some cattle for the catechumen and other Indians. Soon after, the messengers who had just returned from San José del Cabo and Father Támaral, to whom they had carried the news of the revolt, entered the room. Father Carranco was just reading Father Támaral's reply to his message when the murderers rushed into the house and attacked him. Some of them threw him to the floor, they dragged him by the feet toward the entrance of the church, revealing thereby the reason for the revolt and subsequent manslaughter. Before they reached the church, however, Father Carranco's soul had been driven from his body, for some savages had pierced him with arrows, and others had hit him with stones and clubs.

Not very far away stood an innocent little California boy who used to serve the Father at table. When the monsters realized that the child wept for the man who had treated him like a father, one of the murderers grabbed him by his feet and smashed his head against the wall, shouting that, since he felt so much compassion, he should also serve him in the future and keep him company in the other world. As is customary with barbarians, there were some among the assassins whom the padre had considered his most loyal followers and in whom he had placed all his trust. After the murder, they tore his clothes from the body, and horribly abused the soulless corpse. Having satisfied their barbaric instincts, they threw the body on a burning pyre. Then they set fire to the church and house, and burned everything they disliked—sacred as well as other vessels, the altar pictures of our Saviour and of the saints, all were reduced to ashes. Meanwhile those who had gone to bring back the cattle and the two unarmed soldiers returned. They were forced to dismount and slaughter the cows for the criminals, whereupon they were rewarded with a shower of arrows.

On the following day, Father Támaral met the same fortunate fate of martyrdom as Father Carranco at Mission San José del Cabo, twelve hours distant from Santiago. As soon as the criminals had cooled their wrath, which was directed more against the Christian religion than against its preachers, they marched from the one mission to the other. Father Támaral was in his house—untroubled, for he did not believe the warning of his neighbor—when the savage army, augmented by new recruits from among Father Támaral's own parishioners, appeared at the mission. As was customary, they demanded something or other (I do not know what) of the Father, with the intention of starting a quarrel should he deny the request. But from their gestures and the weapons they carried, the Father immediately guessed their true intentions. Therefore, he granted their requests and gave them even more than they had asked. The failure of their plan enraged them to such a degree that they put aside all shame and pretense. Without further delay, they seized the Father, threw him to the floor, dragged him under the open sky, and began to shoot arrows at him. One of them (who had just recently received a big knife as a present from the Father) added ingratitude to cruelty by mercilessly thrusting this same knife through the Father's body. Thus, after having spent many years in California, the two, Father Támaral and Father Carranco, ended their lives, slaughtered by their own sheep, after having proved themselves worthy of such an end by their blameless conduct and their great devotion.

The natives' savagery and lust for destruction of the priests, the church, and everything else went much farther and lasted longer in this place than at Santiago because the number of murderers and rebels was greater and because this was the second victory they had achieved.

One more priest was to be destroyed—the third and last one—but he escaped their hands. Father Sigismundo Táraval, missionary at Santa Rosa, was at that time in Todos Santos, an annex to his mission, on the

Of the Arrival of the Spaniards

western shore of California and a two-day journey from San José. Through some Indians, he received the news of all that had happened just in time. Whether these natives informed him out of a natural love and sympathy for their pastor or whether not all of them had a part in the conspiracy, I do not know. He hurriedly packed a few necessary things, and on the night of October fourth, he and his two soldiers rode on horseback across the country to the other shore. Near Mission La Paz he embarked on the small craft which had been sent there as soon as the first rumors of the impending rebellion had been circulated. With God's help he luckily arrived at Siete Dolores, which at that time was built along the sea. He left behind four missions which had been completely destroyed and leveled to the ground in less than four days. Later, it cost much effort, blood, and many people to rebuild them and make them flourish again.

The rebels did not fare well and were not allowed much time in which to glory in the crimes they had committed. God and man made them pay dearly. These southern tribes, which numbered about four thousand souls at the beginning of the revolt, were finally reduced to four hundred. Wars fought against them by the California and foreign soldiers, internal dissension among the tribes themselves, and above all, ugly diseases and epidemics reduced them to this number. Even among these four hundred, there are today very few who are free from this general disease and who can boast of possessing a healthy body.

On the other hand, let us give a thousand thanks to God's kindness which has never failed to give to individuals among the Catholic priests, and particularly to members of the Society of Jesus, even in these days, the heart and courage to spread the Christian Faith without thinking of personal gain. These men expose themselves to deadly dangers among all kinds of barbarians and are willing to shed their blood when the opportunity for such a sacrifice arrives. These two California missionaries are by no means the only members of this Society who in this century have lost their lives while preaching the Gospel and converting the heathen.[39] Besides others whom I could name by the dozen, there were in 1751 two missionaries who lost their lives among the rebellious Pimas on the east coast of the California gulf. They were Father P. Tomás Tello,[40] a Spaniard, and Father Heinrich Ruhen,[41] a German Jesuit from Westphalia. The previous year (1750) I had traveled with the

Observations in Lower California

latter across the ocean to America, and again on land to Pimería only six months before his death.

CHAPTER NINE : *Some Questions Directed to Protestants and Particularly to Protestant Ministers*

ALTHOUGH I am writing a report and not a controversy, I may be permitted to interrupt my narrative and address myself to the gentlemen of the Protestant faith (it may happen that this small volume will get into their hands). In connection with the two California martyrs whose fate was described in the preceding chapter, I should like to ask some questions of the Protestants, and particularly of their ministers, concerning the lack of zeal these gentlemen show in converting heathen. Such conversions are, however, characteristic of the True Church of the New Testament, which does not say: "In viam gentium ne abieritis" (Do not set your feet into idolatrous provinces and lands), but on the contrary: "Go into the world and preach the word of God to all men." The Holy Scripture frequently and emphatically demands of Christian preachers to seek converts. This work of conversion must be carried on in order to conform with the many prophecies. The neglect of missionary work on the part of the Protestants must be due either to prejudice on the part of all non-Catholic sects, or it must prove the truth of the Roman Catholic religion.

The Protestants have the best opportunity of carrying out the work of converting nonbelievers in both the West and the East Indies, for there, as everyone knows, their trade and power is very great. It would be much easier for them and they would be more successful than the

Of the Arrival of the Spaniards

Catholics, for they have nothing else to preach to the pagans but their doctrine of faith. They would permit the natives, in the spirit of Luther, to practice their wickedness thousands of times a day; they would allow them to kill, and yet throw the gates of Heaven wide open for them, thanks to faith alone.* This doctrine (especially if fortified by miracles of men like Xavier, Ludovico, Bertrando, Anchieta, and others) should not fail to win millions of proselytes a day for the Protestant preachers. The Catholic clergy, on the other hand, has to preach St. Paul, the Holy Scripture, early Christianity, and venerable antiquity to the heathen, as well as Faith, the observance of the Ten Commandments, and the necessity of good works. The Catholic priests did not make the desired progress among the idolatrous in the Orient and in America, especially at the beginning of their missions. There are not so many good Christians as there are baptized natives. Nevertheless, I have not heard or read anything up to now about Protestant missions or missionaries in the East or West Indies.†

For a long time Catholic circles have been waiting for the first volume of edifying letters from Protestant missionaries, or for a martyrology of Lutheran and Calvinistic preachers who became martyrs in India. However, so far no one knows or can guess when one or the other volume will go to the press or see the light of day. Yet, on the Catholic side, more than thirty volumes of edifying letters have already been published by the Jesuits alone, although this collection was not started until toward the beginning of this century and contains less than a third of the total letters. In their book of martyrs, almost a thousand blood-witnesses can be counted. Yet this order is not so old as Protestantism, and there are perhaps a hundred Protestant preachers to one Jesuit priest. This does not include all those whom Luther considers ministers and bishops and, therefore, as

---

* "Be a sinner and sin bravely, but let your Faith be stronger for it, and rejoice in Christ, who vanquished sin, death and the world; we have to sin as long as we are in this world. It is enough that we, through God's wealth and grace, have seen the Lamb, who bears the sins of all the world. No sin will separate us from Him, although a thousand and another thousand times a day we whore or murder." Thus writes Luther in the first Latin volume printed at Jena by Coelestium, page 345, in a letter to Melanchthon.

† For an answer to possible objections which will be raised here by some who are deceived by the Hallensian *Continuatores*, see the end of this chapter.

Observations in Lower California

preachers too. All these, as he writes, have been baptized, including the Devil himself and his mother.*

Therefore, with their permission, I ask these Protestant gentlemen:

First: If the Apostles had remained in their fatherland, sitting at home behind the stove, where would the world and especially our Germany be today? And since the Apostles could neither live forever nor go to every part of the world, they alone could not convert all the heathen, and the growth of the Christian church was thereby limited. But under the guidance and foresight of God, who watches over His Church, the Apostles left successors who would always follow in their footsteps and carry on their work of conversion in accordance with Psalm XLIV: "Pro patribus tuis nati sunt tibi filii." Now where in the Protestant church are such apostolic twigs, such successors of the first Fathers of the Church, who, like the Apostles, would zealously dedicate themselves to the conversion of idolaters and to the growth of the kingdom of Christ? When will one be able to say of the theologians of Wittenberg and Geneva: Their call went out into the world and they have been heard in all the corners of the earth preaching the Gospel to the pagans. (Psalm XVIII.) Daily preachers are born to take the place of Luther and Calvin, but none to convert the heathen; Luther and Calvin were not missionaries either.

Second: I ask, does the definite command of Christ, "Go ye into all the world and preach the Gospel to every creature" (Mark XVI), include the Protestant preachers, or does it not? If it does, why do they not obey, and why do they wish to remain idle spectators of the Catholics, resembling those who buried their talent of silver or those found by the Father to be idling in the market place? On the other hand, if Christ's command has no meaning for them, then they cannot be counted among successors of the Apostles, but only as followers and partisans of Luther and Calvin. That the aforementioned command of Christ does not really concern them seems to be proved, partly by their behavior and their own secret admission, partly by the fact that Christ would endow them with spirit and courage to fulfill this command as he did His Apostles and others. In more than two hundred years, as experience has shown, this has not come

---

* In the first and sixth volume of the German edition, Jena, printed by Winkel-Mess.

Of the Arrival of the Spaniards

to pass; for whatever task God chooses a man, He will give him the means, talents, and strength needed to accomplish it.

Third: I shall not speak of the hundred other prophecies concerning the conversion of heathens. (They would all have to be false if it depended upon Protestants and those who ever separated from the Roman Church.) But, may I ask, what of the particular prophecy of Christ in Matthew xxiv that, before the end of the world arrives, the Gospel shall be preached everywhere and to all nations? * It is certain that if, on the one hand, the Protestants have the only true Gospel and religion in their possession, and on the other hand, their preachers will not do better in the future than they have done in the past two and a half centuries in preaching the Gospel among the heathen, then the Judgment Day will never dawn. They want no part in the work of converting heathen and, to all appearances, will do even less of it in the future. Among them, indifference and tolerance for all religions and superstitions are increasing from day to day, including theism and atheism. These deformities, which originated among the Protestants, are nothing but "mali corvi malum ovum," that is, evil fruit from an evil tree. Of course these gentlemen know quite well how to scatter their seed on the already plowed and seeded field of the Catholic Church, by sowing weeds among the wheat. They catch the fish which are near to the shore and swim voluntarily into their net because it is not tight. Yet they eagerly avoid sailing on the high, raging sea of idolatry, or clearing a forest of heathen in Canada, China, Japan, Malabaria (India), or in the land of the Caffres. For such work they have neither courage nor imagination.†

Fourth: I am asking you what do you think of Christ's saying in Luke xi: "Qui non est mecum, contra me est, et qui non colligit mecum, dispergit," that is: he who is not with Christ is against Him, and he who does not help Him to gather, scatters and destroys? The Protestant gentlemen, their clergy as well as their worldly authorities, truly do not

---

* "Prædicabitur hoc Evangelium regni in universo orbe, in testimonium omnibus gentibus: et tunc veniet consumatio. (Matthew xxiv:14.)

† The occupation of non-Catholics is not to convert heathen, but to pervert Christians, said Tertullian more than fifteen hundred years ago (*De præscript. adv. hær.* cap. 4).

help Christ to bring all the pagans into the fold of the Church. They let the good shepherd sweat and run, but they themselves do not lift a foot to lead the erring sheep on the right path and to unite them under the shepherd's staff of Christ. Their pilots and seamen have been trying to find a northern route to the Orient for almost two hundred years, so that their merchant ships may reach Japan and China in less time; but their preachers do not search for any ways to penetrate into Abyssinia, Tibet, the Great and Lesser Tartary, there to enlighten age-old heretics or to baptize idolaters or other unbelievers. What conclusion may be drawn from that? As was said before, and as Christ Himself has said, the Protestants are not for Christ; therefore they are against Him. In no way do they help to gather the heathen into His Church; they disperse, destroy, and lay waste. The results of their so-called Reformation in the sixteenth century, and from 1517 until now, were nothing but dissension, destruction, and devastation in the sheepfold of Christ and in the field of the Church of God.

Fifth: Good merchandise can be sent into every part of the world; it will find buyers everywhere. The old philosophic-theological proverb says: "Bonum est communicativum sui." Why then, if their religion is so evangelical and good, do the Protestants not seek to introduce it into all parts of the world and bring the light of Faith to so many nations who live in darkness and in the shadow of death? Why do the Dutch not only omit preaching the Heidelberg catechism or the canons of their Dordrecht synod in Japan, where they monopolize all trade, but eagerly conceal their Calvinistic religion before the Japanese? They deny their religion; they do not wish to be known as Christians, but solely as Dutchmen. The image of Him, whom they consider their God and Saviour, they even trample underfoot. How shameful! Never has any greed and avarice brought any Roman Catholic nation to this! Before the rise of the two new evangelists of Wittenberg and Geneva, no one would ever have believed it possible that a Christian nation could go so far. This brings no honor to the Calvinistic (or as they wish to call it, Reformed) religion or its adherents, but should rather cause them to doubt the quality and truth of this sect which leads the subjects of a great state to commit such a fantastic, un-Christian, and blasphemous deed. The English and the Dutch (in particular the latter) trade in all things in all the corners of the globe, and they will do anything for

Of the Arrival of the Spaniards

a profit.* Should even Satan himself have a shipment to any of the four continents, he surely would find much courtesy in Amsterdam and soon have a ship ready to sail at his service. The one thing they do not wish to export and bring to the market, however, is their religion, for which they rebelled and led wars against the Spanish kings for a long time. It is certain that all the preachers in Holland have as little desire as Satan himself to convert one single pagan to Calvinism, or to lead him to Heaven.

Sixth: If Protestant preachers fear misfortune and death, and perhaps for this reason lack courage and do not dare to venture among foreign nations and barbarians, why then do they not show any concern for the eternal salvation of their colonial slaves in America and the Negro slaves from Guinea and elsewhere? Surely from them they have nothing to fear. Why do they let them perish like dogs? †

If those preachers of the Augsburg and Geneva Confession are kept at home by their wives and children, if family and house prevent these gentlemen from a voyage to the pagan kingdoms in the East or West, why do they grumble about the Catholic Church and curse her so mightily because she demands celibacy of all those who voluntarily enter her priesthood? Why does their church not wish to remember St. Paul's saying (1 Corinthians VII): "I have no command from the Lord as to chastity, but I do advise it"; nor Christ's utterance (Matthew XIX: "Whosoever forsakes his house or field in my name . . . ?" Both celibacy and voluntary poverty, though not indispensable, are of service in promoting the conversion of pagans in far distant lands according to the will and command of the Lord. Two big obstacles are thereby removed. The Protestant preacher, however, speaks, as in Luke XIV: "I took a wife, or wish to take

---

* The captain of the Dutch ship which took me from Cadiz to Ostend plucked the chickens and scummed the soup himself.

† There is not one inhabitant (in these colonies) who does not have a slave; some own as many as thirty or more. Up to now little effort has been made to convert these heathen; only a few are baptized; and yet, with small effort, a wonderful community could be assembled from those people, considering that many of the slaves have already a good deal of understanding (of the Christian religion) after so many years of contact (with their masters). Some even have the desire to become Christians, as I have heard from them. But their masters do not permit it, for baptized slaves cannot be resold. Thus writes the Danish Lutheran pastor Boeving in his description of the Dutch colony near the promotory of Bonaespei.

one, I have a house, etc., and it is full of children; therefore I cannot . . ."

Hence among the Roman Catholic clergy, Christ has His helpers and the Apostles have their faithful successors, in the persons of the missionaries, dedicated to the conversion of heathen. To teach and baptize the unbelievers, the missionaries travel throughout the world, penetrating into regions where no profit-hungry merchant nor daring pioneer has ever been before. They work and sweat with Christ for the salvation of souls; they want to see their Faith spread into all the corners of the world and make Christians of all men, no matter who they might be. Some they instruct and baptize, others they prepare for Heaven; they preach the kingdom of God to those who are nothing to them, from whom they get nothing, and from whom they can expect nothing but death and martyrdom. For the sake of this work, they leave their homeland and, with it, everything, to sail over the seas. Like St. Paul, they fear no dangers, but suffer shipwreck, hunger, and thirst, and dwell in deserts, exposed to ugly vermin. They live among wild beasts and such human beings as are only distinguishable from beasts by their bodies. They risk their lives a hundred times, and spill their blood in a hundred different ways. Meanwhile, the Protestant lip servant puts his hands in his pockets and watches indifferently the horrors of idolatry in so many lands. He lets millions of black and white pagans perish and end in Hell, not in the least bothering or thinking of coming to their aid, in spite of God's explicit command to help them and save them from eternal damnation.

Now I beseech the modest and truth-loving Protestant reader to lay aside all prejudices and, in honor of God, draw his own conclusions and tell me in all sincerity: Where and on which side is the love of neighbor, the true mark of the disciple of Christ? On which side, pray, the Catholic or the Protestant, is the spirit of the True Church? Compared with the stand taken by the Protestant preachers in religious zeal and missionary work, does not the attitude of the Catholic clergy appear to be a good test for Catholic priests and the truth of their religion, as against Protestants and the falsehood of their sect? The Church which has the spirit of Christ and of the Apostles can certainly not be the Church of the anti-Christ.

I hope nobody will seriously challenge me by mentioning the one and a half Danish missionaries in Tranquebar,[42] a Royal Danish town in

Of the Arrival of the Spaniards

East India. Within this city, the missionaries conceived the idea of converting the few pagan subjects of his Danish Majesty to a pietistically transformed Lutheranism. Nor should I be challenged in mentioning either a certain Dr. Dellius [43] of New England, who, accompanied by a little Iroquois woman, tried with little success to convert the Iroquois Indians to the English Church, or a few other Protestant would-be converters of this same caliber. Mr. Weislinger [44] has already exposed the pietistic Mr. Ziegenbalg [45] and his helpers in Tranquebar (and possibly others like them) in the second part of his work "Theological Charlatans"; likewise, Father Charlevoix has given a description of the mission of the Englishman Dellius in his "History of Canada." *

---

* He [Mr. Dellius] discharged his duty as a missionary in a way that gave him little inconvenience, but brought him a yearly income of no less than twelve hundred French pounds. He remained almost constantly in Oranienburg (a city in New England), and had all the newly born children brought there for baptism. An Iroquois woman, who lived in his house and accompanied him on his short and very infrequent apostolic journeys, served him as interpreter when instructing adults. The number of these, however, was very small, and the preacher did not try very hard to increase it. I cannot tell with certainty how long this mission lasted, but my documents assure me that a few years later Mr. Dellius was told to vacate the house and was chased out of Oranienburg. One fact is evident beyond a doubt: the Protestant religion made very little progress among the Iroquois.

This attempt of Mr. Dellius to convert pagans into Protestants is not the first which shows our religious opponents that they are not the people to spread Christianity among the heathen, and that their sect neither brings forth that virile and industrious zeal for the salvation of the unbelievers nor produces the fruit which is one of the most visible signs of the True Church of Christ.

The method used by the oft-mentioned Mr. Dellius in making the Iroquois friends of the English nation through the bonds of religion was more likely to produce contrary results. This actually happened. These savages soon saw the difference between the mode of life of this preacher and that of previous Catholic missionaries; wherefor, after a short time the Indians asked the latter to return. (Charlevoix, *Histoire de la Nouvelle France*, tome 3, p. 366.)

A few Dutchmen who lived in the neighborhood of this country decided to spread their gospel among the new converts. They began with the women, thinking it would be easier to change them. . . . Later some of the preachers tried to stir up among the Indians a distrust of their missionaries. They had even less success, for these brave Christian women answered these predicants in a tone which made them blush with shame. The women told them that no devotion, no contempt for selfishness, no modesty or edifying morals were noticeable among them—qualities which made their priest so worthy and

Observations in Lower California

It is and remains irrefutably true that the Protestants of today follow zealously all those who, since the beginning of Christianity, have deserted the Roman Church, and, as everyone knows, have made poor efforts in bringing the pagans to their side, thus making their church in universal conformity with the ninth article of their faith. Luther and Calvin, who probably never thought of the pagans, must have foreseen this, for they eliminated the title "universal," which the Apostles and the first council at Nicaea in 325 had given to the Church, and which is one of the *insigniæ* of the True Church. As a substitute, they adopted the word "Christian," which is as meaningless and as superfluous in this case as a fifth wheel on a wagon. How can a Church not be Christian when,

---

honorable, and which always had appeared to be signs of the truth of the religion these priests were preaching. (*Idem*, tome 2, p. 222.)

He who is casting doubt on the testimony of a Catholic priest may hear what the following Protestants have to say about their mission in East India.

From the beginning of the missions up to this day (i.e., within twenty-four years), one thousand and twenty-three people have been partly converted from paganism to Christianity, partly accepted as children into the community. Thus writes Samuel Urlsperger,[46] Senior of Augsburg, in his "Historic Notes" from the report, printed in 1730, of the Royal Danish missionaries in East India. Surely an impressive number of heathen turned Lutheran within twenty-four years! The worst of it is that these few became Lutherans for the love of money, as will be shown later.

In 1710 several missionaries were sent from Denmark to Tranquebar. They tried hard to convert pagans, but the time of their divine inspiration had apparently not yet come, because the number of new converts amounted to only a few hundred. Thus writes Johann Huebner in 1736 in his *Geography* under the word "Tranquebar."

In 1734 the number of converts had increased to two thousand, nine hundred and twenty, according to the *Continuatores* of Halle, the thirty-eighth continuation of the report on Protestant missions in East India. This includes, however, all minor children and Catholics who had deserted their faith. The Danish Mr. Boeving, who is one of the East Indian Protestant missionaries, says that as far as he knows not one of the converts had been moved or induced to change by preaching. The *causa impulsiva* (i.e., the motive) for their being converted to the Lutheran religion was usually poverty.

This was the state of Protestant missionary work in East and West India thirty and more years ago, and it is no better today. Huebner should not have written that the time for the natives' conversion had not yet arrived, but rather that the Protestants are not suited for such a task and have no calling for it. For during the same years in which the Tranquebarian missionaries had caught so few and such poor fish, the Catholics, like the Apostles, caught thousands and thousands right in the neighborhood of Tranquebar, as they did in hundreds of other places. (St. John XXI and Acts II.)

Of the Arrival of the Spaniards

according to the second article, it believes in Christ and is holy?

Finally, I beg of the non-Catholic as well as the Catholic reader not to take amiss this prolonged digression, which he probably considers superfluous to this book. All this has been written by a well-meaning heart, following the advice of St. Paul to Titus: "Insta opportune, importune": Speak to them whether the time is opportune or inopportune. Not every day do I have an opportunity, oral or written, of offering a good thought to the Protestant gentlemen. I wanted to seize this opportunity the more so because I know that the character of the mission work of the Roman Catholic clergy among the heathen has induced more than one Protestant to take his leave of Protestantism and return to the fold of the Catholic Church, which his ancestors so unwisely had deserted. How happy would I esteem myself if, with my few remarks, I had the good fortune to cause the imperative return of one or the other of these gentlemen.

CHAPTER TEN : *Of the Arrival of Don Gaspar Portolá and the Departure of the Jesuits from California*

THE FATE which befell the Jesuits in Spain [47] was inevitably shared by those in America, and consequently by those in California. From a purely material point of view, no greater favor could have been done for them or for many other missionaries than to get them out of such misery and back to Europe, their homeland. However, I can assure the reader there was not one among them whose heart did not ache at the thought of leaving California and who, even if the position of his brethren in the Spanish monarchy had not changed, would not have gladly turned back in the middle of the homeward journey.

Observations in Lower California

During the months of June and July, 1767, all the Jesuits of the many Mexican colleges and the not-too-distant missions were suddenly seized at night by armed forces, made prisoners, and led by dragoons to the port of Vera Cruz. It happened just as it did in Europe; at times entire regiments were used as though the Moors had to be faced in battle. To save the expense of a long, overland journey, the rest of the missionaries on the mainland (about fifty in number, from the missions of Sonora, Sinaloa and Pimería) were first led to a region in Sonora called Guaymas, on the shore of the California Sea below the twenty-eighth degree latitude, north. At the first opportunity, the missionaries were to be shipped south to Matanchel (below the twenty-first degree), then overland three hundred hours to Santa Cruz. This was done.

Guaymas is a desolate field (a former mission at this place was destroyed by the Seri Indians). No one lives there, and there is no human habitation within many hours of traveling. I saw it from a distance on my overland journey to the Yaqui creek. The heat in summer is very great, many rain and thunderstorms occur, and the cold in winter is such that at times a warm stove would be very welcome. The fifty missionaries spent nine months in this place under heavy military guard, living in a hut made of sticks and branches, which looked more like a cattle barn than a shelter for human beings. They were fed nothing but Indian corn, sun-dried beef, and mutton. After this encampment, they were finally put, like prisoners, in a small frigate where they could not even find ample sleeping space. The journey from Guaymas to Matanchel, which at another season with a north wind blowing is made in five or six days, lasted no less than forty-eight days.

The first day's travel, after they had landed, was even worse than the seven weeks at sea. The march led through a great, low, swampy forest. It was summertime, the rainy season in that region, and it poured all day.* Many of the missionaries, overcome by fatigue, fell off their horses several times; others who preferred to walk often had to wade through water up to the knees. They reached the first cold shelter, thoroughly soaked by the rain, without having had anything to eat all day. After several more days of marching, they arrived in the region of the two Spanish-Mexican villages Aquatitlán and Istlán. Within a few days, twenty of the fifty

---

* I have traveled on this route, but in the middle of February.

Of the Arrival of the Spaniards

missionaries died and had to be buried. The hardships of Guaymas, the endless and thoroughly uncomfortable sea voyage, and the exhausting march of the first day brought on an attack of poisonous fever, and only seven escaped the sickness. Even those who survived suffered a long time afterward.

On July 8, 1769, two years after their arrest, only thirty missionaries arrived in the Bay of Cádiz (Spain), and two of these soon died.*

The Spanish gentlemen tried their best to hide the news of what had happened to the Jesuits in Mexico and on the other side of the California Sea from their colleagues in California. Thus we would not be induced to bury our treasures or escape with them to Shambadia (where, so the Jews say, the Kings of Judah live!). Nor would we be tempted to arm the Indians with the eight thousand rifles which, as the rumor had it, we were supposed to be hiding in our houses. Therefore, contrary to custom, we did not receive any news from the other side for half a year, and during that summer the pearl fishers were not permitted to sail to California.

Don Gaspar Portolá,[48] the duly appointed Governor of California,† was to sail to California. He had full instructions to build cities and fortifications there, and expel the "first conquerors of the land," if I may use this term. With two vessels he twice attempted to sail from Matanchel[49] to California, once in June and again in August, 1767. Both times, however, adverse winds forced him to turn back. With him

---

* These twenty-eight and five others who had lived on the Isle of Chiloë, opposite the Chilean coast, are the only ones out of five thousand Jesuits who to this day are still in Spain. They are closely confined and well guarded. The five Chileans have already been imprisoned for the fourth year, and the twenty-eight others for their third. Their opponents hope that some great crime against the state (or who knows what other villainy) might be uncovered in America and held against them. It is probable that such a plan will not succeed. (I should say, it is quite certain that it will not succeed, for in both of these countries where these thirty-three missionaries have lived no such crime can be committed, even if any wished to perpetrate it.) All the Jesuits who had lived in Paraguay (about whom for more than a century all kinds of rumors had been spread all over the world) had long ago been sent back freely and without any restrictions to their homes in Germany and Italy. "Quare (ergo) fremuerunt gentes? . . . qui habitat in cœlis, irridebit eos." (Psalm II, 1, 4.)

† Until then, there had not been any other authority in California but the captain of the soldiers, who received no higher pay than a common private. However, for his salary of eight hundred and fifty guilders he could demand commodities directly from Mexico at the prices prevailing there.

Observations in Lower California

were twenty-five dragoons, an equal number of musketeers, and fourteen priests. His vanguard, however, sailing in a sloop, had the good luck to land toward the end of September three hours below Loreto. This group was seen by some local travelers and, by their uniforms, recognized as foreign guests. The strangers, however, would not tell what their intentions were, where they came from, or why they had come. They remained silent, reëmbarked at once, and sailed down the coast toward the territory in the south called La Paz. There, too, they kept absolutely silent. When, after some time, Portolá did not arrive and the provisions they had brought with them had been used, they sent to the mines for more, announcing that they were forbidden under penalty of death to reveal the reason for their arrival. Rather a superfluous precaution! With all that secrecy, the Spaniards did not find any more silver in California than if it had been known ten years earlier what was to happen in 1767.

In the middle of October, Portolá tried a third trip across the water. This time he finally succeeded, though it took him forty-two days to cover a distance of about one hundred and fifty hours. He landed near Mission San José del Cabo, at the southernmost point of California. The real objective of his expedition had been to reach Mission Loreto, a hundred and fifty hours away, where he had hoped to surprise the missionary who was also the superintendent of all the missions, and by seizing him during the night, capture the treasures. Instead, he had to undertake this Loretan pilgrimage by land, which gave him the best opportunity (more than he liked) of observing with his own eyes on his arrival in this promised land how this beautiful and noble kingdom of California is level, shady, green, fertile, rich in water, and populous.

Nobody enjoyed the landing at San José del Cabo more than the new soldiers. They had envisioned California as a land paved with silver, and had thought pearls could be swept up with a broom. Their joy did not last long. They soon cursed the country and would have liked to leave it right away. Six only, together with the ensign, had this good fortune, however. Portolá commissioned them to guard us, glad at the same time to have seven mouths fewer in his company.

The captain of the old California militia, Don Fernando Rivera y Moncada,[50] a man of great virtue, scrupulously conscientious and a faithful servant of the King of Spain, happened to be in this region when the Governor arrived in San José. Portolá secretly conferred with him

Of the Arrival of the Spaniards

for several hours and was rudely shaken out of his dreams of California treasures, of the wealth of the missionaries, and of other such things. To tell the truth, there was some silver in all the churches, as I have mentioned before; but in the houses of the missionaries there was either none at all, as it was in mine and others, or if there was any, it represented values received for goods recently sold to the miners. This too I explained in Part Three, chapter seven. Such silver had already been designated for the churches or was to be used for the needy California natives. For this reason, the food for the Viceroy was served by the missionaries, not in silver as it was said he had expected, but in earthen vessels or in porcelain, of which every year the ship from the Philippines left a few pieces at San José del Cabo in payment for provisions. From that place the porcelain was freely distributed among the other missions.

Gratitude as well as respect for his good name compels me to state here that Governor Don Gaspar Portolá (and all the other Spanish officials and non-officials wherever I met them on water or land on my return journey) treated the Jesuits, considering the circumstances, with respect, honor, politeness, and friendliness. He never caused the least annoyance, sincerely assuring us how painful it was to him to have to execute such a commission. On several occasions tears came to his eyes, and he was surprised to find Europeans willing to live and die in such a country.

After having inspected the misery of San José and Santiago, he visited the poverty-stricken mines sixteen hours from there. There, too, he was astonished to see the poor huts and the apparent poverty of the miners. Then he completed all the necessary preparations for a land journey to Loreto. With more than forty people in his company he hastened his departure for Loreto, his future residence. He saw it with little comfort for the first time on December 17, after ten days of travel and forced marches. Only once on his journey did he find human beings and shelter at a mission; otherwise, his eyes saw nothing but stones and thorns, barren hills, dry rock, and waterless creeks.

The daily march was not just four or five hours, as is customary among soldiers, but ten and more. In California miles are not counted, only places where water is available for men and horses, and some hay or brush for the latter.

At Loreto, Portolá sent for Father Ducrue,[51] at that time Superior of all the missions, and who was then staying at his own mission,

Observations in Lower California

Guadalupe. He handed him a very polite letter from the Viceroy of Mexico, ordering him and all the other Jesuits by command of his Catholic Majesty to leave California in order to bring peace to the Spanish monarchy (although there was no war!). Portolá took over the accounts of the soldiers' pay and dispatched people to all the missions to inventory and take over all household goods, church fittings, and everything else. Spiritual care of the poor natives was omitted, for our clerical successors and the regular soldiers were still floundering somewhere on the sea. The Superior also sent a letter to each missionary, written in accordance with the will and desire of the Governor. All missionaries were ordered to assemble for embarkation at Loreto on January 25, 1768. The letter also requested that the missionaries keep the natives calm and preach the maintenance of peace. Since not enough time had been allowed for the journey to Loreto from the furthermost missions in the north, and also because an epidemic was raging among the Indians at San Borja, the missionaries did not arrive at Loreto until the second day of February. Portolá received all of them, as was the Spanish custom in greeting priests, by kissing their hands and embracing them with great politeness.

Much could be told of the lamentations and tears of the Indians when the missionaries left their missions. They considered this departure a penalty (as it was meant to be), but knew of no previous crimes and had heard of none committed at any of the missions. They, like millions of others, did not know what to think or say. Among other causes for their alarm and distress was the fear that in the future they would no longer be provided with food and clothing.* It is a fact that, at least during the year of the departure of the Jesuits, the thousand guilders annually received from the endowed estates were not conceded to their successors. Moreover, in Mexico, hundreds and hundreds of mules which belonged to the California missions were now used for other services, since they were considered Jesuit property. In addition, our first successors, who were all Spanish Americans and had heard false rumors of the wealth of California, had invited many of their friends and relatives to sail with them to California. The natives did not know when their new shepherds

---

* Letters from America make it clear that this fear of the California natives had not been empty and unfounded.

Of the Arrival of the Spaniards

would arrive; many of them were afraid lest they die without receiving the Holy Sacraments, and so it really happened. It is enough to say that at Mission San Xavier (where, seven priests in all, we had assembled before we started our last day's journey to Loreto), after we had celebrated High Mass on the day of the Purification of St. Mary, such general crying and pitiful lamenting arose among all the natives present that I, too, was moved to tears and could not restrain myself from weeping all the way to Loreto. Even now, while I am writing this, tears enter my eyes.

The natives did not know what to think of such an unexpected and sudden departure, and similarly, we did not know how to explain it to them. To speak of the persecution of the Jesuits would have meant as much to them as telling the inhabitants of New Holland or Novaya Zemlya something about the Westphalian peace or the papal bull *Unigenitus*. However, the twentieth chapter of the Acts of the Apostles, where St. Paul's farewell from the people of Miletus is described, would, in part at least, not be above their understanding. And these passages, together with some commentaries, were told to them by one of us as a farewell speech.

The fourteen religious, our successors, and the twenty-five soldiers had even less luck during their sea passage than Don Portolá and his twenty-five dragoons. After sailing around a good deal, they finally had to land on the coast of Culiacán in Sinaloa and arrived at San José del Cabo shortly before we sailed from there. Exposed to adverse winds, they proceeded on the sea to Loreto. There they would find all the sick natives we left behind, blessed by the Holy Sacraments, but very much in need of the daily visits and help of a priest. And others they would find rotting in their graves.

The fourteen new missionaries did not long remain in California. We met their successors two days' journey from where we landed on our way to Vera Cruz, looking for an opportunity to cross over to California. Thus the poor California Indians had three different shepherds of as many different orders within three to six months. Among these, only the members of one order could understand them and speak to them. The cause for this second change is well known to me, indeed far better than the reason for the first. I consider it, however, best to keep silent about the matter, although it would bring honor to those who departed first.

Observations in Lower California

On the third day of February, we celebrated a solemn High Mass before the exceedingly beautiful picture of the Virgin of Loreto, which was draped in black as though it were Good Friday. Father Díaz,[52] a Mexican, delivered an excellent sermon, well adapted to the present circumstances, although a few hours before he had not thought of preparing it. On the same day, at nine o'clock in the evening, after a last and very friendly embrace by Don Portolá, we boarded, by royal order and in God's name, the ship. Although the march to the boat was supposed to proceed in silence, all the Loretans of both sexes were assembled at the shore to bid us their last farewell, and everyone, black and white, natives and Spaniards, was lamenting and weeping.

We were sixteen Jesuits in all, fifteen priests and one lay brother; six were Spaniards, two Mexicans, and eight Germans. The latter were: Lambert Hostel, of Münstereifel in the Duchy of Jülich; Xavier Bischoff, of Glatz in Bohemia; Georg Rheds, of Coblenz; FranzInáma, of Vienna in Austria; Benno Ducrue, of Munich in Bavaria; Ignatz Tirs, of Komotau in Bohemia; Wenceslaus Linck, of Joachimsthal in Bohemia; and I myself, from the upper Rhine. Exactly the same number, that is, sixteen Jesuits, one brother and fifteen priests, we left behind, buried in California.

The journey on the sea, God be thanked, was a lucky one. We covered a distance of three hundred hours in five days. On the eighth day of February, we sighted the green shores of Matanchel with its high, dense forests and many green cedar trees. On the same day we disembarked.

FINIS

APPENDIX ONE : FALSE REPORTS ABOUT CALIFORNIA AND THE CALIFORNIANS

False Reports about California and the Californians

ALL REPORTS which deal favorably with California, her wealth, fertility, or other things necessary to make life comfortable belong without exception to the category of false reports, regardless of who the authors are. Except for her pearls, her two and a half kinds of fruit, her almost permanently blue sky and, at least in the shade, her not too hot and never too cold air, California has nothing which deserves to be praised and esteemed or needs to be coveted by even the poorest of inhabited lands of the globe. The words of Woodes Rogers quoted in Part One, chapter four, about a small part of the land are more than true of all of California from Cabo San Lucas to the Río Colorado. Cluverius [53] states in the following few words: "California solo est arido, sterili atque deserto." (California is an arid, barren waste land.) Therefore, neither I nor all those who have lived with me in California could understand how it could happen that certain people would speak with so much praise of this peninsula and make of it one of the most beautiful countries on earth. Did they perhaps dream of their own fatherland? Were they under the spell of a vision of a paradise on earth? Did they use special magnifying or some other extraordinary glasses when they put their reports on paper? Did California at that time experience the seven fruitful years of Egypt or the golden age of which the poets dream? Or did California at a later time turn completely upside down and change into an entirely different land?

It is absolutely incorrect, as is stated here and there in original writings or in copies, that "it rains in California from November until March," that "the flatlands are flooded during the rainy season," or that "there are beautiful rivers, full of fish and fresh-water lobsters, enchanting valleys, lush meadows, and there is no shortage of plants and grain," that "geese, ducks, partridges, and other fowl are found in great abundance, as well as lions, tigers, etc., etc."

It is false to state that "the air is cold or very hot on the two shores but moderate in the interior," that there are "cities and villages" and

Observations in Lower California

"in Loreto or other places a fort with bastions and trenches," etc., etc., that "Otondo built a fort and a church there in 1683." [54]

It is false to claim that California is thickly populated and that her inhabitants dwell under the trees during summer, and in ground shelters or in subterranean caves during the winter; that they engage in animal husbandry and agriculture, weave carpets, spin woolen cloth and linen, and make pots, kettles, pans, and spoons; that they pray to the moon or other idols and are ruled by princes; that profitable trading could be arranged between New Spain or Mexico and California, etc., etc.

It is false to state that the Californians engage in spirited arguments with the missionaries about matters of Faith, that the natives built a wide pier of heavy piles at the Bay of Santa Magdalena, reaching almost half an hour into the ocean, to facilitate their fishing and to make it possible to catch fish with a net. The natives' language and limited mentality do not rhyme with such arguments; the territory around Santa Magdalena Bay is even poorer in wood than the rest of the country. Native fishermen, says Rogers, have neither nets nor fishhooks, but only a kind of spear (i.e., a long, thin, hard, and pointed stick of wood), which they operate very skillfully, spearing sea fish and turtles alike. All this is true; but again it is not true that the water of the California Sea has a reddish color, etc., etc.!

After quoting these false reports extracted from various books, I shall now present in their order others, though these will by no means be all of them. I found them while reading the first two volumes of the French "History of California," a translation from the English language, published in Paris in 1767. I have already referred to this book in the introduction and other places in this volume. These falsehoods, as well as the others mentioned above, have been sufficiently refuted by what I have written in this little book; therefore it will not be necessary again to contradict them with many words.

Let me begin with the title of the book itself. It reads: "Natural and Civil History of California, containing an exact and true description of this land, its soil, mountains, rivers, lakes, and seas; its animals, plants, minerals, and its famous pearl fishing; also a description of the customs of the inhabitants, their religion, their government, etc." * This entire

---

* *Histoire naturelle et civile de la Californie, contenant une description exacte de ce pays, de son sol, de ses montaignes, lacs, rivières et mers; de ses*

False Reports about California

title is, first of all, pure wind, intended to call attention to the book and attract buyers. Second, pure mendacity, because the promised "exact descriptions" are nowhere to be found in this book. Third, *de subjecto non supponente,* as we say in school, that is, a description is promised of things which, generally, are without substance and never existed in California. There are no rivers, no lakes, and hardly any animals, plants, or minerals in California; therefore, the author or translator does not use any words to describe them in his book. Also, there was neither religion nor government among the pagan Californians. How then could anyone write an impressive natural and political history of California? "Sunt multa fucis illita." There certainly are barren mountains and rocks, but little can be said of them and of the poor plants and animals. The Spanish work, of which the French and English editions are partly a copy, is entitled *Noticia de California.*[55] A translation of this title should have been sufficient.

And now a few details. In the first volume, page 35, it says: "In some places, California is forty miles wide." This is true only if we think of Italian miles, which are but half an hour long and do not include the grades of the road over mountains and hills.

Page 37: "A great number of brooks flow forth from the mountains. Springs are found frequently which serve as drinking water as well as for irrigating the fields." I wish to God it were so!

Page 49: "There are few coyotes." I refer my reader to Part One, chapter seven.

Page 52: "There is an infinite number of bird species. . . . A great number of song birds . . . birds of prey . . . And the *auras,* which help to keep the cities clean, for at daybreak they devour all the refuse which had been thrown into the streets." * Such eagles or hoopoos could earn money in some of the Spanish cities. In California, however, where there are neither cities nor streets nor houses, and much less (with your

---

animaux, vegeteaux, mineraux, et de sa fameuse pêcherie de perles; les moeurs, de ses habitants, leur religion, leur gouvernement, etc., etc.

* "... les auras, lesquelles contribuent a tenir les villes propres, mangeant des le point du jour les charognes, qu'on a jettées dans les rues." *Charogne* really means "carrion." However, I cannot believe that the author meant to talk about carrion, because in none of the European cities is such a thing thrown into the streets. The natives of California, however, industriously search for carrion, wherever they see *auras* rise, and stuff it into their own stomachs. *Auras* are a kind of vulture.

Observations in Lower California

permission) nightstools, nothing of the sort is thrown or poured into the streets. And if the bird species are countless, where will the particular or single birds find their food and enough trees in which to build their nests? It is possible to be or to travel in California without ever seeing or hearing a bird, except ravens or bats.

Page 56: "Near the Bay of Santa Magdalena there is a piece of land covered with stout trees, which the natives use for building their ships." I have often been at this bay and saw nothing but miserable shrubs a few feet high. The Indians who live there are actually worse off than the others for want of firewood to keep warm, for the nights are always cool in that region. Of ships and boats the California Indians, all of them together, knew nothing until the Spaniards arrived on the peninsula. The wood which is now used for building ships and boats at Loreto comes from the forests near Matanchel.

Furthermore, we read: "One finds rare and precious kinds of fruit, some of which are also found in Europe." If this refers to precious acorns, the statement is correct, because there are a few of them in California. Two of them were shown to me at one time as a rarity. These grew in the district of my neighbor's mission on a small oak tree no more than a few fingers thick.

"The amount of fruit is greater on the coasts, for there is more water; and on the banks of rivers and lakes." Water is scarce all over California, but even more so along the two coasts. Where there are no rivers and lakes, no fruit can grow on the banks. It is true that more sour pitahayas are found along the two coasts than in the interior, but they need as little water as those that grow in the interior.

Page 57: "The pitahaya fruit is the staple food of the natives. It is found nowhere except in California." All of Mexico and the territories across from California are full of these pitahayas. As for the sour variety, I have already mentioned all that is necessary at the proper place. By the way, the pitahaya season lasts only a little more than two months, and nothing is preserved for a later time. Hence the pitahaya could not possibly be the principal food of the people.

Page 58: "There are plum trees which secrete a very fine kind of incense instead of rosin or gum. I do not know how these plums taste, but I do know that those who have been in California praise them very highly." Neither do I know how they taste, but I do know that those

False Reports about California

who have been in California do not praise them. In size and shape this fruit resembles more our sloe than our plum; therefore I care neither to see (for they are very scarce) nor to eat them. The so-called incense does not flow from this sloe bush, but from an entirely different plant. It is not so fine as the Arabian incense; otherwise the merchants would fetch it and part of it would not be used for calking California vessels. To be sure, this "incense" is used in churches, but not outside of California.

Page 59: "Among other plants there is also the *pita*, out of which the Indians pull threads." The name of this plant is not *pita*, but in the Mexican language *maguei, mescále*, or in Californian *pui, kenjei*, because there are many varieties. It is nothing else but an aloe plant, and out of its branches a kind of thread is pulled which the Spaniards in Mexico call *pita*. This thread is so coarse and rough that a string made of it is like horsehair unless it is treated with gypsum or lime and softened by beating with stones. I am describing this fiber so that no uninformed person can get the idea that so-called cambric cloth comes from California or that California missionaries sold fine linen in Morocco or in China.

On the same page: ". . . the natives cut the *yucca* into thin, round slices, squeeze out the juice, and bake cakes from it which serve them in place of bread." This would be too much work for the Indians. When they have yucca, they dig it out and throw it directly on the fire or on hot embers. Yucca takes the place of bread, meat, cheese, soup, salad, *bœuf à la mode*, and everything else. If a native is offered meat and bread, he eats one after the other—never the one with the other.

Page 60: "Rivers, canals, and ponds are on both sides planted and bordered with olive trees, fig trees, and grapevines." Again a brave exaggeration! The olive oil which feeds the eternal light in the church of Loreto (the only one in California which is kept lighted at all times, for only in Loreto is the Host kept) is annually imported from Mexico! There are that many olive trees in California! Almost the same can be said about the fig trees and grapevines. There were only five missions with grapevines and fig trees, and these were not by a river, for there are none! These trees and vines are irrigated in the same way as wheat or corn fields.

Page 62: "Although the soil in California is infertile throughout, yet no want is felt in California, for the sea is close and to the right and left

Observations in Lower California

is exceedingly rich in fish." * Even if this last statement were true, one may ask whether a man needs anything else but fish. Do the Laplanders, Samoedes, the inhabitants of Novaya Zemlya, or the islanders of Ormus in the Persian Gulf, and hundreds of others lack nothing simply because the sea is nearby? California lacks nothing except everything. Most natives never see fish soup all year, and others who live among them never choke on fish bones because on days of fasting they have to be satisfied with dried beans. This "general infertility," by the way, does not conform with the report already quoted of so many rivers, fruits, birds, and so on.

Page 68: "At times the shore is covered with turtles, cast out by the sea." I have never heard of this "casting out" in California, much less have I seen it. It is absolutely incorrect.

Page 65: "A great number of people, eager for pearls, have settled in California and are settling there every day." Up to February 3, 1768, not a single person had done so, and nobody ever had such intentions. The pearl fishers come and go every year, like merchants visiting the Frankfurt fair.

Same page: "Many nations are interested in this pearl-fishing industry." † The English and Dutch will know this best, for California is so close to them! And as for all the other nations, I presume that they will also know in which year the Court of Madrid granted them the privilege of fishing for pearls in the California Sea or letting them have a share in that industry.

Page 76: "Many other tribes have been discovered in the Pimería, and since they belong to California, I shall not ignore them." The Pima Indians belong as little to California as the Greeks to Italy, or the Scotch to France or Norway.

Page 78: "They (the natives) would have rather handsome faces if they did not pierce their noses and ears." I have seen many old and middle-aged people with pierced ear lobes, but no one with a pierced nose.

Page 90: "They know nothing about stealing. Their affability is unsurpassed and they are easily led, either for good or evil." Let it be well understood it is true of the latter alone—the evil.

---

* "Quoique le terrain de la Californie soit generalement sterile, cependant le voisinage de la mer fait, qu'on n'y manque de rien etc. ..."
† "Plusieurs nations se mêlent de cette peche. ..."

False Reports about California

Page 96: "The native women were much annoyed to see the girls or daughters of the Spanish soldiers go about naked." * Indeed, they would have been surprised and angered had this been the case, for it would even have been contrary to the custom of the native women!

Page 101: "Their houses are only poor huts on the river's edge ... which they carry from one place to another whenever their search for food forces them to move." The natives do not need to carry their houses from place to place; wherever they go they find living quarters ready, since their homes are nothing but the blue sky and God's earth.

Page 103: "The women pierce their ears and attach to them a big pouch in which they put everything they have to carry." † If all the native women could sew and if the author had not used the adjective "big," I could understand this, thinking perhaps of a small box for needles; otherwise I cannot imagine a pouch big enough to hold small children or a cord of wood, or ears strong enough on which to fasten such pouches, or ear holes in which to hook them!

Page 108: "What we consider the vintage season is to the natives the pitahaya harvest." The pitahayas are neither gathered like grapes or wheat nor stored for a day, much less for a long time. No beverage is made of them as long as they last. Each native picks for himself as many as he can eat that day.

Page 111: The whole account given of native warfare is utterly incorrect. Wars consist of unexpected attacks on the enemy from ambush or at night and of killing as many people as possible. In war the natives have no order, no rites, no war declarations, or anything similar.

Page 339: "The number of Spaniards and others who came from New Spain to settle in California amounted in 1700 to six hundred." Not counting the soldiers, sailors, cow herdsmen, and Mexican Indians working in the mines (all of these people are constantly on the move; they are here today, outside of California tomorrow), the number of Spanish and other permanent settlers amounted in 1768 to one hundred souls.

In the second volume, page 8: "The missionaries and soldiers were greatly worried when their large and small ships, hired to fetch provisions

---

* "Les filles des soldats Espagnols."

† "Les femmes se percent les oreilles et y pendent un gros étui, ou elles mettent tout ce qu'elles portent."

Observations in Lower California

from across the sea, were forced to turn back." * According to that, one might be led to believe that there are as many large and small vessels in the Bay of Loreto in California as in the Texel near Amsterdam, and that there were so many white inhabitants that a whole fleet was needed to bring their food.

Page 213: "The flagship of the garrison bears the captain's name and proper flag." The two small boats which then were, and still are, the whole California navy and sea power are known in and out of California as *los barcos*, the barges of California. One is called *La Concepción* (Immaculate Conception), the other *La Lauretana* (Loreto). They carry similar flags and are of similar size as that market ship which makes the daily route between Mainz and Frankfort, or as the coal barges plying the Maas River between Lièges and Maastricht.

Page 227: "It is certain that of each vessel which went out to fish for pearls, one fifth of the catch (that is, the king's share) was rented each year for twelve thousand *piastres*." † Either the pearls in the California Gulf (on the other side, in the west, no pearls were ever fished) must have enormously decreased or completely disappeared, or this is a monstrous lie! Were it true that only the fifth part of a catch was rented at such a price, what a treasure would a pearl fisher acquire in one year! A certain miner who was still living in California when I left had rented the royal share of all the ships together for a period of five years for sixteen hundred Rhenish guilders; another purchased the slaughtering rights and all the other tithes (the missions were exempt from these) for two hundred guilders a year.

And finally, the cities, capital cities, hamlets, villages, forests, and garrisons so often mentioned by the author are nothing but *entia rationis*,

---

* "Les gros et petits vaisseaux qu'on avoit freté, pour aller chercher des provisions."

† "Il est certain que le quint de chaque barque a été affermé 12,000 piastres par an." There are two kinds of large-sized silver pieces in Spain: the *peso duro* or *fuerte*, and the *peso sencillo*. The first is valued at five French *livres* (pounds), the latter at three *livres* and fifteen *sols*. Which of the two is called *piastre* by foreigners, somebody else may know better than I. Throughout this little book I thought of the *peso duro* as the equivalent of a *piastre* because it is the only one in circulation in America, where it is coined. Formerly it was worth two Rhenish guilders or, as I said, five French pounds.

False Reports about California

or things which never existed. Likewise untrue is the remark about the arrival in California of Father Thyrso González,[56] General of the Society of Jesus, mentioned on page 281 in the first volume; nothing is said about what he is supposed to have done there.

APPENDIX TWO : FALSE REPORTS ABOUT THE MISSIONARIES IN CALIFORNIA

False Reports about the Missionaries in California

Who would imagine, after reading my reports, that slander would also try its teeth on the Jesuits of California and persecute them with its libels? And yet, it so happened.

In the first place, in October, 1766, the Provincial of the Order presented the California Jesuits with eight complaints and a request for an answer. Some "good friends" [57] had sent the complaints to Madrid and from the court they were forwarded to the Viceroy of Mexico. The eight points of accusation were:

1. That the captain of the California-Spanish militia and the soldiers in his command were nothing but slaves of the Jesuits.

2. That the missionaries sold food and other necessities to the soldiers at prices higher than the official tariff prescribes.

3. That the Jesuits force the natives to work hard and give them nothing but boiled Indian corn as reward.

4. That they have secret silver mines in their houses.

5. That they are responsible for the meager output and poor condition of the silver mines of Santa Ana and San Antonio (actually, the missionaries did not want to deprive the Indians of the little corn some of of them had by selling it to the miners).

6. That the Jesuits will in no way permit Spanish families to settle in California and establish a colony.

7. That they trade with the English.

8. And finally, that they purposely never tell the natives anything about the Catholic King, so that the natives would never know of an overlord outside of California and therefore regard the Jesuits as their kings and honor them as the potentates of California.

Fine kings! In truth, "kings" who, as someone said, drank with their horses, ate corn with the chickens, and slept at night with the dogs on the bare soil! Great honor indeed! Honor such as one could seek among the Indians of California or expect from them!

In addition to these points submitted to us in writing, it was also said that the irrigation ditches (through which here and there water is run to a certain piece of land) were of silver, that the house of the missionary of San José del Cabo received six hundred and twenty-five pounds of silver annually, and that we refuse work to any strangers who come to California, so that the news of our wealth would never spread! These last statements are such palpable lies that they do not deserve refutation.

As to the eight points of accusation, we held that it would be good to leave the answers to the captain himself. He had a complete and full knowledge of California, for he had lived there more than twenty-four years, and fifteen of these as captain. In this capacity he governed land and soldiers, jealously guarding his authority.

Thereupon the captain had his lieutenant and seven soldiers who were stationed at Loreto take an oath, and asked them about each accusation raised against the Jesuits. He then sent their sworn and signed depositions to the Viceroy of Mexico. From Mexico we later learned that these eight accusations were considered to be just so many falsehoods and calumnies without basis or semblance of truth. I wish to God that at all times and places people would have proceeded in such a natural manner!

But still, what should the Spanish immigrants do, for instance, in California? They would have to be resigned either to dying of hunger or to running about naked like the natives when the rags they brought with them rotted on their bodies. Then they would have to hunt for field mice and bats, and thus steal the natives' bread from their mouths, as the saying goes. The only Englishman to arrive in California during the Spanish War of Succession was Woodes Rogers. He landed at Cabo San Lucas before anyone had thought of establishing missions in this land. His report, which I will use, did not, in all probability, much inspire his fellow citizens with the prospect of trading with California.

Only the natives gained when they worked. What is more, they ate, in addition to boiled corn, many hundreds of oxen, cows, sheep and goats, several hundreds of pounds of dried figs and grapes, thousands and thousands of pumpkins and melons, and the like. In addition to this, more than twelve thousand guilders had to be spent annually to clothe them.

There was much lamenting among the soldiers when in 1766 it was rumored that in the future they would no longer receive their pay through the Jesuits, as to that date, but through others. The soldiers knew well

False Reports about the Missionaries

that these "others" would try to enrich themselves by administering the pay, just as they did elsewhere.

As for the Catholic King, what could the missionaries say to the natives about him? Should they preach about the number of his subjects and soldiers, his revenues, his court, palaces, summer residences, and the like? How could a priest speak of these things to a people hardly able to count to six, without knowledge of silver and gold—a people more appreciative of a knife and a pound of meat than a hundred pounds of gold; a people that believed the Jesuits, like the cowherders and soldiers, had come to California for their support, and that, aside from them, there was no one on earth except such cowhands and soldiers? To them there was nothing more elegant in the world than a pair of trousers made of rough blue cloth or of plush. A native once, in all seriousness, asked his missionary, who is still living, whether his father had been a cowhand or a California soldier. Father Clemente Guillén,[58] who died in 1740, told some natives who understood Spanish that he read in the newspaper (it was during the Turkish War of 1716–1717) that His Holiness the Pope had sent a blessed sword and hat to Prince Eugene.[59] Greatly surprised, one of the natives asked, "A sword and hat? Why did he not also have a pair of Palmilla trousers made for him?" *

Since I was more strict than they wished me to be, my parishioners threatened several times to complain to my supervisors, thus to make me lose my mission. They held that nothing could frighten me more, because then I would not know where to turn and where to find my bread.

In the second place the "History of California," which has been translated into French and English and which is often quoted, states on page 140, volume two: "Father N. resigned his mission to Father X." This sounds as if the missions of California were lucrative parishes, rich canonicates or fat priories from which a man occasionally resigns to help out a good friend. But in California, as in other places, each missionary remained at the mission assigned to him by his superiors until he died, unless he was transferred by his superiors because of ill health, old age, or for some other important reason to another mission or to a collegium. This leaves no place for a resignation.

---

* *Palmilla* is the poorest blue cloth sent from Mexico to California. It was customary to give trousers and coats made of this material to native California officials and others whom one particularly wished to honor.

Observations in Lower California

On page 201, we read: "California wine is sent to New Spain in exchange for other goods." That is not true. Even if anyone wished to trade, it would be impossible, for that much wine is not made in California. Because of the shortage, the missionaries in California drank considerably more water than wine. At times some of them had to abstain from celebrating Holy Mass because they had no wine.

Page 248: "The salt mines discussed here are found on the isle of Carmen near Loreto. Father Salvatierra asked for them several times, but never received them." These salt mines and all others in California—and there are quite a few—are tax free. Everyone takes as much salt as he wishes, without asking anyone or paying for it. Even so, there are few customers, for the natives eat everything without salt or fat. Furthermore, there is plenty of salt in New Spain or in the Mexican provinces across the gulf from California, and no merchants ever came to California for salt. Therefore I do not see how and why Father Salvatierra should have made any effort to get possession of the salt mines of Carmen.

So much for the content of this "History of California." However, in the foreword the English or French translator, or whoever it may have been, allows himself to say other, and even worse, things about the Jesuits in California and other places. I am certain that the author of this preface did not understand what he wrote about them. He would have to keep silent if he were asked to show proof from the content of the book on which he based his imprudent remarks. He also leaves the reader in doubt about his nationality; now he writes like a Spanish minister of state, now like an English merchant. When he attacks the Jesuits, he speaks the language of a Parisian lawyer of 1762. All these varieties of style are found in the same introduction. Let us hear now what is fine and new, the short and the long of what rolls out:

On page xv, he says: "The Jesuits alone regulated all public and Church affairs in California." * The Jesuits alone! If the author had only given them at least the help of some assistants and consultants, a *procureur* or some *gens du Roy!* Moreover, to the affairs of State and Church he should have added those of the army and of criminal justice. This would have been no more effort than the first two mentioned, because all four

---

* "Les Jésuites ont eu seuls le direction des affaires tant civiles, qu'ecclesiastiques dans la Californie."

False Reports about the Missionaries

branches of government amount to nothing in California. Just the same, the Jesuits' coat of arms could have carried the shepherd's crook on one side and the sword on the other, as is done by so many princes of the realm!

The good man, however, contradicts himself when he writes on page 213: "The captain of the militia is the highest judge and administrator of justice in all of California, exercising his authority over soldiers, sailors, slaves" (There are no slaves in the land. Whom would they serve there?), "and Spaniards as well as over the Indians. . . . It is he who adjusts claims and sees that his verdict is carried out. He also supervises the pearl fishing, etc." * What, then, is left for the sixteen Jesuits to do? Hardly anything occurs in matters of the Church except dispensations for marriage. But regardless of what happens, the Bishop of Guadalajara mediates and settles everything. The Jesuits had no more power or rights than a parish priest in Germany, except for some privileges shared equally by all missionaries who live too far away from the bishop's residence, regardless of the order they belong to.

In the following elegant text, on page XVI, the author continues to pour out all his venom, smearing blindly: "This history puts before our eyes a perfect example of the policies and practices employed by the Jesuits, ostensibly to subject the Californians to the Crown of Spain, but in reality arrogating to themselves absolute power over such people. Here can also be seen the real motives which induce the Spanish government to use the men of this order in such enterprise and to wink at their deeds, so that with the help of various tricks and deceptions it can acquire what it could not master with force." † These are words, and nothing but words. They could not even make me angry, although they persuaded me and

---

* "Le Capitain de la garnison est juge et justicier en chef de toute la Californie; en premier lieu des soldats, tant pour le civil que pour le militaire, des matelots, des esclaves, des colons et des Indiens, c'est lui qui juge les causes, et qui fait executer ses sentences ... il a la surintendance de la pêcherie des perles."

† "Cette histoire nous fournit un tableau parfait de la politique de l'ordre et de la méthode, dont les Jésuites se sont servis, pour rendre ces peuples sujets titulaires de la couronne d'Espagne, et pour s'arroger sur eux une autorité absoluë. On y voit les vrais motifs qui obligent le gouvernement d'Espagne d'employer ces religieux dans ces sortes d'entreprises, et a leur permettre d'acquérir par artifice ce qu'ils sont hors d'état d'usurper par force ouverte."

Observations in Lower California

gave me cause to write these reports. Yes, they were the principal and almost the only cause. Such passages in the introduction, would lead the reader to expect to find throughout the book all kinds of crookedness and cunning trickery committed by the California Jesuits, even though such inventions had to be forged. What strange intentions the Court of Madrid must have harbored for the last two centuries when it ordered and permitted the Jesuits to preach the Gospel to the heathen in Asia and America, and at the same time allowed them to take possession of Peru and Mexico, Chile and Paraguay, the Philippines and California. Why should the Jesuits have been left to rule there and behave like lords, they alone to use those lands until 1767, without ever having been invested with one of those territories as a fief from the king? All this is implied in the Latin and French words *acquérir* and *usurper*. Yet, after the introductory mention of all these roguish deeds of the Jesuits and of all these plans of the Court of Madrid, nothing more is to be found in these three volumes which make up this history. This led me to believe that the translator or author and the man who hammered out the introduction could very well be two different *messieurs*, and that these passages were inserted in the foreword so the book would find more favor with certain people and find more buyers. Be that as it may, it is certain the reader will not find in the book what was promised in the foreword. Since, however, the Jesuits were incapable of "mastering by force" such an open and uninhabited land as California, their power could not be so formidable or their war chest as well filled as some shameless, brainless, and unscrupulous charlatans dare to assert. These writers believe least of all that which they try to make others believe. They send their messages into the world, having the audacity and insolence to imply that the whole globe is threatened by the chains and slavery imposed by the Jesuits. Yet on one point I have to admit this slanderer is right, and I confess frankly and without reserve that he wrote the pure and plain truth when he says that the California Indians were *sujets titulaires*, that is, Spanish subjects in appearance and name only. In this case this lying slanderer fared like the other one called Caiphas (John xii), who against his own will and knowledge also became a prophet. The California natives give absolutely nothing to the King of Spain because they have absolutely nothing to give; they render no gratuitous service nor serve as soldiers, etc., etc. There is nothing of value in California; and where there

False Reports about the Missionaries

is nothing, there cannot be any servitude or any fear of war or enemy. Therefore, as long as I lived in California, no order, no *decrêt*, no *arrêt* or anything like it has ever been issued to the natives, neither by the Court of Madrid, the Viceroy in Mexico, the Council in Guadalajara, nor even by the Spanish captain in California. Consequently, the natives never showed their dependence upon the Crown of Spain, nor did the Spanish Crown assert its rule and domination over the California Indians. Were the Jesuits to blame for that?

Should, however, this prattler wish to know the real reason why, until a few years ago, the Kings of Spain used the Jesuits in such enterprises, he may consult various royal Spanish decrees, especially the one signed by Philip V on December 28, 1743, at Buenretiro. Here he will find that, in addition to the conversion of the heathen (which always was a matter of great concern to the Catholic Kings), the expansion of the kings' dominions and the increase of the royal revenues were also considered. It is also undeniably true that more Americans and Filipinos became and remained subjects of the Crown of Spain through the efforts of the Spanish missionaries (the majority of whom were always Jesuits) than through the Spanish soldiers. Even though California yields no income to the king, many other provinces do so, and more abundantly.

Third and last, just recently a certain writer of repute started a campaign with a large collection of all kinds of beautiful reports against the Jesuits in general and those of California in particular (though against the latter, only *en passant* with two words). He sounded the war trumpet in Spain with a book of two hundred and fifty-nine pages in a quarto size. This book, if it were investigated by a court of justice, might be regarded as libel of the first rank and condemned as such in London or at The Hague. The author, in accordance with his character, gave the book a rather pious title, but it earned little honor in clerical and secular circles and little applause from his own nation. He should have been more discreet and should have published his brain-child under another name; he should not have put his brand on its forehead. In that case it would still be horrible slander and a gross neglect of the truth, but people would not have been so greatly angered. Not even the sinister *Gazettier Ecclésiastique* [60] or the Jansenist [61] journalists of Paris could be more fanciful and farther out of bounds than this Spanish fabulist. As far as I heard in Spain, it is no mystery that he should write in this vein. As the reader can clearly see, he has very little love for the truth! For this book, he had hurriedly collected—without order or system—material condemned by ecclesiastic and secular authorities, material which had been burned in Spain and other countries and contained the most abominable, mendacious, and unbelievable spittle produced by old and new enemies of the Jesuits and the Church. Besides this, the work, written in Spanish and pretending to be pious (to judge from its title), is now and then larded and embellished with Latin and French verses from biting poets and poetasters.*

This book was advertised in the newspapers and openly sold in book shops. I was still in Spain six months after it was published, and in that time the author, whose name was mentioned on the title page, made no protest—a sign that he recognizes the book as his own offspring and not as a substitution. Therefore, he should not be annoyed when I criticize his work a bit and openly refute with all possible fairness the numerous falsehoods he made public against his own better judgment and conscience. On the contrary, he ought to be grateful that I did not and do not intend to divulge his station and name in places where they are not yet known. I have no doubt that his compatriots and colleagues have already told him the truth more forcefully than I could, just as it has happened in similar circumstances to authors in other places.

Wherever I open the book I find a style of writing so contrary to Spanish sobriety and spirited homily, such a revolting, vulgar, and at times irritating, way of joking, jeering, and ridiculing, such unChristian expressions, such manifest falsehoods and impossible tales, that it seems incredible that this work was written by a man who treasures frankness, good taste, and the edification of his fellow men. Some examples may serve as proof.

1. On page 150: He ridicules the world-renowned and world-famous Father Bourdaloue.[62] He calls him a hypocrite and a moral turncoat and accuses him of talking warm and cold in the same breath. After quoting four verses in good French, written by a holy father of Port Royal against

---

* "Amphora cœpit institui, currente rota cur urceus exit?" These lines of Horace are quoted shortly before he ends his pious long-winded hogwash, with a sigh to heaven, the same heaven he calls to witness that he had not written with any feelings of passion, and the *conscia meus recti* must serve as an *excusatio non petita*. Nevertheless, one cannot believe him even if one wished to.

False Reports about the Missionaries

another Jesuit, he states on page 135 distinctly and in good Spanish that "all the bishops of the world are nothing but slaves of the Jesuits and belong to its third order." *

2. On page 145: ". . . that along with the tyrannies the Jesuits committed in Portugal when the order was still in its infancy and had just been started, they dispatched no less than two thousand of the most distinguished secular priests as well as members of religious orders to the other world, causing them to be thrown into the sea. This outrage was so loathsome to the fish that they emigrated to another place and the fishermen caught nothing but the soulless bodies of those clerics until finally the archbishop (of which city the author does not reveal) came to the seashore with a procession and blessed the waters." †

3. On page 20 and 82: "That the war (under King Nicholas) [63] cost the Jesuits of Paraguay thirteen million Roman scudi (or about thirty million Rhenish guilders), and that they had a standing army of one hundred and fifty thousand men." ‡

4. On page 147, he not only charges the Jesuits with the sole responsibility for the revolt in Madrid as reported in the newspapers of Lisbon and with the events in Paris, etc., etc., but demands that this be considered as a fact which permits no doubt. *Ciertamente*, it says, *no puede dudarse*.

---

* "El obispo de Meliapor, que era de los Terciarios Jesuitas y su ESCLAVO, como TODOS."

† "Las tiranías, que executaron en Portugal desde el instante mismo de su fundación ... hizieron arrojar al mar hasta dos mil Eclesiásticos seculares y religiosos de los más distinguidos de aquel reyno, que los pescadores sacaban sus redes llenas de cadáveres, y que los peces admirados de tan sacrílega acción se desviaron del mar, hasta que el arzobispo fue processionalmente á benedecir las aguas." It seems that the Spanish scribbler does not know what German Protestants (among others, the Hamburg predicant Theodorus Heinson, as recently as 1717) have written about the six thousand children of the holy Cardinal, the Jesuit Bellarmini, the killer of sects. Surely he could hardly have restrained himself to use this rare little flower as an ornament in his book. At least these six thousand would not have looked puny alongside of the two thousand, and one truth would have fortified the other—an excellent proof to convince all the Spanish charcoal burners!

‡ These are many more soldiers than the number of people living in the territory (as can be read in the decree of Philip V, mentioned before) between and around the rivers Parana and Uruguay toward Brazil, where these defamed missions of Paraguay are situated, and called on some maps *pays des missions*. NB: One of these missions bears the name of St. Nicholas, which a few years ago gave rise to the well-known fable about Nicholas I.

Observations in Lower California

5. On page 154, he calls on the carpet the mischievous (for honor-loving ears, vexatious) comment made either by an illusionist or a malicious jester about the chapter of the Fourth Lateran Council, which bids all the Faithful to partake of communion during the Easter time. I would be ashamed a hundred times (and my conscience forbids me) to write it down here.

6. On page 139 are the following words: "Father Norbert [64] (that well-known "friend" of the Jesuits) has finally found sanctuary in Portugal, where he also had the consolation of witnessing the execution of Malagrida,[65] etc., etc." * Oh, what a beautiful and superevangelical expression! Those who will may now judge how much of the author's work is Christian, how much is possible, and how much an outright lie! In 1758 a writer could still fool some people about Paraguay. But by 1768 [66] that a literate and well-versed Spaniard still calls up the tale of King Nicholas and the Jesuit-supported army of one hundred and fifty thousand men is simply intolerable, and it is as incomprehensible as the tale of the enslaved bishops under the yoke of the Jesuits or the story of the two thousand noblest Portuguese clerics drowned in the sea. The author must have thought, as so many others, "calumniare, semper aliquid haeret": exaggerate courageously; at least some of the inexperienced common people will be impressed.

I have listed here four or five examples of the honesty and truth-loving spirit of this Spanish braggart in order to show beyond the borders of Spain what monstrous lies are spread behind the Pyrenees about certain people in these times, and that I would not need to refute at length and in detail what he conjured up about California. The reader already knows how much credibility reports from such a pen deserve. If the few quoted examples do not suffice, I can point out some better ones, even a wagon-load full taken from the book itself.

---

* "¿Quien creyera, si no la viese, la persecución de estos hombres al Padre Norberto? le obligazon a vagar incógnito y fugitivo, hasta que halló en Portugal asilo piadoso y tuvo el CONSUELO de asistir al suplicio de Malagrida. According to this version, would it be surprising if someone conceived the idea that nothing could be more comforting to a man like Father Norbert —expelled from his order and excommunicated by Benedict XIV—than to find that Malagrida and many a thousand others had only one neck? Besides, it is ridiculous to pull a sworn enemy of the Jesuits and an apostate out of the mire by making him an anti-Christian.

False Reports about the Missionaries

For instance, on page 82, after babbling at length about the fabulous riches of the Jesuits in Paraguay, he speaks about California: "Every year more than two million Rhenish florins, the income derived from the so-called Paraguaian herb, went to Rome. How many such millions must have reached Rome annually from the excessively rich California?" *

From California! From California! This must have been done in utmost secrecy, for in seventeen years I have never gotten wind of it. When will people become wise and feel ashamed of such stupid lies? Had the Jesuits established missions in Novaya Zemlya or in Spitzbergen, who knows how many millions would have flown from those places to Rome. Who knows how uneasy the author would feel and how he would break out in a cold sweat should anyone take him at his word and make him prove his assertions. I am sure in the future he would no longer enjoy speaking ill of others and slandering them. It is precisely this fact which encourages people to lie—nobody demands proof of an author whose name appears in Gothic letters, as it does on this Spanish book.

However, what should I do with such an author, what reply shall I give him? Shall I tell him to go to California without expecting a profit and see with his own eyes the California misery or the golden mountains of California? He would thank me and decline to accept. Shall I call his attention to these reports? He will undoubtedly call them pure lies. I think we, I and my fifteen companions, who have been in California, should ask the Court of Madrid (where we have some merit as individuals or through rights of succession) that this author be transferred to America either as the lord of California or, if he is not married and longs for some ecclesiastical honors, as primate of America, or first bishop of California.† And he shall have everything which the California missionaries

---

* "De sola la yerba de aquel país iba anualmente un millón de pesos fuertes a Roma; ¿quantos irían de la RIQUISIMA California?" It was mentioned elsewhere that a *peso fuerte* equals five French *livres*.

† Since California had no bishop of her own, because of the few inhabitants and no bishop could live there in a state befitting his rank, the question arose between the two bishops of Guadalajara and Durango as to who should exercise the jurisdiction over the peninsula of California. Thereupon Philip V is said to have given the following modest answer: California shall become part of that territory whose bishop visits the country first and there discharges his duty as a bishop. Since up to that time neither one of them had done it, Pope Benedict XIV permitted the missionaries to administer the sacrament of confirmation to the natives and Spaniards. Actually the country belongs to the bishopric of Guadalajara.

Observations in Lower California

derived from the country for themselves and their general in Rome between 1697 and 1768, except their hard-earned daily bread.

If we succeed, he will be paid and the slander will be avenged, and in the future he will surely no longer blabber about the California millions. I know that the poorest nobleman and hidalgo in Spain is a more impressive figure than the Grand Mogul of California would ever be. No prelate in Catholic lands, not even any canon or parish priest in Spain, would eat more modestly than His Grace, the Most Reverend First Bishop of California. This were so even if Father Laurentius Ricci, then General of the Society of Jesus, or his successor, paid him a hundred per cent interest on all the "millions" Rome derived from California and from Paraguay between 1696 and 1768. But now let me be serious. If so many millions per year had come to Rome, sent from all parts of America and especially from California to the treasury of the Jesuit General, why then does the Spanish Court pay to each of the more than four thousand Jesuits exiled by Spain to the Papal State and to misery one hundred and fifty florins each year? Could they not, even though they deserved an income, live off those millions they are said to have sent each year to the Curia in advance and in anticipation of events to come? Would the Spanish Crown be willing to let its colonial lands be exploited by the Jesuits and then, without necessity and against all merit, spend six hundred thousand florins every year for their support? I think the Spanish government is too intelligent to do that. Besides, we are living in an age when the members of a religious order do not receive too much privileges. The good man did not consider all this, or he believed peasants and old women in Spain would not know anything about that; otherwise he probably would never have mentioned the millions which were never sent.

Besides, if each year so many millions were sent from California to Rome, why then were the California missionaries and those from Paraguay never forced to account for these surprising sums of money? The truth is that neither I nor any of my California colleagues were ever questioned about money or anything else during the eight months of enforced stay in Spain before we were permitted to move on. Nothing more desirable could have happened to us, and nothing more troublesome than such inquiries could have happened to our adversaries.

I stayed with the California millions and the Spanish writer longer than I intended. This would not have happened if I had not been in-

False Reports about the Missionaries

formed in Spain, and had I not other good reasons to believe, that this writer and his voice played a part in precipitating a world-wide event universally known. I leave it to everyone to draw his own conclusions.

As for my readers, some of them may have scruples about believing me and will perhaps doubt my reports about the poverty of California, banishing all the dreams of the oft-quoted scribbler. In this case, I can offer no better advice, for I know they will not go to California and see for themselves, than that they learn the truth from the French astronomer who went to California toward the end of 1768, and who in all probability is now back in Paris.[87] I am sure that he too would not want to sell fairy tales or lies to the world. Or the reader may send to Madrid for a copy of the report which Don Portolá undoubtedly must have rendered regarding the affairs and revenues of his administration in California.

JESUIT MISSIONARIES IN BAJA CALIFORNIA, 1697–1768

Juan Armesto, Cristobal, Spain
Victoriano Arnés, Graus, Spain *
Francisco María Badillo, Spain
Johann Jakob Baegert, Schlettstadt, Alsace *
Juan María Baldasúa, Michoacan, Mexico
Miguel del Barco, Italy *
Johann Xavier Bischoff, Glatz, Bohemia *
Jaime Bravo, Spain †
Lorenzo Carranco, Cholula, Mexico †
Juan José Díaz, Ixtlan, Mexico *
Jacobo Druet, Turin, Italy †
Franz Benno Ducrue, Munich, Germany *
Francisco Escalante, Jaen, Spain *
Francisco Xavier Franco, Spain *
Andrés García, Spain †
Joseph Gasteiger, Leoben, Austria †
Adam Gilg, Römerstadt, Moravia
William Gordon, Scotland
Clemente Guillén, Zacatecas, Mexico †
Eberhard Hellen, Prague, Bohemia †
José de la Hera, Spain
Lambert Hostel, Münstereifel, Germany *
Franz Ináma von Sternegg, Vienna, Austria *
Ferdinand Konschak, Varasdin, Croatia †
Wenceslaus Linck, Joachimsthal, Bohemia *
Agustín Luyando, Mexico
Juan María Luyando, Mexico

---

* = expelled in 1768; † = died in California

Francisco María Masariegos, Mexico
Julián Mayorga, Mexico †
Jerónimo Minutuli, Italy
Julián Mugázabal, Alava, Spain
Ignacio María Nápoli, Italy
Pietro Nascimbén, Venice, Italy †
Karl Neumayr, Bavaria, Germany †
Francisco Osorio, Mexico
Francisco Peralta, Spain
Francisco María Píccolo, Sicily †
Georg Rheds, Coblenz, Germany *
José Rondero, Spain
José María Rotea, Mexico *
Juan María Salvatierra, Milan, Italy
Sebastián Sistiaga, Tepuscolula, Oaxaca, Mexico
Juan María Sotelo, Spain
Nicolás Támaral, Seville, Spain †
Sigismundo Táraval, Lodi, Italy
Anton Tempis, Olmütz, Moravia †
Ignatz Tirs, Komotau, Bohemia *
Joaquín Trujillo, Mexico
Juan María Ugarte, Tegucigalpa, Honduras †
Pedro Ugarte, Tegucigalpa, Honduras
Lucas Ventura, Spain *
Juan Villavieja, Spain *
Franz Xavier Wagner, Eichstätt, Germany †
Bernhard Zumziel, Westkirchen, Germany

---

* = expelled in 1768; † = died in California

TRANSLATORS' NOTES

1 It is well to remember that throughout this text "California" refers only to the peninsula of California, the Mexican territory of Baja (Lower) California; and all references to "Californians" or "California Indians" apply to the native inhabitants of the peninsula.

2 The interior of the peninsula had been explored to about thirty degrees north latitude at the time Father Baegert left Lower California.

3 The work referred to is that of Father Miguel Venegas, S.J., edited by A. M. Burriel, S.J., *Noticia de la California* (3 vols.; Madrid, 1757).

4 Also spelled *quipos, quipee, quipu, quippu*; from the Quechua, "knot." An ancient Peruvian mnemonic device used for counting and for recording facts and events. It consisted of a length of cord from which hung smaller cords of various colors tied in knots. The arrangement of colors and size of knots had special meanings.

5 An imaginary kingdom which Francisco Vásquez Coronado undertook to discover on his expedition in 1541. He thought he had found it when he reached what is now eastern Kansas, but was disappointed when he failed to find the great wealth of gold and silver of which he had been told.

6 Father Jakob Sedelmayr, S.J., native of Bavaria, Germany; sent to Mexico in 1735, and worked as a missionary in Sonora until 1767.

7 Father Ferdinand Konschak (also Consag, Konsak), S.J., born in Varasdin, Croatia, in 1703; sent to Lower California in 1730, and died in 1759. He explored the east coast of the peninsula to the mouth of the Colorado River and led two land expeditions, in 1751 and 1753.

8 Father Wenceslaus Linck (Link), S.J., born in Joachimsthal, Bohemia, in 1736; sent to Lower California in 1762. In his own account of the exploration Father Linck stated that he started from San Borja on February 20, 1766, accompanied by thirteen soldiers in command of Lieutenant Don Blas Fernandez of the presidio of San Borja.

9 The present Cape Blanco, Oregon, lies north of Cape Mendocino, California. Either Baegert was mistaken, or he referred to another landmark of the same name south of Cape Mendocino. Baegert refers here to the expedition of Sebastián Vizcaíno, sent out by the Viceroy of New Spain in 1602 to find a harbor for the Manila galleons. Vizcaíno rediscovered and named Monterey Bay, in Alta California, December 16, 1602.

10 The astronomer was Abbé Jean Chappe d'Auteroche, born in Mauriac, Chantal, France, March 2, 1722; died in San José del Cabo, August 1, 1769. He went to Lower California to observe the transit of Venus (June 3, 1769), and an eclipse of the moon (June 18, 1769). See his *Voyage en Californie, pour l'observation du passage de Venus sur le disque du soleil le 3. juin 1769* ... (redigé et publié par M. Cassini, fils, Paris, 1772).

Observations in Lower California

[11] Johann Huebner, 1668–1731, professor of history and geography. In 1693 he published *Kurze Fragen aus der alten und neuen Geographie* which had thirty-six editions.

[12] Father Baegert's observation on the fertility of the soil under the conditions he mentions is correct. However, at present, with the help of modern methods of irrigation, grain, corn, alfalfa, fruit, and other crops under cultivation show a high yield.

[13] Baegert quotes from Captain Woodes Rogers' *A Cruising Voyage Round the World* (London, 1712). Woodes Rogers was an English buccaneer, one of the leaders of the Edward Cooke expedition (1708–1711), to the South Sea and around the world. While awaiting the appearance of the Manila galleon en route to Acapulco from the Philippines, Woodes Rogers made his observations of Lower California. The galleon was captured by the English off Cabo San Lucas.

[14] This church, after two hundred years, is still well preserved, although little has been done to repair or preserve it. At present it serves the small farming community of San Luis Gonzaga. The mission lands are now part of a privately owned ranch producing grapes, figs, and dates.

[15] Father Franz Ináma von Sternegg, S.J., born in Vienna, Austria, in 1719; sent to Lower California in 1750, and served at Mission San José Comondú until 1768.

[16] Father Ignatz Tirs (also Tiers, Tirsch, Türsch), S.J., born in Komotau, Bohemia, in 1733; arrived in Lower California in 1762, and served at Mission Santiago until 1768.

[17] In 1728 the Bishop of Nueva Galicia, Dr. Carlos Gomez de Cervantes, declared that the two Californias (Alta and Baja) belonged to the diocese of Guadalajara, and not to Durango.

[18] In his original text Baegert used the map of Father Ferdinand Konschak, S.J., which places the southern point of Lower California at twenty-two degrees north latitude, and the northernmost of the Jesuit missions, Santa María, at thirty-one degrees, north. Recent maps show the southern tip of the peninsula near twenty-three degrees north latitude, Santa María near thirty degrees, north.

Concerning the population, Father Baegert wrote, in a letter to his brother (written at Mission San Luis Gonzaga, September 11, 1752), that "from Cabo San Lucas, here in California, to the last mission, almost under the twenty-ninth degree north, in a stretch of more than three hundred hours, we count less than six thousand souls. Although diseases and rebellions have killed many hundreds some years ago—according to a safe calculation—no more than thirteen thousand souls lived in this extended territory at the beginning of these missions and of this century. And that, considering the size of the area, is less than nothing. . . . I count in my mission three hundred and sixty souls, old and young, of both sexes, and there are several [missions] which have even less."

On the same subject, Father Lambert Hostel, S.J., a contemporary missionary in Lower California, wrote in January, 1758: "at the present time we count not many more than six thousand souls in our twelve missions. To be sure, some spreading diseases, which carried off several thousand of our Christians,

Translators' Notes

had something to do with that. This is especially true of the missions toward the South, where two out of four had to be abandoned" [San José del Cabo and La Paz].

[19] Marc Antoine Eidous translated Venegas' work into French (Paris, Durand, 1767).

[20] Señor Fernandez, a secular priest.

[21] Father Francisco María Píccolo, S.J., born in Sicily in 1650; arrived in Mexico in 1688, and served as a missionary to the Tarahumara. In 1697 he went to Lower California in place of Father Eusebius Kino, and arrived there only a few weeks after Father Juan María Salvatierra. At the request of the Real Audiencia of Guadalajara he wrote the *Informe del Estado de la Nueva Christiandad de California*, in 1702. He died at Mission Loreto on February 22, 1729.

[22] Noel Antoine Pluche, 1688–1761, French priest and educator.

[23] The founding of the missions established a more or less regular contact with the mainland and brought newcomers to the peninsula. One unfortunate result of contact with the mainland was the introduction of epidemic diseases into Lower California. In 1698, only a year after the first mission had been started, Father Salvatierra reported a "distemper which carried off many people." In the succeeding years epidemics decimated the Indian population in some of the mission settlements to such an extent that several of the missions, built with great effort, had to be abandoned.

A good example of the devastating effect of an epidemic disease on one community appears in the Abbé d'Auteroche's account of his arrival at San José. The abbé was accompanied on his expedition by an assistant named Pauly, a watchmaker—brought along to take care of the instruments—called Noel, and two Spanish astronomers named Doz and Medina. The party landed at San José, May 19, 1769, to find an epidemic raging. All the members of the party immediately fell ill. Judging from the scanty description of the symptoms and the lingering nature of the illness, it could have been typhoid fever. D'Auteroche wrote that the epidemic had already taken a third of the inhabitants when his party landed at San José. By June 5, the town was a scene of horror, everyone sick, including himself, and no one left to help him. By June 18, three-fourths of the population had died, including the priest, Father Juan Morel, and the rest had fled. D'Auteroche died on August 1, at San José, Noel also died there, and Medina at San Blas.

[24] In his *Storia della California*, Father Francisco Xavier Clavigero, S.J., wrote of an epidemic of smallpox in 1709, the first to have been observed in Lower California, which carried off many adults and nearly all the children.

[25] Father Pierre François Xavier de Charlevoix, S.J., born in Saint-Quentin, France, in 1682; labored in Quebec, Canada, from 1705 to 1709; and voyaged down the Mississippi River to New Orleans in 1720–1722 on a voyage of exploration to find the "Western Sea," supposed to lie west of the Mississippi. He returned to France to teach and write history. His most important work *Histoire et description générale de la Nouvelle France*, was published in Paris in 1744. His other writings included histories of Japan, San Domingo, and Paraguay. Father Charlevoix died February 1, 1761.

[26] Francisco Luzenilla. In 1668 he obtained a license from the government,

Observations in Lower California

permitting him to take an expedition to Lower California. He attempted to establish a settlement in the region of La Paz, but the project had to be abandoned when provisions ran out. After the failure of the Otondo expeditions in 1683, Luzenilla tried to get another license, but was turned down.

[27] Father Eusebius Franciscus Kino, S.J., born in the Tyrol, near Trent, in 1644; studied in Austria and Germany, and became professor of mathematics in Ingolstadt. He was sent to Mexico in 1681, and took part in the Otondo expeditions to Lower California in 1683. From 1687 until his death in 1711 he worked in Pimería Alta (Sonora and southern Arizona). For a complete study of the work of this remarkable and gifted man, see Herbert E. Bolton's edition of Father Kino's contemporary account of the beginnings of California, Sonora, and Arizona: *Kino's Historical Memoir of Pimería Alta* (Berkeley, 1919).

[28] Miquelete, a soldier of the guard of the provincial governor in Spain. Earlier the term was also used to signify a Spanish bandit.

[29] Father Juan María de Ugarte, S.J., born in 1660 (or 1662) in Tegucigalpa, Honduras, of Basque parents; entered the Society of Jesus in 1679. Later he taught philosophy in Mexico City and became acquainted with Fathers Kino and Salvatierra. He was active in raising funds for the foundation of the missions in Lower California. In 1700 he was sent to Loreto and remained on the peninsula until his death at Mission San Xavier on September 29, 1730. Father Salvatierra referred to him as the "Apostle, Father and Atlante of California." Ugarte deserves much of the credit for the survival of mission work in Lower California. A great organizer, architect, builder, explorer, agriculturist, highly intelligent, gifted with artistic and scientific ability and mechanical resourcefulness, he also possessed great physical strength and endurance. See Father Juan José de Villavicencio, *Vida ... de P. Ugarte* (Mexico, 1752).

[30] Father Jacobo Druet, S.J., born in Turin, Italy, in 1698; sent to Lower California in 1732, and served at Mission La Purísima Concepción until his death in 1753.

[31] Father Johann Xavier Bischoff, S.J., born in Glatz, Bohemia, in 1710; sent to Lower California in 1752, and worked as a missionary until 1768.

[32] Father Pietro Nascimbén, S.J., a native of Venice, Italy, born in 1703; sent to Lower California in 1745, died in August, 1754.

[33] Don Juan Antonio Vizarrón, Archbishop of Mexico City, and Viceroy of New Spain, 1734–1740.

[34] Father Lambert Hostel, S.J., born in Münstereifel, Germany, in 1706; sent to Lower California in 1737, and served at Missions San Luis Gonzaga and Dolores until 1768.

[35] See Part One, chapter eight, note 15.

[36] Father Sigismundo Táraval, S.J., born in Lodi, Italy, of Spanish parents, in 1700; studied in Spain and Mexico, and sent to Lower California in 1730. Three years later he established Mission Santa Rosa (later called Todos Santos). In 1750 or 1751 he left Lower California and went to Guadalajara, Mexico, where he died in 1763. He left a great number of manuscripts, some of which contained detailed records of events in California. It is said that Venegas' *Noticia de la California* is based in part on Father Táraval's writings.

Translators' Notes

[37] Father Lorenzo José Carranco, S.J., a native of Cholula, Mexico. He studied in Puebla and made his novitiate in Tepotzotlán; sent to Lower California in 1727 to succeed Father Nápoli at Mission Santiago. Father Baegert gives Saturday, October 2, 1734, as the day of his death; Father Sigismundo Táraval, that it occurred on Friday, October 1.

[38] Father Nicolás Támaral, S.J., born in Seville, Spain, in 1687; sent to Lower California in March, 1717, and founded Mission La Purísima Concepción in 1722, and later Mission San José del Cabo, in 1730. He was murdered by rebellious Indians on October 3, 1734.

[39] In his work *La Obra de los Jesuitas Mexicanos durante la Epoca Colonial 1574–1767* (Mexico, 1941), Father Gerard Decorme, S.J., names fifty Jesuit missionaries who died for the Faith, in New Spain (vol. 1, pp. 408–409). He included Father Juan Bautista Segura, S.J. (born in Toledo, Spain) who, with another father and seven lay brothers "died in the country of Axacán" (killed by Indians), which was in North American territory, between the Potomac and Rappahannock rivers. The list does not mention Father Eusebius Franciscus Kino, who, at least according to one report, was killed by rebellious Indians on March 15, 1711, in Santa Magdalena. Nor does it include Father Johannes Ratkey, S.J. (born in Pettau, Styria, 1647) who is said to have been poisoned by Indians on November 9, 1684, at his Tarahumara mission. To those missionaries, listed by Father Decorme, could be added the names of many other Jesuits who died under similar circumstances in Japan, China, the Marianas, South America, Cochin China, Madura, and other places. See *Der Neue Welt-Bott*.

[40] Father P. Tomás Tello, S.J., born in Almagro de la Mancha, Spain; killed in an Indian uprising at Mission Caborca, Sonora, in November, 1751.

[41] Father Heinrich Ruhen, S.J. (sometimes spelled Rhuen), born in Osnabrück, Germany; slain by Indians at Mission Sonoíta, Sonora, in November, 1751.

[42] Tranquebar, a town in the Tanjore district of Madras, India. Tranquebar was once owned by a Danish trading company which had acquired it in 1620. It became an important trading port. At the suggestion of King Frederik IV of Denmark, a mission was established there in 1706. It was sold to Great Britain in 1845.

[43] Godfreidus Dellius, a clergyman, born in Holland. He arrived in North America in 1683 and became assistant to Gideon Schaats, pastor of the Reformed Church at Albany, New York. He also preached at Schenectady. Later he is believed to have worked among the Indians as a missionary of the Episcopal church. He died in Antwerp about 1705.

[44] Johann Jakob Weislinger, S.J. (1691–1755), an especially gifted German polemical writer; author of several works against Protestant antagonists.

[45] Barthol. Ziegenbalg, a Protestant missionary, born in Ober-Lausitz, Germany, in 1683; went to the Danish colony of Tranquebar, India, in 1705, to establish a mission. He translated the Bible into the Tamil language, and also wrote: *Genealogie der malabarischen Goetter*.

[46] Samuel Urlsperger (1685–1772). German pastor and pietist of note. He was known for his interest in mission work and for his zeal in helping victims of intolerance. He was instrumental in getting Protestants to America

Observations in Lower California

who were expelled from the Salzburg diocese by the archbishop. These Protestant emigrants founded Ebenezer, in Georgia.

[47] On February 27, 1767, King Charles III of Spain signed an order to expel the members of the Society of Jesus from every domain of the Spanish Crown. To allow sufficient time for the royal decree to reach all representatives of the Spanish government, it was kept secret until June 25, 1767. On that day the order was put into effect, simultaneously and immediately, in every part of the Spanish Empire. The same fate had struck at the Jesuits in Portugal, which had decreed their expulsion in September, 1759, and in France, in November, 1764.

[48] Don Gaspar de Portolá born in Balaguer, Spain, in 1723; joined the army in his early youth and became a lieutenant when he was thirty. After twenty years of active service with the Spanish army he went to Mexico and was sent to the frontier presidios of Sinaloa and Sonora. In 1767 he was appointed to direct the expulsion of the Jesuits in California, and to become the first Spanish governor of the territory. In 1769 the Visitor General of New Spain, Don José de Gálvez, ordered Portolá to proceed north, into Alta, California to establish two presidios, one at San Diego, the other on Monterey Bay. Portolá's diary of that expedition, and other contemporary accounts of it are to be found in the *Publications of the Academy of Pacific Coast History* (Vol. I, 1910, and Vol. II, 1911). In 1779 Portolá became governor of the State of Puebla, Mexico. Five years later he returned to Spain.

[49] San Juan de Matanchel, a port on the west coast of Mexico, about a mile south of the present San Blas.

[50] Captain Fernando Rivera y Moncada came to Loreto sometime before 1750. In that year he succeeded Don Bernardo Rodríguez de Larrea as captain-governor of the presidio of Loreto. When Portolá organized the expedition into Upper California, Captain Rivera was sent ahead with a group of men and charged with collecting supplies for the expedition. For a time he was commander of the presidio of Monterey, but later returned to Loreto. In 1781, the rebellious Yuma Indians destroyed two Franciscan missions on the Colorado River, killing the priests and soldiers, as well as colonists who had stopped to rest there on the way from Sonora to California. Captain Rivera, who had led these colonists, lost his life in the same massacre.

[51] Father Franz Benno Ducrue, S.J., born in Munich, Germany, on June 10, 1721; entered the Society of Jesus on September 28, 1738, and sent to Lower California in 1748. After the expulsion he returned to his native city, and died there on March 30, 1779.

[52] Father Juan José Díaz, S.J. (also spelled Díez), born in Mexico, in 1735; sent to Lower California in 1766, one of the last Jesuit missionaries to be sent there. At the time of the expulsion he was serving the newly established Mission Santa María. He died in 1809.

[53] Philipp Cluverius (Klüwer, Clüver), born in Danzig, Germany, in 1580; died at Leyden, Holland, in 1623. The *Allgemeine Deutsche Biographie* (vol. 4, p. 353 f.) calls him the founder of the science of historical geography. Author of *Germania Antiqua*, 1616, and *Italia Antiqua*, 1624.

[54] Admiral Don Isidoro de Otondo y Antillón, who, as the "Superior in command of the Royal Armada" took formal possession, in the name of the King

Translators' Notes

of Spain, of the "Californian Islands" in 1683. His expedition was financed and licensed by the government, and he tried to establish a permanent settlement. But, like the earlier attempts, this one, too, failed for lack of supplies.

[55] The original Spanish title of the Venegas work: *Noticia de California* implies that the book contains "reports from, or information about [Baja] California." The title of the English, French, and German translations *A Natural and Civil History of California*, is more ambitious.

[56] Father Thyrso González was General of the Society of Jesus from 1687 to 1705.

[57] One of the most unrelenting and most influential enemies of the Jesuits in Mexico was Francisco Fabián y Fuero, Bishop of Puebla. Others were the Bishop of Mexico City, Francisco Antonio Lorenzana, and Bishop Abreu of Oaxaca.

[58] Father Clemente Guillén, S.J., born in Zacatecas, Mexico, in 1677; sent to Lower California in January, 1714, and served at Mission Dolores del Sur until that mission had to be abandoned, because most of the Indians had perished in an epidemic of dysentery. In 1721 he started to work among the Guaicura Indians, and persuaded them to collect in small communal groups (rancherías). Three of the rancherías were later part of Mission San Luis Gonzaga. At the same time he began to build Mission Siete Dolores, which he administered for twenty years. He was visitador of the California missions during the troublesome years which followed the Indian revolt in the southern part of the peninsula in 1734. Guillén died in 1748.

[59] Prince Eugène de Savoie-Carignan, born in Paris, France, on October 18, 1663, died in Vienna, Austria, on April 21, 1736. His family had decided that he should become a priest (his mother was a niece of Cardinal Mazarin), but he preferred a military career. King Louis XIV refused his request for a commission in the French army, partly because of a pronounced limp but mostly because of political considerations. Disappointed, the prince left France, in 1683, and turned to Austria to offer his services to Emperor Leopold I, who made the young man (he was nineteen) a colonel in the Austrian army. He proved to be one of Austria's ablest military leaders and statesmen. In 1683, when Vienna was besieged by Turkish troops, he fought with distinction for the liberation of the city. In succeeding campaigns against the French and Turkish armies he achieved brilliant victories for his adopted country. His rise in military rank and public acclaim was continuous and rapid, and he became the national hero of Austria. The decisive defeat of the superior Turkish armies at Temesvár and Peterwardein in 1716, and the capture of the city and fortress of Belgrade, in 1717, led to a treaty of peace with Turkey and Venice, in 1718. Through these victories Prince Eugene discouraged the declared "Holy War" of Turkey against the "Unclean Christians."

[60] The author refers to *Nouvelles Ecclésiastiques* a weekly publication of the Jansenists, printed and circulated secretly in France from 1728 to 1793, then in Utrecht until 1803.

[61] The followers of Cornelis Jansen, Dutch theologian, later Bishop of Ypres, Belgium. He was born in 1585; died in 1683. Influenced by Michel de Bay, a professor at the University of Louvain, Jansen first became known as an advocate of rigid Augustinianism. His famous work (*Augustinus*), which ex-

plained his interpretation of the teachings of St. Augustine, was first published under the auspices of the University of Louvain (1640). A second edition was approved by the Sorbonne in 1641. Although condemned by the pope, because it defended the propositions of Michel de Bay, it was widely circulated in France and became the basis for a reform movement within the Catholic Church. The work was denounced by the Jesuits, who were its most severe and eloquent critics. In 1643 it was condemned by Pope Urban VIII, and again by his successors, Innocent X, Alexander VII, and Clement XI. In France the controversy was carried on openly until 1728, when Cardinal de Noailles, Archbishop of Paris, and one of the defenders of Jansenism, submitted to the papal decree. In the meantime, a group of Catholics that had followed the principles of Jansen had been established in Utrecht, Holland, in 1702. In 1728 this group gave refuge to nuns and priests who refused to follow the example of Noailles.

[62] Father Louis Bourdaloue, S.J. (1632–1704), one of the most powerful preachers of his age. He exercised his gifts in Paris and at the court, and is said to have been one of the greatest orators of the Church.

[63] The tale of King Nicholas is one of the many fables invented by the enemies of the Society. Father Martin Dobrizhofer, a Jesuit missionary in Paraguay, gives an interesting account of this tale in his *Geschichte der Abiponer in Paraguay* (translated from the Latin original into German by A. Kreil, Vienna, 1783).

"In 1753 a royal order caused the rebellion of the Guaraní Indians on the Uruguay River. According to this order, seven of the best villages in Paraguay were supposed to be turned over to the Portuguese. The Indians resisted this order with all their might, not out of hatred for the King of Spain, who wanted to send them into exile, but out of love for their native country. Would not a Spaniard, a German, or a Frenchman do the same, if their ruler were to force them to give their homeland to the enemy? . . . Father Bernardus Nussdorfer, an old missionary and Father Superior, tried to pacify the Guaranís, and it seemed that he had succeeded . . . But when the rumor spread that Gomez Freyre de Andrade, governor of Rio de Janeiro, and originator of the whole sad story, had invaded the country, the rebellion broke out . . ."

"At the very beginning of the rebellion the Guaraní elected a certain Joseph, captain or corregidor of San Miguel, as their leader. He had fleetness of body . . . and courage of spirit, and was a good soldier, but a poor general. After he was killed in combat, the Indians chose the corregidor of Concepción, Nicolás Neenquirù, to be their leader. Nicolás understood more about music than about war . . . which caused the Uruguayans to lose heart. The whole affair took a turn for the worse, and the seven villages were delivered to the royal troups. And that was the same Nicolás who was represented to the Europeans as King of Paraguay. At the time when everyone in Europe talked and wrote about the King of Paraguay (how we laughed when we, in Paraguay, saw the European newspapers!) I saw Nicolás Neenquirù in the village of Concepción. He was barefoot, like the other Indians, sometimes riding herd or driving a herd of steers to the slaughterhouse, or splitting wood. I watched him, and laughed. He came to me to kiss my hand, as the Indians do, and

Translators' Notes

asked me to let him have sheet music and symphonies, so he could copy them, for his violin, which he played very well."

"The story of King Nicholas had its origin in the mind of the man who had for a long time desired to chase us [the Jesuits], the most ardent defenders of Spanish sovereignty, out of Paraguay."

[64] Father Norbert was a Capuchin who published *Mémoires historiques sur les affaires des Jesuites* in which he attacked the Jesuits and accused them, particularly, of illegal commercial transactions. It was the Marquês de Pombal, prime minister of Portugal and deadly enemy of the Jesuits, who had this work widely distributed.

[65] Malagrida (1689–1761), a Jesuit missionary in Brazil from 1721 to 1749. He returned to Portugal and apparently exerted great influence at the Court of Lisbon. Pombal, the prime minister and great enemy of Malagrida and the Jesuits, succeeded in having him banished and all the Jesuits removed from the court. Pombal, however, did not rest until Malagrida was condemned to death by a "packed" court of the Inquisition. "He was strangled at an auto-da-fé and his body burned."

[66] In October, 1768, the *Gazeta de Madrid*, official organ of Spanish governmental circles, states: "It is now well known that everything that had been reported about King Nicolaus was a fable and pure invention."

[67] Baegert refers here to Abbé Chappe d'Auteroches. See Part One, chapter one, note 4, and Part Two, chapter seven, note 4.

INDEX

Agave, 32
Agriculture at missions: land cultivated, 129; livestock introduced, 129; irrigation, 129; crops, 130; vegetables and fruits, 130; wine, 130–131; animal husbandry, 131 ff.
Alligators, 11; eyeteeth antidote for snakebite, 11–12
Animals: hares, 38; coyotes, 39, 177; wildcats, 39; mountain goats, 39; zorilla, 39–40; snakes, 41; toads, 43; bats, 43. See also Insects
Anti-Jesuit propaganda, discussion of, 187 ff.
Apaches, terrorize missions, 112
Appearance of Indians, physical, xvi–xvii, 53, 180–181
Aquatitlán, Jesuits arrive at, 166
Arteága, Don Nicolás de, endows a mission, 116
Arreola, Don Augustín, xv n. 10

Baegert family, xi–xii
Baegert, Father Johann Jakob: early years, xi; baptism, xi; life, xii; education, xii; to Cadiz, xii; journey to New World, xii–xiii; lands at Vera Cruz, xiii; third year of probation, xiii; ordered to California, xiii; account of journey, xv; meals, xvi, 143; arrives at Yaqui, xvi; visits Sonora missions, xvi; crosses Gulf, xvi; arrives at Loreto, xvi; to San Luis Gonzaga, xvi; solemn profession at Mission Dolores, xvii, 140; Superior of California missions, xviii; visits each mission, xviii; reading, xviii–xiv; interests, xix; on life of missionary, xix, 143
Baegert, Maria Magdalena (Scheideck), xi
Baegert, Michaelis Joannes, xi
Baegert, Stanislaus Ignaz, Father Baegert's letter to, xiv–xv
Balsas, 57

Balthasar, Father Johann: Provincial, xiii; orders Baegert to California, xiii
Baptism of Indians, 7, 62–63, 114
Béjar and Gandia, Duquésa de, endows two missions, 116
Birds, fowl and game, 27, 38; cardinals, 38; moucherons, 38; ducks, 38; false reports about, 177–178
Bischoff, Father Johann Xavier, 126
Bisnága, 33; thorns, 33–34
Boton: leads uprising, 152; aim, 152
Bourdaloue, Father Louis, 194

Cabo Blanco, 13, 14
Cabo San Lucas: southernmost point, 11; distance to mouth of Río Colorado, 13; borders, 13
Caborca mission in Sonora, 112
Cadiz, Baegert at, xii
California: derivation of name, 16; origin of, 29, 30. See also Peninsula of California
Calvin, John, eliminates title "universal" from Church, 164
Cardón, 32; fruit of, 32
Carranco, Father Lorenzo, 152; murdered in uprising of 1734, 153–154
Catalána Island, 12
Cavallero y Ozio, Don Juan: donates to Salvatierra's journey, 109; endows two missions, 116
Celibacy, Protestant criticism of, 161
Ceralbo Island, 12
Chahuixtle, 23
Charles II, California forgotten during reign of, 108
Charlevoix, Father Pierre François Xavier de, 54, 55, 81; "History of Canada" describes Dellius, 163 and n.
Chicóri: leads uprising, 152; aim, 152
Chino, 31
Chocolate, 79, 123
Churches, mission: construction, 125, 127; ornaments, 125, 127–128, 143–

213

Churches (continued)
144, 145; bells, 125; organs, 126; altars, 126; vestments, 126; singing, 126; incense, 179
Cluverius, Philipp, quoted on California, 175
Cochineal, 35
Collegium San Gregorio (Mexico City), Baegert completes probation at, xiii
Condé, Baegert a passenger on, xiii
Confession, 123–124
Corn, 27–29
Cortés, Hernán, 107
Cotton, 27 n.
Córas revolt, 151
Creed, Twelve Articles of, in Guaicura language, 100–102

Dellius, Godfreidus, Father Charlevoix describes, 163 and n.
Díaz, Father Juan José, sermon, 172
Diseases of Indians, 77–78; syphilis, 77; smallpox, 77; remedies, 78–79, 90; epidemic at San Borja, 170
Druet, Father Jacobo, 122–123
Ducrue, Father Franz Benno: Portolá sends for, 169; Superior of all missions, 169; letter from Viceroy ordering Jesuits to leave California, 170; sends letter to each missionary, 170

El Carmen Island, salt from, 48, 190
Endowments to missions, 116

Ferdinand VI, orders to soldiers, 147
Fernandez, Don, Portolá's Field chaplain, 118
Fish, 37–38, 180
Fogs, 23; carry chahuixtle, 23; manna, 23
Fourth Continent, 55; purpose in finding, 107
Fourth Lateran Council, 196
Fruits, 27, 34–36, 178

Gálvez, José de, xv n. 10
Gazettier Ecclésiastique, 193
Game. See Animals; Birds
González, Father Thyrso, 183
Grapes: at Todos Santos, 16; vines, 28; wine, 130–131, 190; five missions with vines, 179; irrigated, 179
Grass, 19, 32
Guadalajara: Baegert's description of, xv; California in bishopric of, 47; Bishop of, 191
Guaicuras: Hostel ordered to start new mission among, xiii; language, xiii, xiv, xvii, 94–95, 99–102; clothing, xvi
Guaymas, missionaries at, 166
Guillén, Father Clemente, xiii, 189
Gulf of California: called California Red Sea, 11; islands, 12; color, 176

Hagenau (Alsace), Baegert professor in collegium at, xii
Herbs, 32–33
"History of California," 176 ff.; title of, 176–177; falsehoods refuted, 176 ff.; false impression of missions, 189
Hospitium de las Indias (Cadiz), Baegert at, xii
Hostel, Father Lambert: to California, xiii; at San Luis Gonzaga, xiii; to Mission Dolores, xiii; describes California, xiii; abandons plan for Holy Trinity mission, xiv; history of, xiv n. 10; aids Baegert, xvii; Baegert's gratitude to, 150
Huebner, John, remarks on California weather challenged, 16

Ikas: language, 55; number of, 55
Ináma von Sternegg, Father Franz: examines snakes, 41; Baegert's gratitude to, 150
Indians: baptism, 7, 62-63, 114; beliefs, 7, 58, 91–92, 93, 177; burial customs, 79–80, 88–89; character, 20–21, 80–86 *passim*, 146, 180; children, 74–76, 91; counting method, 81, 189; customs and manner of living, 86, 87 ff., 176; dancing, 89, 91; diseases, 77–90, 170; dress, 61–63; dwellings, 59–60, 176, 181; food, 26, 47, 66–71, 145, 187, 188; household utensils, 63; language, 87, 92, 94–104; life of, 48, 49–50, 59 ff., 92–93; marriage, 72–74, 88; medicine men, 89–90; origin, 57–58; population, 53–56 *passim*, 59; punishment of, 91; tribes, 7, 8, 56, 59; uprisings, 151–155; weapons, 64–65. See also Apaches; Córas; Guaicuras; Ikas; Pericúes; Pimas; Seris
Insects, 40 ff.; scorpions, 42; centipedes, 42; tarantulas, 42–43; wasps, 43; ants, 43; locusts, 44
Istlán, 166

214

Index

Jesuits. *See* Anti-Jesuit propaganda; Missionaries

Kino, Father Eusebius: purpose in conquering California, 108; discusses California with Salvatierra, 108; trip from Sonora to Río Colorado, 112; proves California a peninsula, 112

Konschak, Father Ferdinand: map of California, xi; explores California east coast to Río Colorado, 12; results of exploration questioned, 12

Language, Indian, 87, 92, 94–104; Guaicura, 94–95; Creed and Lord's prayer in Guaicura, 99–102

Linck, Father Wenceslaus: in charge of Mission San Borja, 12; ordered to Río Colorado, 12–13

Livestock, 131 ff.; cattle, sheep, and goats, 132–134; horses and mules, 132; pigs, 132; herders for, 133

Luther, Martin, eliminates title "universal" from Church, 164

Luyando, Father Juan María, endows a mission, 116

Luzenilla, Francisco, request for expedition to California rejected, 108

Mainz, Baegert's novitiate at, xii

Mannheim, Baegert teaches at collegium in, xii

Matanchel, San Juan de: expelled Jesuits at, 166; departure from, 166; wood for boats from, 178

Mendocino, Cape, 13, 14

Mescále, 66, 69, 179

Mesquite, 31; pods, 33

Mines, 45–47 and n.; silver, 46; settlements, 47; missionary and, 47; Rosario, 47; one-fifth to king, 47; San Ignacio sulphur, 47; salt, 48, 190; miners paid in silver, 150

Missionaries: consignments to, 120; all responsibilities, 122–123; in illness, 123; confession, 123–124; houses, 125; vestments, 126; burden of livestock, 134; armed escort, 146; virtues, 150–151; fifty Jesuits shipped to Guaymas, 166, to Matanchel, 166, to region of Aquatitlán and Istlán, 166; twenty die, 167; arrive in Bay of Cadiz, 167; letter from Viceroy and expulsion from California, 170; assemble for embarkation, 170; arrive at Loreto, 170; successors land in Sinaloa, 171; second change, 171; names of, 172; majority of Spanish, always Jesuits, 193

Missions: number of Indians in, 54; need for fifteen, 56; on Mexican side of Gulf, 111; extend to thirty-first degree, 111, 112; eighteen more erected, 112, 114; established by missionaries themselves, 112; royal orders for, 113; 1697–1716 payments, 113, 119; fifteen in 1768, 114; listed in geographic order, 114–116; priest for each, 116; description, 116; endowed, 116; favorable sites, 116, 129; drinking water, 116, 129; meager supplies, 116; revenues, 119 ff.; Philip V's command, 119; March consignments, 120; permanent residents, 120; Mass, 121; bells, 121; holidays and Passion Week, 121; fiscals and magistrates, 121; food distributed, 122; working hours, 122; building, 126–127; treasures imported from Mexico, 127; land cultivated, 129; animal husbandry, 129, 131 ff.; four established in 1733, 151–152; four destroyed in four days, 155. *See also* Churches

Molsheim: Baegert teaches at, xii; Baegert admitted to Holy Orders at, xii

Mountains in California, 25, 125

Nachrichten von der Amerikanischen Halbinsel Californien, published in Mannheim, xi; second edition, xi

Nascimben, Father Pietro, 126

"Navy," California: wood for ships, 178; *La Concepción*, 182; *La Lauretana*, 182; reports about, 182

Negroes, 55

Neustadt, Father Baegert at, xi

Norbert, Father, 196

Nuestro Padre San Ignacio mission: masonry church, 31; sulphur and iron ore in region of, 48; founded in 1728, 115; church pictured, 136

Nuestra Señora de Columna mission, 115–116

Nuestra Señora de los Dolores [del Sur] mission: Father Hostel to, xiii, xvii; Baegert makes solemn profession at, xvii and n. 12; distance from Todos Santos, 115; founded in 1721, 115

Observations in Lower California

Nuestra Señora de Guadalupe, 115
Nuestra Señora de Loreto mission: Baegert arrives at, xvi; Salvatierra's name for first mission, 110; first church consecrated, 114; started in 1697, 115; distance from San Xavier, 115; residence of Governor and Viceroy, 116; site, 116–117; missionary's dwelling, 117; barracks, 117; garrison, 117; native huts, 117; heat, 118; church, 125; bells, 125; tabernacle, 126; picture, 141; workmen at, 149; objective of Portolá's expedition, 168, 169; missionaries to embark at, 170, 172; High Mass, 172; only church at which Host is kept, 179
Nuestra Señora del Pilar de la Paz mission, 152

Palmilla, 189 n.
Paloblanco, 31
Palohierro, 31
Pearl fishing, 44–45, 180; one-fifth to king, 45, 182; behavior of pearl fishers, 108; Salvatierra forbids use of Indians for, 111; no pearl fishers permitted to sail for California in 1769, 167; reports about, 180, 182
Peña, Marquesa de la, endows a mission, 116
Peninsula of California, 11, 12; width, 11, 12, 14, 177; part of mainland? 12; length, 13, 14, 15; latitude, 11, 13, 15; Konschak's exploration confirms, 12; longitude, 14; size, 14, 53–54; origin, 29; Kino's trip to prove, 112; California declared a peninsula, 112
Pericúes, revolt, 151
Philip V: orders regent in Mexico to pay for support of missionaries, 112–113, 193; royal orders for missions, 113; equipment for churches, 113; soldiers and ships to serve missions, 113, 147; payments check hardships, 116, 119
Píccolo, Father Francisco María: cited on seed pods, 66; lays foundations for second mission, 110
Pimas, 112, 180
Pimería, 57, 112, 180
Pirates: Moorish, xii; inhabitants of islands in Gulf, 12; trade ended in 1715, 12
Pitahayas, 23; sweet, 35; harvest, 35, 181; sour, 35–36, 178; seeds, 68; ambía, 87; staple food, 178
Plátanos (bananas), 27 n.
Pluche, M., *Spectacle de la Nature*, mentioned, 74
Population, Indian, 53–56 *passim*; size of tribes, 59; many nations, 56
Portolá, Don Gaspar: first governor of California, 118, 167; salary, 118; instructions to build cities and fortifications, 167; attempts to sail to California, 167; vanguard, 168; lands near Mission San José del Cabo, 168; Mission Loreto objective, 168; confers with Don Fernando Rivera y Moncada, 168–169; friendly to Jesuits, 169; inspects San José and Santiago, 169; visits mines, 169; land journey to Loreto, 169; sends for Father Ducrue, 169; letter from Viceroy, 170; inventories missions, 170; receives missionaries, 170; reports on California, 199
Protestants, neglect missionary work, 156 ff.
Puerto Santa María (Cadiz), xii, xiii
Purísima Concepción mission, 22, 115

Rancherías, xvii
Revenues, mission: from founder, 119; Philip V's decree for, 119; decree not acceptable, 119; from private persons, 1697–1768, 119
Rheds, Father Georg, 172
Ricci, Father Lorenzo, 198
Río Colorado (Red River), 11; Konschak follows upstream, 12; Linck ordered to, 12; distance from San Borja, 12
Río Gila, 112
Rivera y Moncada, Don Fernando: captain of California militia, 168; Portolá confers with, 168–169
Rivers, 21–22
Romero, Felipe, xv n. 10
Royal Council in Mexico: pronounces California unconquerable, 108; Salvatierra reports to, in Guadalajara, 110–111; refers Salvatierra's report to Viceroy, 111; honors Salvatierra, 114
Rousseau, J.-J., *Emile* mentioned, 76
Ruhen, Father Heinrich, 155–156
Russians, land in America, 13

Index

Sailors, 147

Salt mines, 190

Salvatierra, Father Juan María: qualities, 108; visits missions of Sonora as Provincial, 108; discusses California with Kino, 108; permission to sail to California, 108; Viceroy refuses help, 109; friends aid, 109; equips vessel, 109; sails from Sinaloa, 109; relations with Indians, 109; lays foundations for first mission, 109–110; teaches Spanish to Indians and learns their language, 110; sends ship to Sinaloa for provisions, 110; report to Viceroy, 110, and to Royal Council, 110–111; case submitted to Viceroy, 111, to king, 111; captain of soldiers owes obedience to, 111; forbids use of Indians for pearl fishing, 111; idea of land route to California, 111–112; asks Kino to go to Río Colorado, 112; collects payments 1697–1716, 113; envisions entrance of Don Gil de la Sierpe into heaven, 113; leaves California, 114; Provincial in Mexican province, 114; permission to resign, 114; confers with Viceroy, 114; dies, 114; interred in Lauretan chapel, 114; supports soldiers to put down revolts, 146; and report of salt mines, 190

San Antonio silver mine, 46

San Bonaventura, distance from Red River, 12–13

San Dionisio, bay of, Salvatierra lands in, 109

San Francisco Borja mission: Linck in charge, 12; distance to Río Colorado, 12; snowflakes at, 15; distance from Santa Gertrudis, 115; epidemic at, 170

San Francisco Xavier mission: distance to Bay of Santa Magdalena, 12; distance from Mission Dolores, 115; church, 125; only church with glass windows, 125; bells, 125; imported altar, 127; pictured, 137, 138, 139

San José Comondú mission: river at, 22; close to Pacific, 115; bells, 125

San José del Cabo mission: brook at, 22; name, 114–115; founded in 1720, 115; established in 1733, 152; Father Támaral missionary, 152; 1733 uprising, 154; Portolá lands near, 168; successors to missionaries arrive at, 171; report about house of missionary, 188

San José Island: inhabited, 12; salt, 48

San Juan Londó mission, ruins of chapel pictured, 142

San Lucas Mountain, 115

San Luis Gonzaga mission: Baegert arrives at, xi; Hostel's pioneer work, xiii; seven hours from Mission Dolores, 115; established in 1731, 115; picture, 135

Santa Ana silver mine, 46

Santa Cruz, missionaries shipped to, 166

Santa Gertrudis mission, established in 1751, 115

Santa Magdalena, Bay of: distance from Mission San Xavier, 12; Baegert lives opposite, 14; reports about pier, 176, and country around, 176, 178

Santa Rosa de Todos Santos. See Todos Santos

Santa Rosalía de Mulegé mission: brook at, 22; distance from Gulf, 115; founded in 1705, 115; picture, 136; Father Táraval missionary at, 152

Santiago de los Coras mission: river at, 22; distance from San José del Cabo, 115; founded in 1720, 115; established in 1733, 152; Father Lorenzo Carranco missionary, 152

Schlettstadt: Baegert born in, xi; returns to, xi

Sierpe, Pedro Gil de la: aids Salvatierra, 109; Salvatierra's vision of, 113

Siete Dolores mission, prefect of all missions at, 153

Seris, incursions, 112

Shrubs, 32–33

Silver mines, 46

Sinaloa, Salvatierra sails from, 109

Slaves, 161 n., 191

Social classes in California, 49–50; workmen in Loreto, 149; Spaniards, 181

Society of Jesus: royal decree expels from Spanish possessions in New World, xi; notice about Baegert in catalogue of, xviii; Father Thyrso González General of, 183; Father Lorenzo Ricci General of, 198. See also Missionaries

Soil, California, 20, 25; infertility of, 26, 179; with water, 27

Soldiers, xviii; end pirate trade, 12; protest Linck's expedition, 13; nationality of, 49, 146; captain of, slanders padres,

217

Soldiers (*continued*)
111; captain owes obedience to Salvatierra, 111; tired of country, 111; decree for armed guards, 146; Salvatierra maintains, 146; paid by King of Spain after 1716, 146; number, 146; officers, 146; weapons, 146; armor, 146; five mounts, 146; pay, 146–147; duties, 146–147; orders of Philip V and Ferdinand VI to obey missionaries, 147; depositions to Viceroy on accusations against Jesuits, 188; report about captain, 191

Sorcerers, Indian, 89–90

Stahl, Anna Maria (Scheideck), Baegert's god parent, xi

Swamps, 22

Stones and rocks: wacke, 19; kinds and uses, 25–26, 29, 125

Támaral, Father Nicolás, 152; murdered in 1734 uprising, 154

Táraval, Father Sigismundo, 152; escapes from 1734 uprising, 154–155

Tello, Father P. Tomás, 155

Tekakovíta, Catherine, 86

Thorns, 33–34, 64

Tirs, Father Ignatz: and locusts, 44; last missionary to Pericúes and Corás, 157

Toba, Pablo de la, xv n. 10

Todos Santos mission: Guaicura Indians sent to, xv n. 10; weather at, 16; river, 22; almost on shores of Pacific, 115; established in 1720, 115; church, 125

Trade: island Indians acquire boats in, 12; none with English, 19; extent of, between California and other nations, 149; on peninsula, 149; with miners, 150

Trees, 30, 60; mesquite, 31, 33; brazilwood, 31; willows, 31; palms, 31; paloblanco, 31; ironwood, 31; wild fig, 31; espaliered, 31; no shade, 60; reports about, 178, 179; plum, 179

Tribes, Indian: small groups, 7; no contacts, 7; thirty hours apart, 8; names of, 56; size of, 59

Tunas, 34–35

Ugarte, Father Juan María, 122–123

Uchities, 95 n.

Uñagato, 31

Uprisings, Indian: causes, 151, 152; 1734, 151 ff., 181; leaders, 152; plot discovered, 152; six soldiers only obstacle to, 152; natives murder two soldiers, 152; plan first blow against San José del Cabo, 153; priests killed, 153–154; penalties, 155

Velasco, Marqués Luis de: donation for mission, xiii; endows one mission, 116

Venegas, Miguel, *Noticia de la California*: faults of, 6, 177 ff., 194 ff.; comments on campaign against Jesuits, 193 ff.; style of, 194; standing army of Jesuits, 195; revolt in Madrid, 195; wealth of California, 197

Viceroy of Mexico: objects to Salvatierra's journey to California, 108; refuses aid, 108–109; Salvatierra reports to, 110; Royal Council refers Salvatierra's case to, 111; submits it to king, 111; calls Salvatierra to confer about California, 114; food for, served in earthen vessels or porcelain, 169; letter from, ordering Jesuits to leave California, 170; eight accusations against Jesuits forwarded to, 187, and replies, 187 ff.

Villa-Puente, Marqués de la: aids missions, 113; equips regiments for War of Spanish Succession, 113; endows six missions, 116

Viscaya, Sebastián de, 13

Water: rain, 20–24 *passim*, 175; still waters, 22; insufficient for irrigation, 28; missions built near drinking, 116, 129; reports about brooks, 177, about scarcity, 178, about irrigation ditches, 188

Watermelons, 71 n.

Weather: compared with Cadiz', 15; temperature, 16; favorable to vegetables, 16; hot season, 17; cold, 18; differences between north and south, 18; winds, 19; rain, 20–24 *passim*, 175

Weislinger, "Theological Charlatans," exposes Tranquebar missionaries, 163

Wines. *See* Grapes

Wirth, Josephus, Baegert's god parent, xi

Young Workers' Association at Hagenau, Baegert president of, xii

Yucca, 66, 179

Ziegenbalg, Bartol., "Theological Charlatans" on, 163

www.ingramcontent.com/pod-product-compliance
Lightning Source LLC
Chambersburg PA
CBHW021704230426
43668CB00008B/720